Adolf Alt, Albert E. Foote

**A Treatise on Ophthalmology**

for the general practitioner

Adolf Alt, Albert E. Foote

**A Treatise on Ophthalmology**
*for the general practitioner*

ISBN/EAN: 9783337815462

Printed in Europe, USA, Canada, Australia, Japan

Cover: Foto ©Andreas Hilbeck / pixelio.de

More available books at **www.hansebooks.com**

ON

# OPHTHALMOLOGY

FOR THE

General Practitioner.

ILLUSTRATED.

BY

ADOLF ALT, M.D.

J. H. CHAMBERS & CO.
Publishers and Dealers in Medical Books,
CHICAGO, ILL.   ST. LOUIS, MO.   ATLANTA, GA.
1884

Entered according to Act of Congress, in the year 1884, by

JAMES H. CHAMBERS,

In the Office of the Librarian of Congress, at Washington, D. C.

TO

MY FRIEND AND COLLEAGUE.

# JOHN GREEN, M. D.,

OF ST. LOUIS,

MO.,

THIS BOOK

IS RESPECTFULLY DEDICATED.

# DR. JOHN GREEN,

## ST. LOUIS, MO.

Sir—*I have taken the liberty of dedicating this book to you, and I hope you will accept it as a token of my grateful esteem and friendship.*

*You may, however, ask what motives prompted me to write this book, and thus to add one more to the long list of manuals on ophthalmology, which the last few years have produced. Was there any need of another such manual? Or, can this book offer anything new?*

*I confess that I would not have undertaken to write this book, had I not been asked to do it. While considering the proposition made to me by the publishers, and looking again over the excellent English and American manuals on ophthalmology by authors like* Noyes, Nettleship, Macnamara *and others, it appeared to me that, after all, there may be a want which these works do not exactly supply, and which I might, perhaps, succeed in supplying.*

*I mean that a book on ophthalmology, written solely for the general practitioner and his wants, was not among them. I mean a book, which the general practitioner would really peruse, and not lay aside because overburdened with details relating to subjects of little or no use to him; in short, a book which would give the general practitioner a clear idea of the principles of ophthalmology, together with so much only of its practice as he might be reasonably jus-*

tified in attempting. That such a book might be capable of doing a good work, I could not doubt.

The present volume, then, is not intended for specialists, nor does it aim at making an oculist out of every general practitioner. It is, however, intended to serve as a guide for the general practitioner, as to when he may conscientiously take upon himself the responsibility of dealing with an eye affection, and when he had better not do so.

I have, therefore, thought it best, on the one hand, to give all the information necessary for the undertaking of our special work, and on the other hand, to withhold such information as would be likely only to lure him into dangerous paths. I have, furthermore, given most space and labor to such subjects as are likely to be of practical value to the general medical practitioner.

Regarding, therefore, the end which I have had in view in writing this book, you will, I believe, find that it differs materially from other existing manuals on ophthalmology. If it shall prove acceptable and useful to the class of practitioners for whom it has been written, my intention will have been largely realized.

Respectfully yours,     Adolf Alt,
1405 Washington Ave., St. Louis, Mo.
January, 1884.

# CONTENTS.

## CHAPTER I.

### ANATOMY OF THE EYE.

ORBIT.—TENON'S CAPSULE.—EYE-LIDS.—CONJUNCTIVA. SCLEROTIC.—CORNEA.—UVEAL TRACT.—OPTIC NERVE. RETINA.—CRYSTALLINE LENS.—VITREOUS BODY.—EXTERNAL MUSCLES OF THE EYE-BALL.—LACHRYMAL APPARATUS. - - - - - - - - 1 to 19

## CHAPTER II.

### EXAMINATION OF THE EYE.

EYE-LIDS.—CONJUNCTIVA.—CORNEA.—IRIS.—CRYSTALLINE LENS.—FOCAL OR OBLIQUE ILLUMINATION.—ACUTENESS OF VISION.—VISUAL FIELD.—COLOR-SENSE.—INTRA-OCULAR TENSION.—ACCOMMODATION REFRACTION.—OPHTHALMOSCOPE.—MOTILITY.—DIPLOPIA.—INSUFFICIENCY OF THE INTERNAL RECTI MUSCLES. - - - - - - - - 20 to 29

## CHAPTER III.

### DISEASES OF THE EYE-LIDS.

BLEPHARITIS CILIARIS.—PHTHIRIASIS.—CHALAZION.—ABSCESS.—SYPHILITIC ULCER.—WARTS.—XANTHELASMA.—EPITHELIOMA.—SARCOMA.—TELEANGIECTATIC AND ANGIOMATOUS TUMORS.—TRICHIASIS.—DISTICHIASIS.—ENTROPIUM.—ECTROPIUM.—PTOSIS OF THE UPPER EYE-LID.—BLEPHAROSPASMUS.—LAGOPHTHALMUS. WOUNDS.—EMPHYSEMA.—BURNS. - - - - 30 to 45

## CHAPTER IV.

### DISEASES OF THE LACHRYMAL APPARATUS.

LACHRYMAL GLAND.—HYPER-SECRETION. — DAKRYADEN-ITIS.—NEOPLASMS.—CYSTIC DISTENSION (DAKRYOPS). — DRAINAGE APPARATUS. — EPIPHORA. — FOREIGN BODIES IN THE LACHRYMAL CANALICULUS.—DAKRYO-CYSTITIS CATARRHALIS.—DAKRYO-CYSTITIS PURULENTA. STRICTURES.—LACHRYMAL FISTULA.—MELANO-SARCO-MA OF THE LACHRYMAL CARUNCLE. - - - - 46 to 54

## CHAPTER V.

### DISEASES OF THE ORBIT.

PERIOSTITIS OF THE WALLS OF THE ORBIT.—HEMOR-RHAGES INTO THE ORBITAL TISSUE.—CELLULITIS OR-BITÆ, PHLEGMONOUS INFLAMMATION OF THE ORBITAL TISSUES. — INFLAMMATION OF TENNON'S CAPSULE.—EMPHYSEMA.—NEOPLASMS.  - - - - -  55 to 60

## CHAPTER VI.

### MINOR MANIPULATIONS IN THE TREATMENT OF EYE-DISEASES.

COLD APPLICATIONS. — WARM APPLICATIONS. — LEECH-ING.—REMOVING DISCHARGE.—INSTILLATION OF MED-ICATED FLUIDS.—APPLICATION OF ASTRINGENT SOLU-TIONS.—APPLICATION OF CAUSTIC SOLUTIONS.—APPLI-CATION OF REMEDIES IN SUBSTANCE.—APPLICATION OF OINTMENTS.—INSPERGATION OF MEDICINAL POWD-ERS.—ISOLATION.—REMOVAL OF WILD HAIRS.—RE-MOVAL OF SMALL FOREIGN BODIES.—INSERTION OF LID RETRACTORS.—BANDAGING.—HINTS FOR ASSIS-TANCE IN EYE OPERATIONS. - - - - - 61 to 73

## CHAPTER VII.

### DISEASES OF THE CONJUNCTIVA.

HYPERÆMIA.—CATARRHAL CONJUNCTIVITIS. — PURULENT CONJUNCTIVITIS.—CROUPOUS CONJUNCTIVITIS.—DIPHtheritic Conjunctivitis.—Granular Conjunctivitis (Trachoma).—Phlyctaenular Conjunctivitis.—Subconjunctival Hemorrhage.— Injuries. — Burns.— Symblepharon. — Anchyloblepharon. — Pinguecula.— Pterygium.— Cysts. — Epithelioma. — Sarcoma. - - - - - - - - - 74 to 91

## CHAPTER VIII.

### Diseases of the Cornea.

Phlyctaenular Keratitis.—Parenchymatous Keratitis.—Syphilitic Keratitis.—Abscess of the Cornea.—Hypopyum.— Ulcers of the Cornea.—Malarial Keratitis.— Neuro-paralytic Keratitis.—Scars in the Cornea.—Tatooing.—Arcus Senilis.—Staphyloma of the Cornea.—Conical Cornea.—Injuries.—Burns.—Neoplasms. - - - - - 92 to 103

## CHAPTER IX.

### Diseases of the Sclerotic.

Episcleritis.—Scleritis.—Staphyloma of the Sclerotic.—Posterior Scleral Staphyloma.—Neoplasms.—Wounds. - - - - - - - 104 to 107

## CHAPTER X.

### Diseases of the Iris.

Plastic Iritis.—Serous Iritis.—Purulent Iritis.—Gummatous Iritis.—Poisoning by Atropia.—Injuries.—Traumatic Coloboma.—Iridodialysis.— Neoplasms.—Cysts.—Sarcoma.—Mydriasis.—Myosis. 108 to 116

## CHAPTER XI.

### Diseases of the Ciliary Body.

Plastic Cyclitis.—Serous Cyclitis.—Purulent Cyclitis—Neoplasms.—Sarcoma.—Injuries. - - 117 to 119

## CHAPTER XII.

### DISEASES OF THE CHOROID.

PLASTIC CHOROIDITIS.—SEROUS CHOROIDITIS.—PURULENT CHOROIDITIS.— NEOPLASMS.— GUMMA.— TUBERCLE.— SARCOMA.— INJURIES.— ISOLATED RUPTURE OF THE CHOROID.—HEMORRHAGE.

## CHAPTER XIII.

### DISEASES OF THE RETINA.

HYPERÆMIA.— ANÆMIA.— EMBOLISM OF THE CENTRAL RETINAL ARTERY.—THROMBOSIS OF THE CENTRAL RETINAL ARTERY.—THROMBOSIS OF THE CENTRAL RETINAL VEIN.—DETACHMENT OF THE RETINA.—PIGMENTARY RETINITIS. — SYPHILITIC RETINITIS. — ALBUMINURIC RETINITIS.—HEMORRHAGE.—GLIOMA.

## CHAPTER XIV.

### DISEASES OF THE OPTIC NERVE.

HYPERÆMIA. — NEURITIS OPTICA.— ATROPHY.— COLOR-BLINDNESS.—AMBLYOPIA.—AMAUROSIS.—HEMIANOPIA. INJURIES.—NEOPLASMS.—MYXOMA.  -  -  -  136 to 141

## CHAPTER XV.

### DISEASES OF THE CRYSTALLINE LENS.

CONGENITAL CATARACT.—ZONULAR CATARACT.— POLAR CATARACT.—SOFT CATARACT.—CORTICAL CATARACT.— NUCLEAR CATARACT.—DIABETIC CATARACT.—TRAUMATIC CATARACT.—DISLOCATION OF THE CRYSTALLINE LENS.—ECTOPIA LENTIS.—APHAKIA.  -  -  -  142 to 152

## CHAPTER XVI.

### DISEASES OF THE VITREOUS BODY.

HYALITIS.—MUSCAE VOLITANTES.—LARGER OPACITIES.— NEW-FORMATION OF CONNECTIVE TISSUE WITHIN THE VITREOUS BODY.—SYNCHISIS SCINTILLANS.—HEMORRHAGE.  -  -  -  -  -  -  -  -  153 to 156

## CHAPTER XVII.

### Glaucoma.

Chronic Simple Glaucoma.—Chronic Inflammatory Glaucoma.—Acute Glaucoma.—Glaucoma Absolutum.—Secondary Glaucoma. - - - - 156 to 160

## CHAPTER XVIII.

### Injuries of the Eye-Ball and their Consequences.

Injuries without Retention of a Foreign Body.—Injuries with the Retention of a Foreign Body within the Eye-Ball. - - - - - 165 to 168

## CHAPTER XIX.

### Sympathetic Ophthalmia.

Sympathetic Irritation.—Sympathetic Neuritis.—Sympathetic Iritis.—Sympathetic Irido-Cyclitis.—Sympathetic Irido-Choroiditis. — Sympathetic Keratitis. - - - - - - - - 169 to 173

## CHAPTER XX.

### Errors of Refraction and Accommodation.

Emmetropia.—Ametropia.—Hypermetropia.—Myopia.—Astigmatism.— Accommodation.— Presbyopia. —Paralysis of the Accommodation.—Spasm of the Accommodation.- - - - - - - 174 to 187

## CHAPTER XXI.

### Diseases of the External Muscles of the Eye.

Normal Condition and Action.—Diplopia.—Paralysis.—Paralytic Strabismus.—Muscular Strabismus. Convergent Strabismus.—Divergent Strabismus.—Insufficiency of the Internal Recti Muscles.—Nystagmus. - - - - - - - 188 to 195

xii                    *CONTENTS.*

## CHAPTER XXII.

ON THE DIAGNOSTIC VALUE OF EYE-DISEASES IN INTRA-CRANIAL AFFECTIONS.

ANÆMIA AND HYPERÆMIA OF THE OPTIC NERVE AND RETINA.—ŒDEMA OF THE OPTIC PAPILLA.—OPTIC NEURITIS AND NEURO-RETINITIS.—PROGRESSIVE ATROPHY OF THE OPTIC NERVE.—TUBERCLES IN THE CHOROID.—CONDITIONS OF THE PUPIL.—HEMIANOPIA.   -    -    196 to 201

## CHAPTER XXIII.

EYE-AFFECTIONS CAUSED BY DISEASES OF DISTANT ORGANS OR DISEASES OF THE GENERAL SYSTEM.

RESPIRATORY APPARATUS.—CIRCULATORY APPARATUS.—DIGESTIVE APPARATUS.—URO-POETIC APPARATUS.—GENITAL ORGANS.—AFFECTIONS OF THE SKIN.—AFFECTIONS OF THE JOINTS.—INFECTIOUS DISEASES.—INTOXICATIONS.—DIABETES.—SCROPHULOSIS.   -    -    - 202 to 213

## CHAPTER XXIV.

ON THE DETECTION OF ONE-SIDED SIMULATED BLINDNESS AND CONGENITAL COLOR-BLINDNESS.

METHODS FOR DETECTING SIMULATED BLINDNESS.—HOLMGREN'S METHOD FOR DETECTING COLOR-BLINDNESS.   114 to 116

## CHAPTER XXV.

ON THE MOST IMPORTANT OPERATIONS ON THE EYE-BALL AND THE EYE-LIDS.

TENOTOMY. — ADVANCEMENT. — ENUCLEATION. — PARACENTESIS OF THE CORNEA.— ABSCISION OF A CORNEAL STAPHYLOMA.— SCLEROTOMY.— IRIDECTOMY.— IRIDOTOMY.—EXTRACTION OF CATARACT.—DISCISSION OF THE ANTERIOR LENS-CAPSULE.— PTERYGIUM OPERATIONS.—OPERATIONS FOR THE CURE OF SYMBLEPHARON.—PTOSIS-OPERATION.—TRICHIASIS AND ENTROPIUM-OPERATIONS. — ECTROPIUM - OPERATIONS. — CANTHOTOMY AND CANTHOPLASTY.—BLEPHAROPLASTY.   -    -    217 to 227

## CHAPTER XXVI.

On the Drugs Most Commonly Used in Ophthalmic Practice. Atropia.— Homatropia. — Pilocarpine. —Eserine.— Boracic Acid.—Zinc.—Tannic Acid.— Nitras Argenti.—Yellow Oxide of Mercury.—Red Oxide of Mercury.—Iodoform. - - - - - 228 to 230

# ILLUSTRATIONS.

| FIGURE. | | PAGE. |
|---|---|---|
| 1. | Horizontal section through the orbit and eye-ball | 1 |
| 2. | Vertical section through the eye-lids and eye-ball | 3 |
| 3. | The corneo-scleral region | 6 |
| 4. | The corneal nerves | 8 |
| 5. | The ciliary body of a very short-sighted eye | 10 |
| 6. | The ciliary body of a very far-sighted eye | 11 |
| 7. | The optic nerve-entrance | 13 |
| 8. | The different layers of the retina | 15 |
| 9. | The communication between the supra-choroidal and Tenon's space | 18 |
| 10. | The lachrymal drainage apparatus | 19 |
| 11. | The back-ground of the eye, as seen with the ophthalmoscope | 27 |
| 12 and 13. | Knapp's method of blephoroplasty by sliding flaps | 36 |
| 14. | Hotz's method of operating for trichiasis | 38 |
| 15. | Green's method of operating for entropium | 39 |
| 16 and 17. | Operations for ectropium | 40 |
| 18. | Operation for ptosis of the upper eye-lid | 41 |
| 19. | Tarsoraphy | 43 |
| 20. | Bowman's probes for dilating the nasal duct | 52 |
| 21. | Dropping tube | 63 |
| 22. | Cilia-forceps | 66 |
| 23. | Desmarres' lid-retractors | 67 |
| 24. | Wire-speculum | 68 |
| 25. | Fixation-forceps | 69 |
| 26. | Bent needle for the removal of foreign bodies | 69 |
| 27. | Spud or gouge for the removal of foreign bodies | 69 |
| 28. | Bandage for one eye | 70 |
| 29. | Bandage for both eyes | 71 |
| 30. | Purulent conjunctivitis | 76 |
| 31. | Symblepharon | 88 |
| 32. | Pterygium | 89 |
| 33. | Knapp's operation for pterygium | 90 |
| 34. | Epithelioma of the conjunctiva | 91 |
| 35. | Ulcer of the cornea | 97 |
| 36. | Healed corneal ulcer | 100 |

## ILLUSTRATIONS.

| | | |
|---|---|---|
| 38. | Total staphyloma of the cornea | 101 |
| 39. | Staphyloma of the sclerotic | 105 |
| 40. | Posterior scleral staphyloma | 106 |
| 41. | Posterior synechiæ | 107 |
| 42. | Results of iritis | 107 |
| 43. | Crater-shaped iris | 111 |
| 44. | Purulent iritis | 112 |
| 45. | Gummy tumor of the iris | 113 |
| 46. | Iridodialysis | 115 |
| 47. | Results of plastic cyclitis | 118 |
| 48. | Melanosarcoma of the ciliary body | 119 |
| 49. | Disseminate choroiditis | 121 |
| 50. | Panophthalmitis | 123 |
| 51. | Isolated Rupture of the choroid | 125 |
| 52. | Detachment of the retina | 128 |
| 53. | Pigmentary retinitis | 130 |
| 54. | Glioma of the retina | 134 |
| 55. | Interstitial optic neuritis | 137 |
| 56. | Atrophic excavation of the optic papilla | 139 |
| 57. | Lamellar cataract | 142 |
| 58. | Iridectomy in a case of lamellar cataract | 143 |
| 59. | Anterior polar cataract with coloboma of the iris | 145 |
| 60. | Secondary cataract | 149 |
| 61. | The crystalline lens dislocated into the anterior chamber | 150 |
| 62. | The crystalline lens dislocated into the vitreous body | 150 |
| 63. | Glaucomatous excavation of the optic papilla | 157 |
| 64. | Incarceration of the iris | 161 |
| 65. | Prolapse of the iris | 162 |
| 66. | Knapp's hook for removing foreign bodies | 165 |
| 67. | Emmetropic eye | 174 |
| 68. | Hypermetropic eye | 175 |
| 69. | Myopic eye | 175 |
| 70. | Snellen's test types | 176 |
| 71. | The focal interval of light refracted by a cylindrical surface | 184 |
| 72. | The partial decussation of the fibres of the optic nerves | 200 |
| 73. | Basedow's disease | 207 |
| 74. | Strabismus scissors | 218 |
| 75. | Strabismus hooks | 218 |
| 76. | Stop-needle | 220 |
| 77. | Beer's knife | 221 |
| 78. | Knapp's method of applying sutures before removal of a corneal staphyloma | 221 |
| 79. | Graefe's knife | 222 |
| 80. | Iris-forceps | 223 |
| 81. | Wecker's iridotomy-scissors | 223 |
| 82. | Cystotom | 224 |

# CHAPTER I.

## ANATOMY OF THE EYE.

ORBIT. — TENON'S CAPSULE. — EYE-LIDS. — CONJUNCTIVA. — SCLEROTIC. — CORNEA. — UVEAL TRACT. — OPTIC NERVE. — RETINA. — CRYSTALLINE LENS. — VITREOUS BODY. — EXTERNAL MUSCLES OF THE EYE-BALL. — LACHRYMAL APPARATUS.

*The orbit* is a pyramidal cavity surrounded by bony walls, which separate it upwards from the cranial and frontal cavities, downwards from the antrum Highmorii and inwards from the nasal cavity.

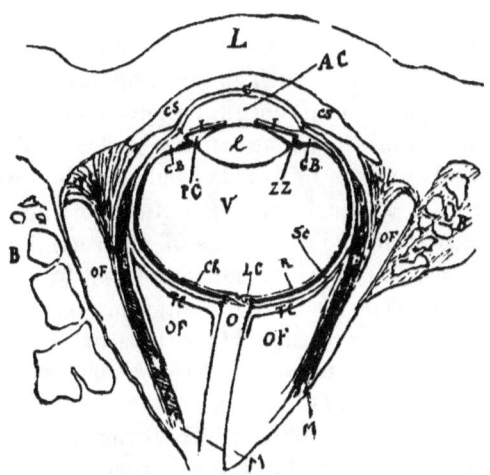

FIG. 1. Horizontal section through the orbit and eye-ball (after Gerlach). L. Eye-lid. B. Bony walls of the orbit. OF. Orbital fat. TC. Tenon's capsule. O. Optic nerve. R. Retina. Ch. Choroid. Sc. Sclerotic. LC. Lamina cribrosa. V. Vitreous body. CB. Ciliary body. I. Iris. l. Crystalline lens. ZZ. Zonule of Zinn (suspensory ligament). AC. Anterior chamber. C. Cornea. CS. Conjunctival sack. PC. Posterior chamber.

The dura mater after having entered the orbit through the canalis opticus and fissura sphenoidea is split into two parts, one of which serves to form the periosteal coat of the orbit, while the other, in the main, forms the dura mater sheath of the optic nerve, and a capsule for the posterior parts of the eye-ball, called *Tenon's capsule*. This ensheathes about four-fifths of the eye-ball and is a serous membrane, lined with a layer of endothelial cells. The serous space, which lies between it and the eye-ball, is called *Tenon's space*. (See Fig. 1).

In this capsule the eye moves very much like a joint in its capsule.

From Tenon's capsule a large number of small trabeculæ run off into the periostium of the orbit. Between these trabeculæ lies the orbital fat, and in the neighborhood of the lachrymal gland they contribute to the formation of its firm fibrous capsule. They, furthermore, help to keep the eye-ball and the other contents of the orbit in position.

Tenon's space can be inflated or injected from the subdural space of the cranium. Such an injection shows that this space ends near the corneo-scleral margin, where the tissue of Tenon's capsule goes over into the tissue of the ocular conjunctiva.

The external muscles of the eye-ball, which must naturally pierce this capsule to reach their insertions in the sclerotic, receive a sheath from it. The sheaths of the recti muscles can be traced backward into the orbital fat where they are gradually lost in the perimysium. The sheath of the superior oblique (*trochlearis*) muscles reaches to the trochlea, and there joins the periosteum, while that of the inferior oblique muscle hardly reaches as far back as the orbital adipose tissue (*Gerlach*).

The layer of the dura mater which forms the *periosteum of the orbit*, runs forward to the anterior margins of that cavity, where it passes over into the periosteum of the surrounding bones. It also gives off a fascial layer for the eye-lids, called *tarso-orbital fascia*. The orbital periosteum is, for the most part, only loosely connected with the bone, but wherever there is an aperture in the orbital walls, and also at the orbital margins, its attachments are very firm.

The *eye-lids* are originally a duplicature of the skin, growing

## ANATOMY OF THE EYE.

down from the upper and up from the lower orbital margins during foetal life. The part of this fold which lies directly upon the eye-ball takes on the character of a mucous membrane, the *palpebral conjunctiva*, and forms with the ocular conjunctiva a cul-de-sac, which is called the *fornix* of the conjunctiva. (See Fig. 2).

At the free margin of the lids this mucous membrane and the cutaneous outer surface pass over into each other, in the same way as they do, for instance, on the lips. The free margins of the eye-lids form two distinct edges, the inner one (toward the eye) sharp, the outer one rounded off. Where the upper and lower eye-lids join each other in the horizontal line, they form the outer and inner angles of the palpebral fissure, (outer and inner canthus). The outer angle is sharp; the inner is rounded. Behind the inner angle of the palpebral fissure lies a small reddish, round body, called the *lachrymal caruncle*. It has the structure of the cutis, and contains fine hairs and sebaceous glands.

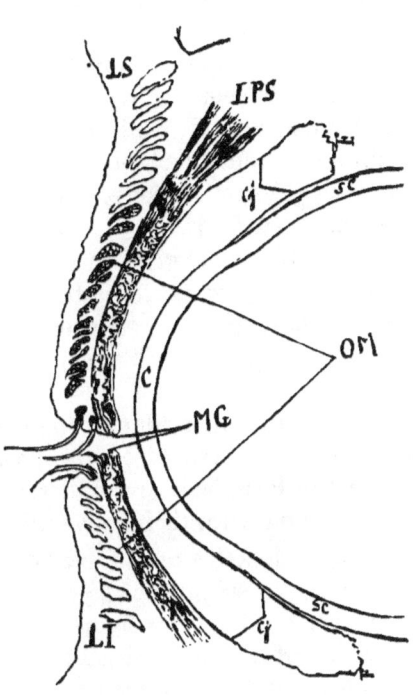

FIG. 2. Vertical section through the eye-lids and eye-ball. C. Cornea. SC. Sclerotic. Cj. Conjunctiva. F. Fornix of the conjunctiva. LS. Upper eyelid. LI. Lower eye-lid. OM. Transverse sections through the bundles of the orbicularis palpebrarum muscle. MG. Longitudinal sections through the Meibomian (tarsal) glands. T. Tarsal tissue. LPS. Levator palpebræ superioris muscle

A little outwards from the inner angle of the palpebral fissure each eye-lid shows at the inner edge of the margin a small papilla-like elevation with a small aperture at its apex. These elevations are the *lachrymal papillæ;* the apertures are the *lachrymal puncta.*

The cutis of the eye-lids is thin and its hairs are very fine and short. The subcutaneous tissue is very loose and contains no fat.

Between the conjunctival and cutaneous surfaces of the lids lie the tarsal tissue, the muscular layer, nerves and blood-vessels.

The *tarsal tissue,* commonly called the tarsal cartilage, lies close upon the conjunctiva. It consists of dense, tendon-like connective tissue and is really no cartilage. This tarsal tissue, freed from its surroundings, has a more or less semi-lunar shape. In the upper eye-lid its convexity is directed upwards, in the lower eye-lid, downwards.

Near the conjunctival surface a number of glands, the *Meibomian* or *tarsal glands,* lie embedded in the tarsal tissue. The orifices of these glands are arranged in a row, at the inner edge of the free margin of each eye-lid. Their secretion is a fatty substance.

Nearer the outer edge of the free margin of the eye-lid grow the *cilia, eyelashes.* They are short, strong hairs, which are curvilinear in form, and are so directed that those of the upper and lower eye-lids turn their convexities toward each other.

The conjunctiva of the eye-lids is closely attached to the tarsal tissue, no submucous layer intervening. Where the tarsal tissue ends, submucous tissue makes its appearance, being very loose and of an adenoid character. This is most pronounced in the fornix of the conjunctiva. In this region the surface of the conjunctiva is wrinkled and folded, and numerous muciparous glands open into it.

The muscles of the eye-lids are embedded in the loose connective tissue on the outer surface of the tarsal tissue. The most important one is the *orbicularis palpebrarum.* This is a very broad, thin muscle, covering the whole area of the eye-lids, and reaching somewhat beyond them in all directions. Its three component parts are called the palpebral, the orbital and the malar portions.

Where the upper and lower halves of this muscle join each other at the outer and inner angles of the palpebral fissure, they form the *ligamentum palpebrale externum and internum.*

The orbicularis acts as a sphincter muscle, contracting the palpebral fissure and closing the eye-lids.

At the upper edge and along the whole breadth of the tarsal tissue of the upper eye-lid the *levator palpebræ superioris muscle* is inserted by a broad, thin tendon. This muscle draws the upper eye-lid upward and backward into the orbit, and thus opens the eye.

The *ocular conjunctiva* begins at the fornix and ends at the corneo-scleral margin (*limbus corneæ*). Its submucous tissue is loosely connected with the sclerotic (*episcleral tissue*). No glands are found in the ocular conjunctiva, although its epithelial layer contains numerous mucoid cells.

The shape of the eye-ball is nearly spherical, and is determined by the so-called hard membranes which together constitute its outer wall, namely, the sclerotic and the cornea.

The *sclerotic* consists, like the tarsal tissue, of a dense connective tissue, the fibres of which are irregularly interwoven, and are held together by a protoplasmic cementing substance. Embedded in this latter is a system of lymphatic canals, which enlarge at intervals and contain large, flat, stellated connective-tissue cells.

The fibres of the sclerotic run mostly in an approximately longitudinal (meridional) direction. Fibres running in a circular (equitorial) direction are found in larger quantities only around the optic nerve entrance and near the corneo-scleral margin.

At the optic nerve entrance the sheaths of the nerve become merged in the sclerotic. There is no large opening in the latter membrane to admit the optic nerve, as a whole, into the eye-ball, but a large number of small holes, each admitting a bundle of nerve-fibres. This sieve-like region is called the *lamina cribrosa* of the sclerotic. The tendons of the external muscles of the eye-ball are lost in the tissue of the sclerotic near their insertions.

The sclerotic has an endothelial coat on its outer and inner surface, and is pierced by the ciliary nerves and arteries, and by the *venæ vorticosæ*, with their respective lymph-sheaths.

At the corneo-scleral margin the tissue of the sclerotic, which is only translucent, passes over into the transparent tissue of the cornea, but in such a manner that the sclerotic tissue slightly overlaps the cornea at its periphery.

The *cornea* consists of fibres of a perfectly transparent modified connective tissue, which are regularly arranged in bundles, and these again in lamellæ, which lie more or less parallel to each other, and are all united by the same protoplasmic cementing substance, which is found in the sclerotic. In this substance are enclosed the lymphatic canals of the cornea, which, like the lamellæ, are more numerous and lie closer together toward the

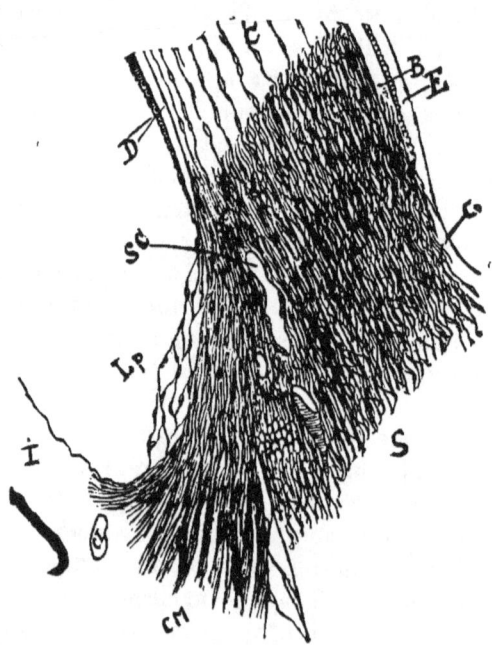

Fig. 3. Meridional section through the region of the corneo-scleral margin. C. Cornea. D. Descemet's membrane. B. Bowman's layer. E. Ephithelial layer. Co. Conjunctiva. Lp. Ligamentum pectinatum. SC. Schlemm's canal. S. Sclerotic. I. Iris. CI. Large arterial circle of the iris. CM. Ciliary muscle.

anterior surface of the cornea. They have, like the scleral canals, numerous ampulla-like enlargements (lacunæ), in which are contained the large, flat, many-branched connective-tissue cells of the cornea (corneal corpuscles). At the corneo-scleral margin this system of canals goes directly over into the similar system of canals in the sclerotic.

Near the outer (anterior) surface the layers of the cornea become more compact, and finally coalesce to form a layer, which by its lack of cellular elements appears like a distinct hyaline, elastic membrane. This is called *Bowman's layer*. At its posterior surface the cornea is lined by a thin vitreous membrane called *Descemet's* membrane. This is an elastic membrane, and rolls upon itself, when divided or separated from the corneal tissue.

Upon the anterior surface of *Bowman's* layer lies the corneal epithelium. *Descemet's* membrane is also lined by a single layer of endothelial cells on its posterior surface.

At the corneo-scleral margin (See figure 3), where the ocular conjunctiva ends, its epithelium goes directly over into the epithelium of the cornea, and *Bowman's* layer, together with the nearest corneal lamellæ, is split into fibrillæ and becomes merged in the subconjunctival tissue. *Descemet's* membrane, with the adjoining layers of the cornea, is similarly split into fibrillæ at the periphery of the cornea, and is lost partially in the tendon of the ciliary muscle and partially in the iris. On their way these fibres form what is called the *ligamentum pectinatum* of the iris. Between the fibres of this so-called ligament lie a large number of cavities, which are called *Fontana's* cavities. These cavities communicate toward the outer surface with the canalicular system of the cornea and sclerotic, and with *Schlemm's* canal, a larger lymph-canal embedded in the corneo-scleral tissue; on the other side they open into the anterior chamber.

The corneal tissue contains blood-vessels only at its periphery, where a system of loops of capillaries reaches into it for the distance of about one millimeter. The arterial vessels which take part in the formation of these loops come from the anterior ciliary arteries, and anastomose with the blood-vessels of the conjunctiva. The blood is carried away from these loops by small veins which empty it into the episcleral and so into the anterior ciliary veins.

The cornea at its periphery is, furthermore, supplied by about fifty larger nervous branches which come from the conjunctival and anterior ciliary nerves. They enter near the posterior surface of the cornea and lie in a special system of canals. Soon after having entered the corneal tissue, the nerve-fibres lose their double contour, and the main stems give off branches which soon form a network, called the deep stroma-plexus. From this plexus smaller branches rise toward the surface of the cornea, split into axis-cylinders and axis-fibrillæ, and after having formed another network under Bowman's layer, called the superficial stroma-plexus, they pierce this layer nearly at a right angle, and form a third network between the epithelial cells (the intra-epithelial plexus), and are there lost. (See Fig. 4).

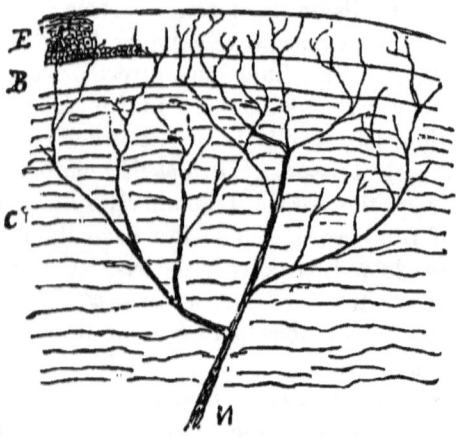

FIG. 4. Shows the manner in which a larger corneal nerve branches off, and is finally lost within the epithelial layer of the cornea. E. Epithelium. B. Bowman's layer. C. cornea. N. Nerve.

Next to the inner surface of the sclerotic lies the *uveal tract*, the vascular membrane of the eye-ball. Although the uveal tract consists, in the main, of the same tissue from one end to the other, it is divided into three distinct parts, the *choroid*, the *ciliary body* and the *iris*.

The uveal tract firmly adheres to the sclerotic around the optic nerve entrance and at the cornea-scleral margin. Between these two attachments it is slightly separated from the sclerotic by the supra-choroidal space. This space is traversed by innumerable fibres going from the uveal tract into the sclerotic and vice versa, which thus form a delicate, spongy tissue containing a great many endothelial cells. When the choroid is forcibly detached from the sclerotic these fibres are torn, and the part of them which then adheres to the sclerotic has been called the lamina fusca, while the part adhering to the choroid, is known as the lamina supra-choroidea. In this spongy tissue the ciliary nerves run forward to the ciliary body, after having pierced the sclerotic near the entrance of the optic nerve.

The *choroid* proper consists of a loose network of connective-tissue fibres, which contains a large number of stellated pigmented and unpigmented cells. The pigmented cells are more numerous in the outer two-thirds of the choroid, their pigment varying considerable in tint in different eyes. In albinos it is slightly yellowish; in negroes deep brown, or even black, and all intermediate shades may be seen in different eyes, corresponding in a general way with the pigmentation of the skin and hair of the individual.

In this loose network of connective tissue lie embedded the innumerable blood-vessels of the choroid. The veins which collect the blood and empty it into four or six larger trunks, the venæ vorticosæ, lie in the outer two-thirds of the choroid. The inner third contains the capillaries (*chorio-capillaris*).

The choroid contains, moreover, a large number of nerves and ganglionic cells, and some organic muscular fibres. On its inner surface it is lined by a thin elastic hyaline membrane called the lamina vitrea of the choroid. Upon the inner side of this hyaline membrane lies a single layer of large hexagonal cells, containing pigment-granules in the whole body of the cell. This is the pigmentary epithelium layer, which formerly was counted as a part of the choroid and later as a part of the retina. Its cells have brush-like offsets on their inner surface which enter between the outer segments of the rods of the retina. The retinal purple, a substance which gives the outer surface of the retina a purple tint during life, is exuded by this layer, which is therefore to be considered as a special glandular organ interposed between the choroid and retina.

Near the firm attachment of the uveal tract to the sclera, at the corneo-scleral margin, the former becomes somewhat abruptly thicker, and thus forms the ciliary body with the ciliary processes on its innner surface. This thickening of the uveal tract is especially caused by the presence of the ciliary muscles. The tendon of this muscle, by its insertion in the corneo-scleral tissue, forms the firm attachment between the uveal tract and the sclerotic. The fibres of this muscle, which are organic, spread fan-like backwards and a little inwards in the ciliary body and are finally lost in the choroid.

There are two distinct sets of muscular fibres, the one lying superficially and running in a longitudinal (meridional) direction,

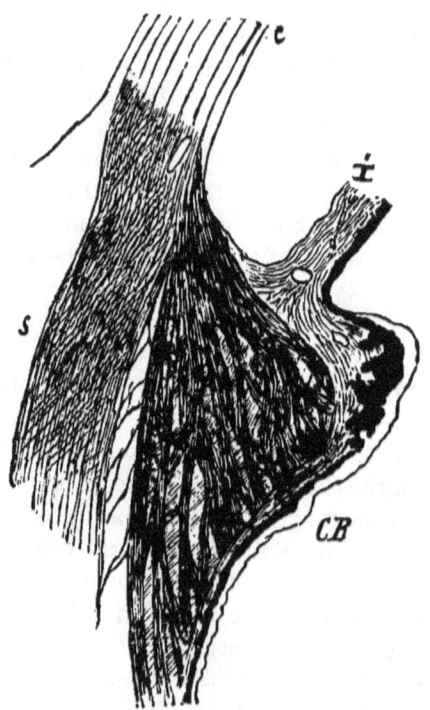

FIG. 5. Meridional section through the ciliary body of a very short-sighted (elongated) eye-ball. The fibres of the ciliary muscle run almost exclusively in a meridional (longitudunal) direction. C. Cornea. S. Sclerotic. I. Iris. CB. Ciliary body.

the other lying more deeply and running in a circular direction. The former kind prevails in elongated (short-sighted) eyes, while the latter kind predominates in short (far-sighted) eyes. (See Figs. 5 & 6).

The ciliary muscle lies embedded in the outer part of the ciliary body. Its inner surface is covered by the tissue proper of the uveal tract with its vitreous lamina. Upon the inner side of the latter lies the thick, dark uveal layer, the continuation of the pigmentary epithelium layer, and further on, on the inner side of this lies one layer of cylindrical cells, which gradually decrease in height toward the insertion of the iris. This layer is a continuation of the retinal tissue and is called the ciliary part of the retina (*pars ciliaris retinæ*).

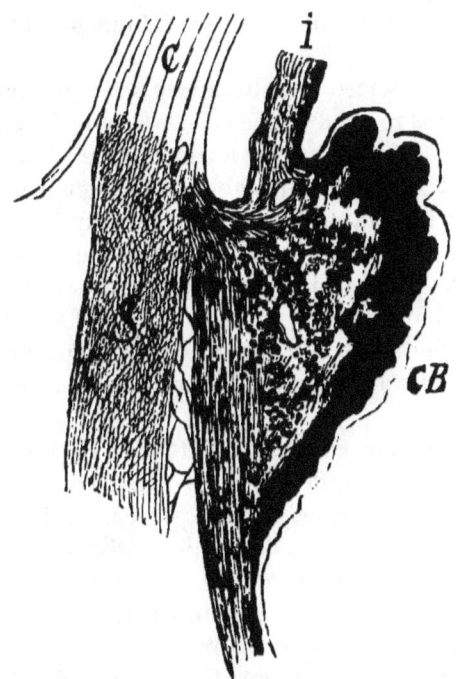

FIG. 6. Meridional section through the ciliary body of a very far-sighted (short) eyeball. The fibres of the ciliary muscle run to a very great extent in an equatorial (circular) direction and are, therefore, cut transversely. By comparing figs 5 and 6 it will be noticed that in the far-sighted eye the distance between the cornea and the origin of the iris is but small, while in the short-sighted eye this distance is much larger. The initials denote the same parts of the eye, as they do in fig. 5.

On the inner surface of the ciliary body, we can distinguish between its posterior smooth part, the pars non-plicata, and its anterior wrinkled part, the pars plicata. These folds and wrinkles are caused by small irregular offsets called the ciliary processes.

These latter, about seventy in number, project toward the axis of the eye-ball, and form a circle or wreath upon the inner surface of the globe behind the insertion of the iris.

The arterial blood-vessels of the ciliary body come from the anterior and the long posterior ciliary arteries; the veins carry the blood back partly into the conjunctival veins and partly into the venæ vorticosæ.

The ciliary nerves form a coarse network on the inner surface of the ciliary muscle and send small branches into it and to the iris.

The *iris* is inserted into the ciliary body just before the tendon of its muscle is merged in the corneo-scleral tissue, and the plane in which it lies forms nearly a right angle with the axis of the eye-ball. It forms an adjustable diaphragm across the eye-ball and is pierced by a central opening, the pupil.

The bulk of the tissue of the iris is the same as that of the ciliary body. Near its anterior and posterior surfaces, it becomes more dense, however, and consists largely of spindle-shaped cells. On its posterior surface it has the darkly pigmented, thick uveal layer and on its anterior surface a delicate layer of endothelial cells.

Near the pupillary margin and toward the posterior surface of the iris, we find embedded in the iris tissue a ring of organic muscular fibres, the *sphincter pupillæ*, which, by its contraction, reduces the size of the pupil. Some authors maintain, also, the existence of an antagonist muscle, which is said to lie along the posterior surface of the iris and to run in a radial direction; it is called the *dilator* muscle of the pupil.

The arteries of the iris come from a large circular blood-vessel, which lies near the insertion of the iris into the ciliary body, and is formed by the anastomosis of the ciliary arteries. This is called the large iris-circle. From this arterial ring branches run toward the pupil in a radial direction. After having formed another ring, the small iris-circle, and just before reaching the sphincter muscle of the pupil, they form a network of capillaries within the fibres of this muscle.

## ANATOMY OF THE EYE.

The veins of the iris run back to the ciliary body, and finally empty their blood into the venæ vorticosæ.

The arteries of the iris have a much thicker muscular coat than any other arterial blood-vessels of their calibre in the human body.

The nerves of the iris come from the ciliary nerves.

The *optic nerve* when it reaches the sclerotic is enclosed in three sheaths. The outer sheath is formed by the dura mater and closely applied to and lining this is the arachnoid sheath.

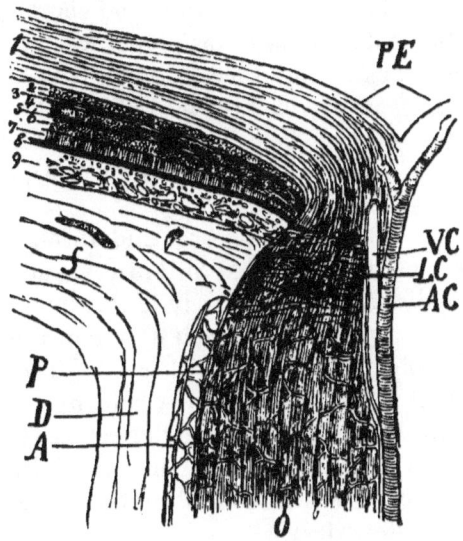

FIG. 7. Meridional section through the region of the entrance of the optic nerve into the eye-ball (after Schwalbe), showing one-half only. O. Optic nerve. AC. Central retinal artery. VC. Central retinal vein. LC. Lamina cribrosa. PE. Physiological excavation. 1. Nerve-fibre layer of the retina. 2. Ganglionic layer. 3. Inner molecular layer. 4. Inner granular layer. 5. Outer molecular layer. 6. Outer granular layer. 7. Rods and cones. 8. Pigmentary epithelium. 9. Choroid. S. Sclerotic. P. Pia mater. A. Arachnoid. D. Dura mater.

These two sheaths become merged in the sclerotic as soon as they reach its posterior surface, and do not enter the eye-ball. The third or inner sheath is a continuation of the pia mater of the brain. It encloses the nerve directly, and also forms the network of connective tissue in which the fibres of the optic nerve lie embedded. It enters the globe with the nerve, joins the inner layers of the sclerotic and ends in the lamina cribrosa, through which the bundles of nerve-fibres pass on into the eye-ball. (See Fig. 7).

Just before entering the lamina cribrosa the optic nerve becomes a little thinner, and its nerve-fibres lose their double contour. As soon as the nerve-fibres have reached the inner surface of the choroid, they bend nearly at a right angle with their former direction and expand to form the inner (nerve-fibre) layer of the retina.

After passing through the sclerotic and choroid (lamina cribrosa), and before entering the retina proper, the nerve-fibres form a slight, roundish elevation called the optic papilla or optic disc. Owing to the manner in which the nerve-fibres thus enter the eye and immediately change their direction, the normal optic papilla shows a more or less centrally located, funnel-shaped depression, the so-called physiological excavation.

In the center of the optic nerve, and through this funnel-shaped depression, the central retinal artery and vein enter the eye-ball, to be distributed exclusively to this tissue.

The *retina* is separated from the inner surface of the choroid by the pigmentary epithelial layer. The retina proper reaches forwards to the ciliary body, where it ends with a scolloped edge, called the *ora serrata* of the retina. A thin membrane continuous with the retina, and morphologically a part of it extends further forward, and forms the retinal layer of the ciliary body, as already described.

The retina is the light-perceiving organ, and has a very complicated structure. If we do not count the pigmentary epithelial layer, it consists of nine distinct layers. (See figure 8)

The most external layer is that of the rods and cones, then follows the (doubtful) external limiting membrane. The third layer is the outer granular layer, then comes the outer molecular layer. Then follow the inner granular and inner molecular layers. The seventh and eighth are the ganglionic and the nerve-fibre layers, and these are separated from the vitreous body by the ninth and last layer, the inner limiting membrane.

While the last three layers are called the brain-layers of the retina, the other six are designated as its neuro-epithelial layers.

All the elements of which the retina consists, are held together and in position by supporting connective-tissue fibres, called *Mueller's* fibres.

While a direct connection between the optic nerve-fibres and cones within the retina has been anatomically demonstrated, the existence of such a connection between nerve-fibres and rods has so far not been shown. The retinal purple gives its tint only to the rods; the cones are untinted.

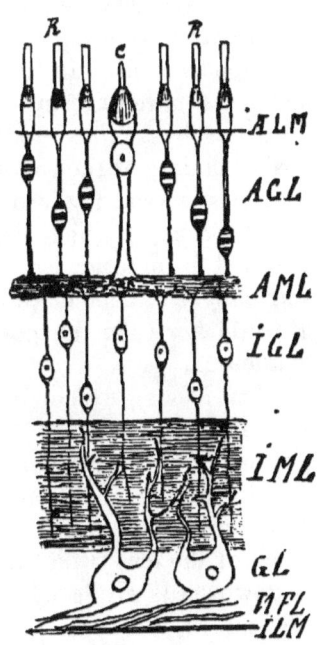

FIG. 8. Diagram showing the different layers of the retina (after Schwalbe). ILM. Inner limiting membrane. NFL. Nerve fibre layer. GL. Glangionic cell layer. IML. Inner molecular layer. IGL. Inner granular layer. AML. Outer molecular layer. AGL. Outer granular layer. ALM. Outer limiting membrane. R. Rods. C. Cone.

To the outer side of the optic papilla and slightly below its horizontal diameter lies the yellow spot (*macula lutea*), the point of acute vision. It has a small depression, the *fovea centralis*, excentrically situated. The retinal tissue at the periphery of the yellow spot is somewhat thickened, while in the fovea centralis it is exceedingly thin. Moreover, in the yellow spot the cones are thinner and longer, and consequently more numerous than in any other part of the retina, and the rods are almost altogether wanting. The proportion between the rods and cones grows in favor of the former from the macula lutea to the ora serrata. These two facts seem to prove that, for distinct vision, the cones are of much greater importance than the rods.

The blood-vessels of the retina, branches of the central retinal artery and vein, lie chiefly in the nerve-fibre and ganglionic layers, but sometimes they reach even into the inner molecular layer. The outer layers have no blood-vessels. In the periphery of the retina the arteries and veins unite to form terminal loops.

Behind the iris lies the *crystalline lens*, a transparent lentil-shaped body. It consists mainly of the so-called lens-fibres, and is inclosed in a hyaline, elastic sack, the lens-capsule.

That part of the lens-capsule which lies anteriorly to the equator of the lens is called the anterior lens-capsule. It has on its inner surface a single layer of cuboid epithelial cells, the capsular epithelium. It is thicker than the posterior lens-capsule, which is devoid of epithelium.

The lens-fibres (or. lens-bands), which form the main part of its structure, are also epithelial elements. Where their ends join each other beneath the lens-capsule, they form sutures, which are seen to run in a radial direction from the anterior and posterior poles of the lens, forming angles with each other of about $120°$. On the anterior surface of the lens two of these sutures run upwards while one runs downwards, while on the posterior surface the conditions are reversed.

The crystalline lens is suspended from the ciliary body by the zonule of *Zinn*, or suspensory ligament. This consists of tough, transparent fibres, which come from the vitreous body. While on their way forwards they are bound down to the ciliary body and follow all the depressions and elevations of the ciliary processes until they reach the inner anterior angle of the ciliary body. From here they bend abruptly inwards and, partially crossing each other, are inserted on the anterior and posterior lens-capsules, a short distance from the equator.

In the normal eye-ball the pupillary margin of the iris rests, and, when moving, slides upon the anterior lens-capsule.

The space between the posterior surface of the cornea, the anterior surface of the iris, and the central portion of the anterior lens-capsule, is called the *anterior chamber*. It contains a clear, watery fluid, without organized elements, the *aqueous humor*.

The space bound by the peripheral part of the anterior lens-capsule, the zonule of *Zinn*, the anterior surface of the ciliary body, its tendon, and the posterior surface of the iris is called the *posterior chamber*. It also contains aqueous humor.

The whole space backwards from the lens and zonule of *Zinn* is filled with a transparent gelatinous substance, the *vitreous body*. This has on its anterior surface a depression, the fossa patellaris, in which the lens lies. In the region of the optic disk a small fissure can be traced in the vitreous body from behind forward towards the patellary fossa, called *Stillings'* canal; the hyaline artery lies in this fissure during embryonic life. The vitreous body, especially in its peripheral parts, contains a moderate number of cells.

We have stated above that the sheaths of the optic nerve are direct continuations of the meninges of the brain. The inter-vaginal spaces of the optic nerve are in fact in direct communication with the intra-meningeal spaces in the cranium, and can be injected from them.

The course of the fluids within the eye-ball is at present thought to be from behind forwards through the vitreous body, the zonule of *Zinn*, and the posterior chamber into the anterior chamber; and the exit of these fluids is thought to take place through *Fontana's* cavities into *Schlemm's* canal and the lymphatics of the sclerotic and conjunctiva.

There are direct communications between the supra-choroidal space and Tenon's space where the venæ vorticosæ and the ciliary arteries and nerves pierce the sclerotic, and fluids may escape by these channels from the eye-ball into Tenon's space. (See figure 9).

The *external muscles* of the eye-ball are six in number. Five of these, the four recti muscles and the superior oblique muscle, together with the levator muscle of the upper eye-lid, take their origin from the apex of the orbit around the canalis opticus. The inferior oblique muscle comes from the inner margin of the lachrymal canal.

The *lachrymal apparatus* consists of the lachrymal gland, the puncta lachrymalia, the canaliculi lachrymales, the lachrymal sack, and the nasal duct.

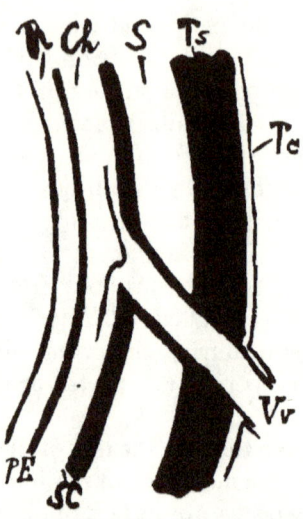

FIG. 9. Shows the communication between the supra-choroidal space within the eyeball and Tenon's space outside of it (after Schwalbe). R. Retina. Ch. Choroid. S. Sclerotic, SC. Supra-choroidal space. Vv. Vorticous vein. Ts. Tenon's space. Tc. Tenon's capsule. PE. Pigmentary epithelium.

The puncta lachrymalia, as stated above, lie near the inner angle of the palpebral fissure at the apex of the lachrymal papillæ, and are the external orifices of the lachrymal canaliculi. The latter, after having run into the lid for a little distance at a right angle to the lid margin, turn abruptly towards the nose and converge towards the lachrymal sack. Just before reaching the latter they unite into one short canal. The lachrymal sack forms an oblong receptacle for the tears lying behind the ligamentum palpebrale internum. Its upper portion (cupola) lies higher than the entrance of the canaliculi. (See figure 10). The lachrymal sack is about twelve millimeters long, and ends below in the nasal lachrymal duct. The latter opens upon the mucus membrane of the inferior nasal meatus, just under the insertion of the inferior turbinated bone.

The lachrymal sack is surrounded by bone at its posterior surface only, the nasal duct is enclosed in bone.

The lachrymal gland, which secretes the tears, is divided into

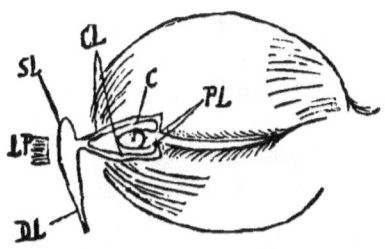

FIG. 10. Shows the lachrymal drainage apparatus. PL. Lachrymal puncta. C. Lachrymal caruncle. CL. Lachrymal canaliculi. SL. Lachrymal (nasal) duct. LP. Palpebral ligament.

two portions, an upper, larger, and a lower, very much smaller one. The upper portion enclosed in its tough capsule, lies in the lachrymal fossa of the frontal bone, just behind the upper outer margin of the orbit. The lower portion, which consists only of a few loosely connected acini, rests upon the fornix of the conjunctiva, just below the upper one. Small ducts lead the tear-fluid from these glands into the conjunctival sack, whence it flows into the nose through the lachrymal puncta, and the remainder of the drainage part of the lachrymal apparatus. Around the base of the lachrymal papillæ lies a minute muscle—*Horner's muscle*—whose function it is to assist in sucking up the tear-fluid.

# CHAPTER II.

### EXAMINATION OF THE EYE.

EYE-LIDS. — CONJUNCTIVA. — CORNEA. — IRIS. — CRYSTALLINE LENS. — FOCAL ILLUMINATION. — ACUTENESS OF VISION. — VISUAL FIELD. — COLOR-SENSE. — INTRA-OCULAR TENSION. — ACCOMMODATION. — REFRACTION. — OPHTHALMOSCOPE. — MOTILITY. — DIPLOPIA. — INSUFFICIENCY OF THE INTERNAL RECTI MUSCLES.

For all examinations of the eye good light is absolutely required. In day-time it is therefore best to put the patient near a window and opposite to it, avoiding, however, bright sunlight. After the patient has been properly seated, a systematical examination should begin with the inspection of the cutaneous surface of the *eye-lids*. Then the eye-lashes and their position, the orifices of the *Meibomian* glands, the motility of the eye-lids and the size of the palpebral fissure should be carefully noted. To get a good view of the outer and inner canthus, the puncta lachrymalia and the caruncula lachrymalis, it is best to slightly raise the upper eye-lid with the forefinger, while the thumb of the same hand gently pulls down the lower lid. This little manipulation, which has to be used very frequently in examining eyes, should be executed without exerting the slightest pressure on the eye-ball. If it is impossible to make a perfect inspection with the aid of this manipulation, it will be best to draw the upper eye-lid upward with the thumb of one hand and the lower eye-lid downward with the thumb of the other hand. If the skin of the lower eye-lid is too slippery for this manœuvre, a towel or piece of linen cloth wound around the thumb will be of great assistance. In thus separating the eye-lids all pressure upon the eye-ball must be carefully avoided. This is most surely accomplished by laying the thumbs on the skin of the eye-lids near the orbital margins and drawing them apart by dragging on the skin only.

If there is any complaint about *stillicidium lacrymarum* (teardropping, lachrymation), the first point to be examined into, is, whether the puncta lachrymalia lie in contact with the ocular conjunctiva at the caruncle. Then, making pressure on the lachrymal sack, while the puncta lachrymalia are closely watched, the escape of fluid into the conjunctival sack will give us an indication of any obstruction to the proper drainage of the tears into the nostril.

If there is an escape of fluid from either punctum, its character, whether watery, mucous or purulent, will be of importance with regard to the diagnosis of an inflammatory process in the lachrymal sack. The further exploration of the lachrymal sack and duct by means of probes will be detailed in Chapter IV.

To inspect the *ocular conjunctiva* we draw the lids apart in the manner just described, and notice whether it appears hyperæmic. If it appears hyperæmic, we should make sure whether this hyperæmia is confined to the conjunctival blood-vessels, or whether it involves also the ciliary blood-vessels in the sclerotic near the cornea-scleral margin. This is best done by sliding the conjunctiva slightly upon the sclerotic by means of the eye-lids. A hyperæmia confined to the moveable tissues concerns the conjunctival blood-vessels only. These vessels are, moreover, comparatively large and convoluted, and are easily distinguishable as separate vessels, whereas the deeper-lying ciliary vessels are much finer and appear rather as a ring of diffuse redness, densest next to the cornea and shading off into the sclerotic.

If the symptoms complained of refer to the conjunctiva of the eye-lids, or if a foreign body has entered the conjunctival sack, we must next inspect the *inner surface of the eye-lids*. The conjunctival surface of the lower eye-lid and the lower fornix of the conjunctiva are easily exposed to view by directing the patient to look upward and drawing the skin of the lower eye-lid downward toward the cheek with the thumb. In deeply set eyes, the lower fornix is most perfectly exposed by drawing the lower lid downwards, while the patient also looks downwards (*Arlt.*) The exploration of the conjunctival surface of the upper eye-lid and the upper fornix of the conjunctiva requires more skill, and is accomplished in the following way: Place the thumb of the right hand (when examining the patient's left eye) against the brow above the outer angle of the palpebral fissure, then take hold of the cilia with the thumb and forefinger of the left hand and direct the patient to look downwards. Next draw the eye-lid, thus held by the cilia, gently downwards and forewards, at the same time shifting the thumb of the right hand into the depression, which appears between the eye-brow and the tarsus, and lastly turn the lid-margin upwards, using the right thumb to keep the upper edge of the tarsus in position, while the whole tarsus is being turned around its upper edge as a fixed center. Instead of the thumb a smaller round object (such as a probe, a pencil, or a match) may be used to fix the upper edge of the tarsus. Examining the patient's right eye, the hands should be reversed. When the eye-lids are very forcibly shut and the patient is unable to assist in looking down, or when the conjunctival sack is considerably shrunken, it may be very difficult to bring the conjunctival surface of the upper lids to view. When the eyelashes are absent, it is often sufficient to direct the patient to look strongly downward, to lay the end of a probe along the upper edge of the tarsus so as to press it gently downwards and backwards, and to draw the lid margin upwards by means of the ball of the thumb applied to the dry skin of the eye-lid near its free margin (*Desmarres*).

In young children the inspection of the lids, as well as of the eye-ball, is best effected by taking the child's head in the lap, or, if necessary, between the knees, while its legs rest on the lap of another person. Sometimes an anaesthetic may be necessary.

When the lids and conjunctiva have thus been explored, we next inspect the *cornea*. A healthy *cornea* is perfectly transparent and polished, reflecting the light like a mirror. These two peculiarities allow us to distinguish all affections of this membrane easily.

If there is any form of inflammation, or an abrasion, a scar, or a foreign body present, the tissue of the cornea will be seen more or less affected, either in its transparency, or in the perfection or polish of its surface. Any considerable changes in the curvature of the surface of the cornea will be easily detected by putting the patient in such a position that we can see the reflected image of a window or a flame on his cornea. By then directing the patient to move his eye, say in a horizontal direction, so as to allow the reflected image to move, so to speak, over the cornea, it will become distorted as soon as it reaches the part in which the curvature is altered. The sensibility of the cornea is examined by touching it with a camel's hair brush or a small roll of tissue paper.

After examining the cornea, we inspect the contents of the anterior chamber, the *aqueous humor*, which, in the normal condition, is also perfectly transparent. Any lack of transparency in this fluid, is due to an affection of the deeper portions of the eye-ball.

In examining the *iris*, we have first to pay attention to any anatomical changes in its tissue, and then to its function as a moveable diaphragm. The pupil ought to expand promptly on shading the eye and to contract on exposing the eye again to the light.

If the iris is inflamed, there is hyperæmia of both the conjunctival and ciliary blood-vessels. The latter show as a pink or bluish-red zone around the corneo-scleral margin and are not moveable with the conjunctiva. The tissue of the iris appears swollen and loses its lustre. The color of the iris is also changed, in blue eyes taking on a greenish shade, in dark eyes a dirty brown. After iritis has become established, the pupil is nearly or wholly immoveable.

The function of the iris may also be disturbed when there are no inflammatory symptoms present. In order to test this, we cover the healthy eye so as to exclude all light from it, and then, alternately shading the other eye with the hand and exposing it to light again, we watch the size of the pupil. While this examination goes on, the patient must keep his eye-lids well apart and look steadily in the same direction. If the pupil remains unchanged, under the influence of alternate light and shade, we must see whether it contracts, perhaps, during the effort to accommodate for a near object.

We should, furthermore, see whether the iris trembles when the eye-ball is moved. The size and shape of the pupil, when at rest, are also to be noted.

The position of the plane of the iris is also of importance. We must see, whether its periphery is bulged forwards or drawn backwards, or whether any particular part of it is protruding, etc.

If the pupil is immoveable, or acts imperfectly, it is best to test its dilatability by the instillation of a mydriatic. The simplest one for a mere examination is a one per cent. solution of homatropinum hydrobromatum, as its action disappears very readily (in from 8 to 12 hours). If a stronger mydratic is needed, as is generally the case in inflammation of the iris, a one per cent. solution of atropinum sulfuricum is sufficient.

An inflammatory process of the *ciliary body* is recognized by a deep blueish-red zone of injection around the corneo-scleral margin, and by pain on pressure upon the ciliary region. The latter symptom is easily ascertained, by pressing slightly upon the ciliary region through the closed eye-lids with a pencil or any rounded small object, or even with the finger. (Tenderness of the ciliary region on pressure may also be present in iritis).

Inspecting the *crystalline lens*, we have chiefly to notice its transparency. If the lens is wanting, or is dislocated from the patellary fossa, the iris will tremble (*iridodonesis*), except, when the whole lens lies in the anterior chamber, a condition which presents otherwise characteristic appearances. See chapter xv.

If the lens is transparent enough, we may also be able to see changes in the anterior portion of the vitreous body through it.

For the examination of the anterior third of the eye-ball, we make use of the so-called *focal* or *oblique illumination*, which enables us to detect, for instance, slight changes in the cornea, which, in the diffuse illumination, may escape our notice altogether. The patient is seated opposite the examiner and a lamp is placed at the side and somewhat in front of the eye under examination, a convex lens of two and a half or three inches focus is used to throw a pencil of light obliquely upon the cornea. By moving this lens nearer to or farther from the eye the focus may be thrown upon deeper or more superficial parts. It is sometimes a decided help in making a diagnosis to view the illuminated parts with a magnifying lens held in the other hand.

# EXAMINATION OF THE EYE.

Tumors, abscesses, etc., within the *orbit* may be detected by the protrusion and displacement of the eye-ball and can be located by palpation.

Thus far, we have treated of the visible changes occurring in affections of the anterior part of the eye-ball only. Eye affections, not accompanied by changes, visible to the naked eye, call for the testing of vision subjectively.

The *acuteness of vision* is tested by means of test-types, and when it is very much reduced, by the outstretched fingers of one hand. The test-types in use are constructed in such a manner that their limbs are seen by the normal eye under a visual angle of one minute, while the whole letter is seen under an angle of five minutes. Of these letters one set is used for distant vision and contains letters to be seen by the normal eye distinctly at from 200 to 20 feet distance. The other set is constructed for near vision. The acuteness of vision is expressed in the form of a fraction, the denominator of which gives the distance at which the letters ought to be recognized, while the numerator gives the distance in which they are actually seen. The normal eye, must see the letters called XX, in our set of test-types, at 20 feet, and this is noted in the following way, V, visus $= \frac{20}{xx}$. (If the patient sees the letters, which a normal eye recognizes at 100 feet, at 20 feet only, we write $V = \frac{20}{c}$, and his visual acuteness is said to be only $\frac{1}{5}$ of that of a normal eye. In making such examinations the test-types must be well lighted and the patient must sit or stand with his back to the light.

When no letters can be distinguished, we may examine the acuteness of vision by means of the outstretched fingers. In doing so, we should be careful to hold the fingers against a dark back-ground.

The whole region within which an eye, when perfectly at rest, can perceive objects, is called its *visual field*. This can be projected on a plane surface and thus accurately mapped. A simpler method is, to let the patient cover one eye and to direct him to gaze steadily, with the other one, into the observer's opposite eye. Then move the fingers, or a small staff, with a white tip from different directions towards the line connecting his eye with that of the observer, keeping always at an equal distance from both, and notice when he first recognizes it. If your own eye is normal and gazes steadily into the patient's eye during this procedure, the extent of your own visual field will allow you to notice at once any defect in his.

If the patient's sight is so poor, that he can no longer recognize the fingers, or other small objects, as in a case of cataract, the visual field is best examined with a candle-flame in a dark room. This is done exactly in the same way, directing the patient to look straight ahead and not to change the position of his eye. Care should be taken to shade the patient's eye whenever the direction of the candle is changed.

These two methods will suffice for ordinary purposes. Sometimes we have to examine a patient in regard to his *perception of colors*. A great many methods for this purpose have of late come into use since the subject of color-blindness has received especial attention in connection with the marine and railroad service of almost all civilized countries. Holmgren's method, in which skeins of variously colored wool are employed, is the most convenient. The patient is first shown a light green skein and asked to match it with similar tints. If he is color-blind, he will make strange mistakes, selecting gray-green, brown, yellowish, pink and grayish red, etc. For further details, see chapter XXIV.

The *intra-ocular tension* is best examined by directing the patient to look down, and then gently laying the tips of both index fingers upon the upper lid, and alternately pressing them upon the globe, as we are accustomed to do in searching for fluctuation. We determine in a general way, whether an eye is harder or softer than normal, by comparing it with its fellow. When both eyes are affected, the tension should be compared with that of the healthy eyes of another person.

The *accommodative power* of an eye is examined by directing the patient to look at a small object (finest test-types) and moving it so close to the eye that he can but just recognize it. If the accommodation is defective this near-point (*punctum proximum*), will be farther from the eye than it should be, taking into account the age of the patient. (See chapter XX).

This examination will at the same time give us a hint with

EXAMINATION OF THE EYE. 27

regard to the state of *refraction* of the examined eye. If it can read finest print for a prolonged period and at a smaller distance from the eye than the age of the patient would warrant, the eye is short-sighted. If it is unable to read smallest print at all or for any length of time, it is probably far-sighted or astigmatic.

In order to see any changes in the conditions of the posterior portions of the vitreous body, the optic nerve, the retina and the choroid, we have to make use of the *ophthalmoscope*.

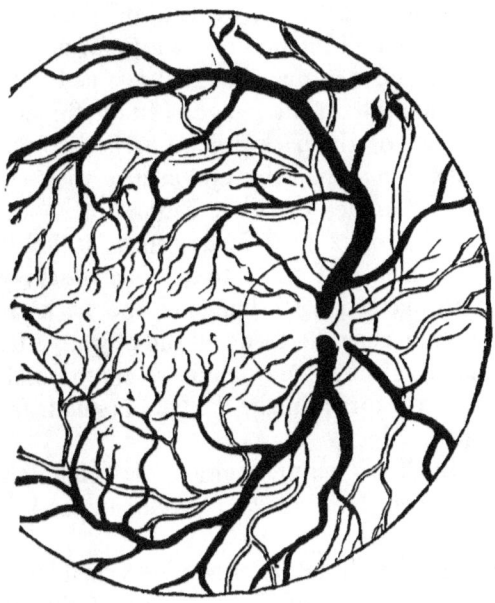

FIG. 11. The ophthalmoscopic appearance of the back-ground of a normal eye showing the optic papilla and the retinal blood-vessels. The veinous vessels are dark.—

Light thrown into an eye will not only be perceived there, but it is also reflected. The reflected rays return to the source of light by the same way by which they have entered the eye.

When the pupil of an examined eye is very large the observer's unaided eye is sometimes able to catch such rays returning to their source, and then he sees the usually black pupil appearing shining red. In this way, of course, no details of the back-ground of the eye are to be distinguished. To make this possible it is necessary to bring the observer's eye into the axis of the returning pencil. This is done by throwing light into the eye by means of a mirror, perforated by an opening, through which the observer looks. Armed with such a mirror, with suitable correcting glasses behind the central opening, the observer's eye is enabled to view all the details of the back-ground of the examined eye. (See figure 11).

In examining eyes with the ophthalmoscope, we make use of two different methods, called the direct, and the indirect method.

In the direct method the observer's eye, armed with the mirror, is brought as near to the examined eye as is possible, without excluding the light. The image seen by this method is the virtual erect image of the back-ground of the examined eye.

In the indirect method, the eye armed with the mirror, is moved from the examined eye to a distance of 1½ or 2 feet, and a convex lens of from 2 to 3 inches focus is held before and within about 2 inches of the latter. The observer's eye now catches the real inverted aerial image of the back-ground of the examined eye at or near the focus of the objective lens.

In the indirect image the details seen are smaller, but the field is larger, in the direct image the field is small, but the details are much larger.

In both methods we may use either artificial light or diffuse daylight. The former is more convenient, and is generally employed.

By means of the ophthalmoscope we are enabled to scan very closely the largest part of the back-ground of the eye and detect anything abnormal. The ophthalmoscope may further be used to examine the transparency of the anterior parts of the eye and for the determination of errors of refraction.

We should further examine into the *motility* of the eyes, especially noticing whether the movements of one or both eyes are restricted or excessive in any direction. This mode of examination is mostly called for in cases of strabismus and in paralysis of one or more of the external muscles.

Direct the patient to fix his gaze upon your forefinger, and while moving it toward and from his nose in the middle line, observe whether his binocular fixation is preserved within the whole range of his accommodation. Next cover one eye and let him look straight at your finger with the other, then quickly removing the cover from the first eye, note whether it makes any movement to come back to the point of fixation. Then direct him to follow your finger in different directions with both eyes and pay particular attention to the excursion of each eye.

If one or more muscles of one eye (or both) refuse to act or act to an undue degree *double vision* (*diplopia*) must result, as binocular vision is no longer possible. The patient will see a true image with the healthy eye and a false one with the diseased eye.

The examination for double images is best made with a candle flame. This is moved before the patient's eyes at a distance of six or eight feet in all directions, and the patient is directed to say when he sees double. In order to enable him the better to distinguish the second image, one eye, usually the healthy one, is armed with a colored glass.

Particular attention has sometimes to be paid to the action of the *internal recti* muscles during convergence, as in some people these muscles refuse continued work. Moving the forefinger towards the patient's nose, while his gaze is fixed on it, will often enable us to detect such a weakness, one eye presently diverging. To make sure of such an observation, it is then best to let the patient look at a small object at reading distance, while a weak prism with base up or downwards is held before the suspected eye. If the false image thus produced does not stand directly above or below the real one, but stands also to one side, an insufficient action of one or both recti interni is shown. The prism, by means of which, with its base inward, we can bring the two images into the same vertical line, gives us the degree of insufficiency.

# CHAPTER III.

### DISEASES OF THE EYE-LIDS.

BLEPHARITIS CILIARIS.—PHTHIRIASIS.— HORDEOLUM. — CHALAZION. — ABSCESS.— SYPHILITIC ULCER.— WARTS.—XANTHELASMA.—SARCOMA.— EPITHELIOMA.—TELEANGIECTATIC AND ANGIOMATOUS TUMORS. —TRICHIASIS. —ENTROPIUM. — ECTROPIUM. — PTOSIS. — BLEPHAROSPASMUS.— LAGOPHTALMUS.— BLEPHAROPHIMOSIS. —WOUNDS.— EMPHYSEMA.— BURNS.

The most frequent affection of the lid-margin is *blepharitis ciliaris* or *blepharadenitis*.

The prominent symptoms of this affection are scales or larger crusts along the lid-margin, at the roots of the eye-lashes ; also redness and swelling, which latter are usually also confined to the lid-margin.

When the disease progresses, the original small scales are replaced by larger crusts, in which the eye-lashes are often totally embedded. The swelling increases sometimes to such an extent that the lid-margin is turned outward from the eye, thus giving rise to an ectropium, especially of the lower eye-lids. Such an inflammation cannot exist for a long period without affecting the eye-lashes also. They fall out, their bulbs become atrophied, and when the inflammation has finally passed away, the eye-lids remain more or less destitute of eye-lashes (*madarosis*). Blepharitis ciliaris is mostly, in its severer or chronic forms, always combined with some degree of catarrhal conjunctivitis.

From the beginning the disease causes a disagreeable feeling of heat, irritation and weakness, when the eyes are used for small objects. In the morning the eye-lashes are glued together by the dried secretion.

The affection is chiefly one of childhood, although it is observed in adults also. Children of a strumous habit and of a fair complexion are perhaps oftenest subject to it.

Blepharitis ciliaris does not, as a rule, yield easily to treatment, and in its worst forms a restitutio ad integrum is almost impossible. Where a strumous habit exists, internal treatment should be combined with the local one.

The treatment, which yields the best results in mild cases of blepharitis, is the following : Bathe the eye-lids with luke-warm water until the scabs are well soaked. They can then readily be removed by rubbing along the lid-margin back and forth with a dry, rough towel. If luke-warm water does not seem to soak them sufficiently, the application of fresh lard or vaseline will do so. When all the scabs have been carefully removed, apply a small quantity of an ointment, containing from 2 to 4 grains of yellow or red oxide of mercury to 3 or 4 drachms of vaseline. This is to be rubbed into the eye-lashes while the eye-lids are kept closed. After having allowed it to remain there for about ten minutes, the surplus ought to be gently wiped off. This application must not be made just before the patient retires, but several hours earlier. If any of the ointment gets accidentally into the conjunctival sack it may cause considerable smarting, but it will do no harm. If the catarrhal conjunctivitis is at all pronounced, it should also be treated. (See Chapter VII).

In severer cases where large crusts glue the eye-lashes together and cover an ulcerated lid-margin, it is best to soften the crusts with fresh lard or vaseline. We are often obliged to remove such crusts with the forceps. This should be done very carefully and gently. When we have succeeded in thoroughly removing the crusts, the ointment of oxide of mercury may be applied. It will, however, but rarely suffice in these forms of blepharitis, and we are often compelled to resort to a caustic treatment. The application of a 2 or 3 per cent. solution of nitrate of silver with a camel's hair brush, while carefully shielding the eye-ball, is highly to be recommended. In some cases the solid nitrate of silver stick must be used. In other cases tar or oleum rusci, either pure or mixed with vaseline, is very useful.

Such applications should not be discontinued at once, when the ulceration is healed, but be continued for a longer period, until all swelling and irritability of the tissue of the lid-margin have disappeared.

This treatment, which, to ensure perfect success is, at least in the severe cases, best applied by the surgeon himself, may be greatly assisted by the patient. He ought to bathe his closed eye-lids frequently with cold water, or apply cold compresses to them. He must refrain from using his eyes for all occupations, which are likely to irritate them, especially by artificial light. Children should be kept from school. Adults should not smoke in a close room or stay in rooms where others are smoking. Fresh air is not injurious. If blepharitis ciliaris is observed in a patient, whose eyes are ametropic (show an error of refraction), and especially, if they are hypermetropic or astigmatic, the correction of the ametropia by glasses may have a beneficial influence on the result of the treatment. Myotic agents, the best of which is a solution of muriate of pilocarpine of $\frac{1}{2}$ per cent., may also sometimes be used with advantage. (*Green*).

*Phthiriasis*, an affection of the lid-margin which may simulate blepharitis ciliaris, is caused by the presence of crab-lice (pediculi pubis) upon the eye-lashes. The patient, who is usually unaware of their presence, feels a great irritation on the lid-margin, and by repeated scratching, often produces such a condition of the lid-margins as may easily be mistaken for blepharitis ciliaris. On closer inspection the eggs of the parasite are seen adhering to the eye-lashes, and the parasites, themselves may be recognized.

The treatment consists simply in the application of a mercurial ointment. Among them the common blue ointment is as good as any. About a quarter of an hour after this has been rubbed into the affected lid-margins, the parasites will have come out of the glandular orifices, into which they have burrowed their heads, and can then be easily removed with the forceps. The application may be repeated if necessary. The eggs ought to be seized singly between the teeth of the forceps and gently pulled along the eye-lashes, to which they are adherent. This is the easiest method of removing them, and much better than cutting off the eye-lashes. As soon as the irritating cause is removed, the inflammatory symptoms disappear.

The acute inflammation of the orifice of a *Meibomian* or tarsal gland, and later of the gland itself, is called *hordeolum*, commonly stye. It begins with a slight circumscribed redness and swelling at the lid-margin, which is often exceedingly painful. The swelling gradually increases and may lead to an œdematous swelling of the whole affected lid, so that it may appear like a very serious affair. Soon, however, the swelling comes to a head at the orifice of the gland, or perhaps on the conjunctival surface of the lid, and, if it breaks and the pus is discharged, the inflammatory symptoms will subside. This result will be hastened by hot fomentations.

The best way to treat a stye is to split the swelling in its beginning with a narrow knife or lancet in a direction at right angles to the lid-margin. The depletion and consequent decrease of tension in the affected part, and sometimes the removal of an actual obstruction, will cut short the inflammatory process and the patient's suffering.

A weakened constitution or strumous habit seems often to be a predisposing cause of this affection, and such patients sometimes suffer habitually from styes. Tonic treatment is therefore sometimes indicated.

A similar affection is caused by an obstruction, distention, and inflammation of the deeper (tarsal) parts of a *Meibomian* gland, and is called *chalazion* or tarsal tumor. The formation of such a cystic tumor is usually comparatively painless, and so long as it remains small it may cause no inconvenience.

These tarsal tumors sometimes disappear without surgical interference by absorption, and then leave no trace behind. In most cases, however, they remain stationary, or even grow steadily. When they have attained a considerable size, and especially when they lie in the upper eye-lid and near the lid-margin, they are not only disfiguring, but cause disagreeable symptoms, and become very annoying. They may even obstruct a part of the visual field.

These larger tarsal tumors are usually no longer cystic, the contents of the cyst having become organized, and forming a granulation tissue, which may nearly or quite fill the whole cyst cavity. In some cases the tumors are firm and of a fibrous or even enchondromatous character.

The best way to deal with the tarsal tumors is to enucleate them. This is done by means of a horizontal cut through the cutaneous surface of the eye-lid. Such a cut will leave no visible scar. Only a clean and perfect removal of the whole cyst-wall will afford security against a relapse.

Some surgeons prefer to remove tarsal tumors from the conjunctival surface of the eye-lid.

The smaller tumors, when of a soft consistency, may be opened from the conjunctival surface of the eye-lid by an incision at right angles to the lid-margin and parallel to the direction of the *Meibomian* glands.

*Phlegmonous abscesses* in the subcutaneous tissue of the lid are comparatively rare. They cause redness, heat and swelling, and fluctuation soon can be felt. As soon as the diagnosis is secured, a knife should be plunged into the swollen part in a horizontal direction, and the pus thus be evacuated.

*Syphilitic ulcers*, primary as well as from constitutional syphilis, have been observed on the eye-lids. They call for no other treatment than the manifestations of syphilis do in other organs.

*Warts and horny excrescences* on the lids are of ittle importance, and may be simply cut off with the scissors.

*Xanthelasma* is a yellowish or brown tumor of the skin. It usually lies near the inner margin of the orbit in the integument of the upper eye-lid. It appears often in symmetrical spots on both upper eye-lids and forms only a slight elevation. This growth is perfectly harmless, but if the patients, mostly females, desire its removal, a clip of the scissors will easily accomplish it.

*Sarcomatous* growths are but very rarely observed in the eye-lids as a primary affection, but *epitheliomata* quite frequently originate in this region. They appear most frequently on the lower eye-lid, near one of the angles, more frequently on the inner angle, of the palpebral fissure.

These malignant tumors often take their origin from a preexisting wart, or, if not, they resemble such a harmless growth, very much in their early stages. Gradually the wart becomes somewhat sore on the surface, and a little scab is formed which grows, and soon, when removed, reveals an ulcerated surface underneath. The tumor slowly spreads and eats away more and more of the lid-margin, and it soon produces an irregularly shaped, nodular hard swelling of the adjacent tissues. The eversion of the lid-margin caused by its presence, or perhaps the destruction of the lachrymal canaliculus, allows the tears to drop continually. This and the irritation from the partially unprotected state of the eye-ball, become more and more annoying. Sometimes a very distressing shooting pain accompanies the growth of the tumor.

In case it is not interfered with, the epithelioma may extend to the ocular conjunctiva, and thus an epitheliomatous symblepharon may be formed. In this way the newformation may even enter the interior of the eye-ball and spread there.

The growth of these tumors is slow, and a patient may suffer from them a very long time before they attain a fatal development.

The only treatment which promises a radical cure in sarcomatous or epitheliomatous tumors of the eye-lids is their early removal by excision. This operation must be done, of course, according to the general surgical rules for the removal of malignant tumors.

According to the size and situation of the newformation, its removal will cause a more or less important loss of substance of the affected eye-lid, which may have to be made good by means of a plastic operation. In most cases a part of the lid-margin and a piece of healthy eye-lid will be left after the removal of the tumor, and these should be carefully made use of.

In such cases I consider the method for repairing the loss of substance by sliding flaps (*Knapp*) (See figures 12 and 13), as generally the most satisfactory and least disfiguring operation. It consists in the following procedure: If the newformation involved, for instance, the inner two-thirds of the lower lid-margin and eye-lid, we shall have, after its removal, an extensive gap between the inner canthus and the remaining healthy part of the eye-lid. To fill this gap, we make an incision through the outer canthus in a horizontal direction towards the temple, allowing its end to run slightly upwards, and a similar incision from the outer lower angle of the loss of substance outwards towards the ear, allowing its end to run slightly downwards. The nearly rectangular flap thus formed contains at its nasal end the remaining healthy portion of the eye-lid. When this flap is carefully dissected from the underlying tissues, it is best to try whether, without dangerous stretching, it will cover the flap. This is usually not the case, and another small flap must be dissected from the

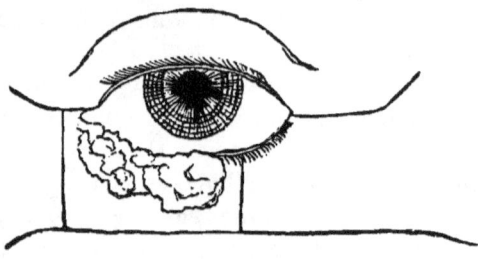

FIG. 12. A malignant tumor involving the inner two-thirds of the margin of the lower eye-lid. The diagram shows the incisions made in order to supply the gap resulting from the removal of this tumor in Knapp's method of operating by sliding flaps.

inner canthus, and from the side of the nose. These flaps are drawn over the gap and are carefully stitched together and to the skin below. Although this newly-formed eye-lid presents now a raw wound-surface towards the ocular conjunctiva, it gradually

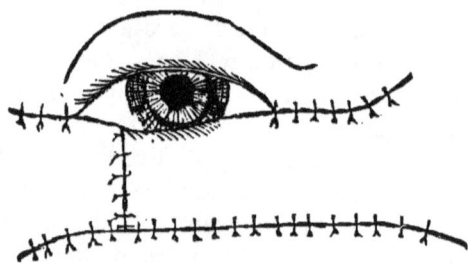

FIG. 13. Diagram showing how the flaps are united by sutures after this operation. The newly formed eye-lid consists near its nasal side of the former outer third of the eye-lid.

becomes lined during the healing process by an epithelial coat, derived from the part of the conjunctiva, which has been preserved, and soon its inner surface appears like that of the normal eye-lid. The disfigurement caused by the scars is trifling, when the wound-lips have united well.

In some cases it may be necessary to supply the loss of substance by means of twisted flaps.

The same methods may be applied, whenever a part of the eye-lid is destroyed by some other cause. Care must, however, always be taken to preserve whatever is left of a healthy lid-margin and eye-lid.

*Teleangiectatic and angiomatous* growths are not infrequent on the eye-lids, especially on the upper lids. They form reddish or dark bluish, soft tumors under the skin of the eye-lid and are usually congenital. They are compressible and increase in size when the patient stoops, cries or coughs. These tumors ought to be removed as early as possible, and the knife or scissors is the preferable means for their removal. Injections of sesqui-chloride of iron, the actual and galvano-cautery, etc., are less liable or are followed by a more disfiguring scar.

Different forms of disease of the eye-lids and of the palpebral conjunctiva cause the eye-lashes to grow in an abnormal direction. This condition is called *distichiasis* or *trichiasis*. It becomes very annoying as soon as the eye-lashes touch the eye-ball, as the cornea is continually scratched by them.

This constant irritation of the corneal tissue causes it to become inflamed and often to partially or totally lose its transparency by the formation of scars. The trouble is most easily remedied in its incipiency.

It is very common for such patients to pull out the offending cilia, as well as they can, with all sorts of instruments and thus to relieve themselves for a time. The surgeon should, however, not be satisfied with such a palliative remedy, the effect of which vanishes after a few days. A lasting effect can only be produced by a surgical operation, that forces the eye-lashes to stand in a direction from the eye-ball.

If there is only one or if there are but a few eye-lashes which rub against the cornea, they may be removed with their bulbs by the simple excision of a small wedge of tissue from the lid-margin, including their bulbs.

When, however, the trichiasis involves a larger part or the whole of the lid-margin, we have to perform more extensive operations.

The method of *Hotz* (See figure 14) is a very effective one. Its main point is that the skin of the lid is forced to adhere to a punctum fixum, for which he has chosen the tarso-orbital fascia, in the upper eye-lid just above the tarsal tissue, in the lower one just below it. An incision is carried through the skin and muscle down to the fascia along the upper edge of the tarsus. A strip of the muscular tissue is then removed and the parts are united by four or five sutures, going first through skin and fascia, and then through fascia and skin on the opposite side. This simple method yields good and apparently lasting results even in bad cases of trichiasis.

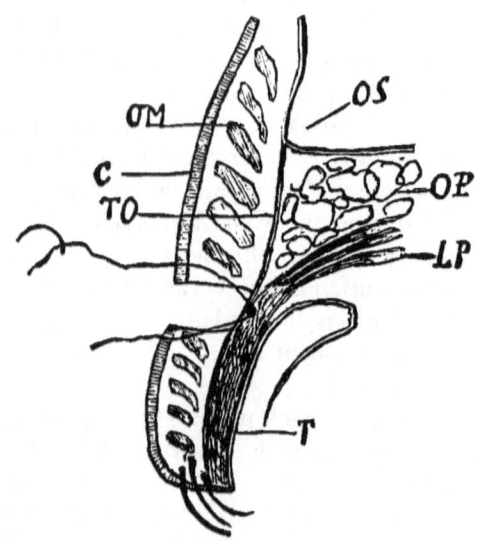

FIG. 14. Diagram showing Hotz's method of operating for trichiasis, etc. OS. Upper margin of the orbit. OF. Fat tissue of the orbit. LP. Levator palpebræ superioris muscle. T. Tarsal tissue. OM. Orbicularis palpebrarum muscle. C. Cutis. TO. Tarso-orbital fascia.

Although trichiasis may be observed as the only result of an inflammation, which requires an operation, it is much more frequently complicated with a change in the curvature of the tarsus, so that the lower edge of the tarsus also rubs against the eye-ball. This condition is called *entropium*.

The affection referred to is mostly the result of trachoma of the conjunctiva, commonly called granulated eye-lids.

# DISEASES OF THE EYE-LIDS.

A large number of operations have been devised and are used to remedy this troublesome affection, which endangers the usefulness of the eyes. A very useful method is to cut a wedge-shaped piece out of the tarsal tissue, near and parallel to the lid-margin, after having removed the corresponding strips of skin and muscle. Then the wound-lips are united by sutures, the lid-margin is turned outwards and thus relief is obtained. Relapses are comparatively rare after this operation, which, however, shortens the eye-lid.

*Hotz's* operation, just described, does also well enough in milder cases of entropium. In severer ones I now prefer

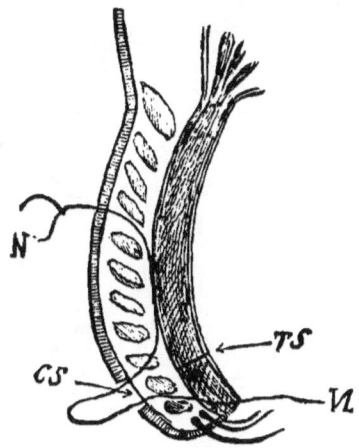

FIG. 15. Diagram showing Green's method of operating for entropium, etc. TS. Incision through the tarsal tissue. CS. Strip of skin removed from the outer surface of the eye-lid, opposite the tarsal incision. NN. The sutures.

*Green's* operation to all others. (See figure 15.) The lid-margin in this method is freed by an incision through the conjunctiva and tarsal tissue, running parallel with and about two millimeters removed from it. When by this incision all tough bands of tissue have been severed, the patient feels at once relieved. To render this momentary effect permanent it is usually necessary to remove a narrow strip of skin opposite the tarsal incision and to insert a few sutures, which are entered near the posterior edge of the lid-margin, brought out at the lower wound-lips, then entered again at the upper wound-lip and running along for some distance on the tarsal tissue are brought out through the muscle and skin. These sutures may be removed the next day, or they may be allowed to remain a few days. The requirements of each case may alter the procedure slightly.

When the lid-margin is turned outwards, away from the eyeball, the condition is called *ectropium*. This concerns mostly the lower eye-lids, while entropium is observed on the upper eye-lids especially. It very frequently affects chiefly the nasal part of the eye-lid, but it may, of course, involve the whole of it.

The stillicidium (dropping of the tears), the irritation and often very great swelling of the conjunctiva, caused by its continued exposure to the air, call for surgical interference, and often

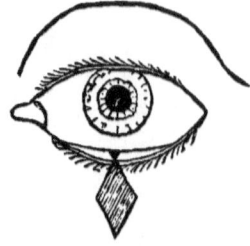

FIG. 16. Diagram showing the method of remedying ectropium of the lower eye-lid by the excision of a rhomboid piece of tissue from the eye-lid.

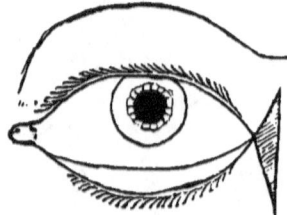

FIG. 17. Diagram showing the method of remedying ectropium of the lower eye-lid by the excision of a triangular piece of tissue from the outer angle of the palpebral fissure.

the operation required seems very extensive in comparison with the seeming triviality of the affection. This is especially the case in that most frequent form of ectropium, when it is due to the retraction of cicatricial tissue.

If the ectropium is small it may often be remedied by the excision of a rhomboid piece of the whole thickness of the eye-lid with the long diagonal in a vertical direction. (See figure 16.) If the wound-lips are now sewed together, the formerly everted part of the lid-margin will at first be raised considerably above the neighboring parts of the lid-margin. Later on the retraction of the scar will bring it down to the proper level.

In other cases the removal of a triangular piece of tissue from the outer angle of the palpebral fissure and stitching the corner of the lower eye-lid into the upper corner of the wound will serve to overcome the eversion. (See figure 17.)

When the ectropium is, however, very extensive, it may require a plastic operation for its removal. In this we may make use of twisted or sliding flaps, or flaps without a pedicle, according to general surgical rules and as it seems best for the case under consideration.

Drooping of the upper eye-lid with a total or partial inability to lift it enough, to expose the pupil for convenient sight, is called *ptosis*. It may be either congenital or due to an acquired paralysis of the levator palpebræ superioris muscle. If congenital, it usually concerns both upper eye-lids and the levator palpebræ superioris muscles are atrophic or totally wanting. The paralytic ptosis is frequently one-sided.

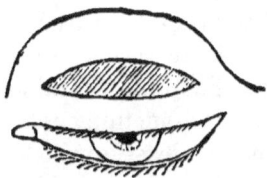

FIG. 18. Diagram showing the method of remedying ptosis of the upper eye-lid by the removal of a horizontal fold of skin and muscle.

There is another affection very similar to ptosis, which is chiefly observed in older people and which is not due to a muscular affection but to a superfluity and excessive looseness of the skin of the upper eye-lid. It is called prolapse of the skin of the eye-lid or *ptosis atonica*. In this affection *Hotz's* method of operating, as described above, appears to be satisfactory.

The method of operating, usually resorted to in cases of congenital or paralytic ptosis, (See figure 18), consists in the removal of a horizontal fold of skin and muscle from the upper eye-lid conjoined with stitching of the wound. The aim must be to shorten the eye-lid sufficiently for convenient vision and yet, to leave it long enough to cover and protect the cornea during sleep. The result of these operations is usually rather inadequate, and ptosis-operations have consequently fallen somewhat into discredit. *Macnamara* recommends to combine with the excision of the skin and muscle an artificial elongation of the pupil downwards (by iridectomy), and this seems to me a very reasonable procedure and calculated to make ptosis-operations more successful.

In the paralytic form of ptosis an operation must, of course, not be resorted to, until internal and galvanic treatment have been tried and proved unsuccessful. It is most frequently due to syphilis and then usually yields to anti-syphilitic treatment.

The orbicularis palpebrarum muscle is sometimes subject to clonic spasms, called *blepharospasmus*. In the incipient stage such spasms may concern only a few muscular fibres, and they are then felt and seen, as a slight tremor of the skin of the eyelid near the lid-margin. This slight degree of blepharospasmus is not rare and it is often observed after excesses in venere or in baccho, and will then disappear without treatment. In other cases it develops into a more serious form, in which the patient is forced to wink his eye-lids almost continually, especially, when trying to gaze steadily at something when watched by another person, or, when in the least excited. In such cases the blepharospasmus is, as a rule, combined with similar clonic spasms of the facial muscles and may be unilateral. This affection is, of course, a most annoying one and it is very difficult to cure. Subcutaneous injections of morphine and local electric treatment seem to yield the best results. In very severe cases neurectomy of the supra-orbital and infra-orbital nerves have been successfully resorted to.

*Spasmodic entropium* of the eye-lids and chiefly of the lower lid is the consequence of a tonic spasm of the orbicularis palpebrarum muscle, and is frequently observed in affections of the cornea and conjunctiva. It generally disappears when the irritating cause is removed, but may sometimes necessitate canthotomy or other operations. (See later on).

*Paralysis of the orbicularis palpebrarum muscle* causes inability to close the eye or even to wink the eye-lids, so that the cornea remains unprotected even during sleep. This affection has been called *lagophthalmus*, (hare eye) as it has been said, that the hare sleeps with open eyes. It is one of the symptoms of paralysis of the facial nerve and may be either a paresis or a total paralysis. The dangers arising from the continued exposure of the cornea are evident. If the paralysis is of long standing, and no longer curable by the treatment for the nervous disease, these dangers to the eye-ball will call for aid from the ophthalmic surgeon.

The cornea may be partly protected and the eversion of the lower lachrymal punctum, which always occurs in the later stages of this affection, may be relieved to a certain extent by shortening the palpebral fissure. This little operation, which is called tarsoraphy, consists in removing a small strip of skin including the hair-bulbs from the lid-margin of both eye-lids to an equal distance from the outer angle of the palpebral tissue. (See

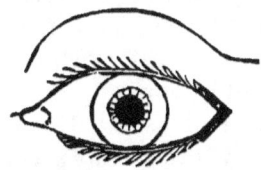

FIG. 19. Diagram showing how to pare the -lid-margins in the outer angle of the palpebral fissure for tarsoraphy to remedy lagophthalmus.

figure 19.) The pared edges are then sewed together. In some cases it may be necessary to shorten the palpebral fissure from the inner angle also, and then care must be taken not to interfere with the lachrymal apparatus.

When the palpebral fissure has become shortened in consequence of the shrinkage of the conjunctival sack, and of changes in the curvature of the tarsal tissue, the condition is called *blepharophimosis*. This affection is nearly always due to chronic trachoma.

In order to extend the palpebral fissure, canthotomy is performed. This consists either of a simple cut through the outer canthus with one clip of a strong pair of scissors, or the cut is followed by stitching the conjunctiva into the corner of the wound. In the former case care must be taken, that the wound does not heal per primam, or the effect will be lost again altogether. Even, if the healing per primam is successfully prevented, part of the effect of the canthotomy will be lost. To prevent any such loss, it is best to undermine the conjunctiva near the wound with fine scissors and then to sew it into the gap, caused by the canthotomy. Three sutures, one in the corner and one on each side, are usually sufficient.

In severe cases of blepharophimosis *Noyes* has recommended to take a small flap from the temple near the canthotomy-wound and to twist it and sew it into the gap (canthoplasty).

*Wounds* of the eye-lid, which involve only the skin, or the skin and orbicularis muscle, heal, as a rule, readily. Only when they are very extensive, they may give rise to ectropium by the subsequent contraction of the scar-tissue.

When the wound extends through the whole thickness of the eye-lid, and reaches the lid-margin, it usually remains more or less open, the wound-lips become covered with epithelium, and a traumatic coloboma of the eye-lid is the result. Such a coloboma in the upper eye-lid may, if extensive, affect the eye injuriously by depriving it of its normal protection, as in the case of paralysis of the orbicularis muscle. If it is situated in the lower eye-lid, it forms a very disagreeable ectropium, over which the tears continually trickle down the cheek.

By paring the lips of the coloboma and sewing them together, the deformity may be greatly lessened, and in most cases entirely cured.

If a wound severs the fibres of the levator palpebræ superioris muscle, a traumatic ptosis must result. *Green* had once occasion to sew such a torn levator muscle to the tarsal tissue again, and thus to cure the ptosis.

Other injuries of the eye-lids have to be treated according to general surgical principles.

Sometimes we have occasion to see a case of *emphysema* of the eye-lids. It is almost always due to an injury with fracture of the inner wall of the orbit, (lamina papyracea ossis ethmoidei or os lachrymale) establishing a communication between the nasal cavity and the areolar tissue of the orbit. The patient must be guarded against blowing the nose for a few days. No other treatment, except, possibly, a compressive bandage, will be required.

*Burns* of the outer surface of the eye-lid are very frequently the cause of ectropium from the retraction of the scar.

Burns of the conjunctival surface of the eye-lid and eye-ball will mostly result in an attachment between the two. If this is only partial, it is called symblepharon, if total or nearly so, anchyloblepharon. (See chapter VII). The name of anchyloblepharon is also applied to a union of the lid-margins only.

# CHAPTER IV.

## DISEASES OF THE LACHRYMAL APPARATUS.

DISEASES OF THE LACHRYMAL GLAND. — HYPER-SECRETION. — DAKRY-ADENITIS. NEOPLASMS. — CYSTIC DISTENTION. — DISEASES OF THE DRAINAGE APPARATUS.— EPIPHORA. — FOREIGN BODY IN THE CANALICULUS.— DAKRYO-CYSTITIS CATARRHALIS AND PURULENTA.—STRICTURES.—LACHRYMAL FISTULA.— MELANO-SARCOMA OF THE LACHRYMAL CARUNCULA.

The diseases of the lachrymal apparatus must be divided into diseases of the organ, which secretes the tears, the lachrymal gland, and those of the drainage apparatus, which consists of the lachrymal puncta and canaliculi and the lachrymal sack and duct.

The lachrymal gland in the normal condition secretes continually a small quantity of a clear, alkaline fluid, the tears. An *excessive secretion* of tears is brought about by nearly all inflammations of the membranes of the eye-balls and eye-lids, by the presence of a foreign body in the conjunctival sack, and under the influence of emotion, as in crying.

In paralysis of the trigeminus nerve the secretion of tears may be stopped.

It happens, although comparatively seldom, that the lachrymal gland becomes the seat of an inflammatory process. This is called *dakry-adenitis*, and is usually an acute inflammation.

In this affection the gland is painful to the touch; it swells, and the temporal half of the upper eye-lid becomes œdematous. Soon the eye-lid swells more, and can no longer be raised sufficiently to open the eye, and the eye-ball is pushed gradually downwards and toward the nose, and somewhat out of the orbit. Any movement of the eye in an upward and outward direction is attended with great pain, or such movements may become altogether impossible. It may now be possible to feel by palpation a hard tumor in the outer upper part of the orbit through the upper eye-lid, or even to see it protruding into the upper fornix of the conjunctiva, if the swelling permits the upper eye-lid to be everted. Soon the tumor becomes softer, and it may then perhaps be possible to detect fluctuation in it. When not interfered with, the abscess may point through the upper eye-lid, or through the conjunctiva, and thus be evacuated into the conjunctival sack. The wound heals quickly as a rule, and is but seldom followed by a fistula. In some cases no pus is formed, and the inflammatory symptoms subside gradually.

If the patient is afraid of the knife, all that can be done in this affection is to apply hot fomentations to hasten the formation and evacuation of the pus. The best method of dealing with a dakry-adenitis, however, is to make an early incision into the swelling, either through the upper eye-lid, or, which is preferable, through the fornix of the conjunctiva. This incision should be followed by the application of hot fomentations.

A chronic non-suppurative inflammation of the lachrymal gland has been observed, but it is extremely rare.

The lachrymal gland is sometimes the seat of a *neoplasm*. Quite a number of such tumors of the lachrymal gland have been described by the older authors, and their histological diagnoses vary greatly, and are little creditable. More recent investigations seem to show that the tumors of the lachrymal gland are usually either of an adenoid or of an epitheliomatous character. By the gradual and mostly painless swelling of the lachrymal gland the eye-ball is more and more pushed downwards and inwards and out of the orbit, and the movements of the eye in an upward and outward direction become restricted. As the upper eye-lid is usually but little swollen, although apparently stretched and elongated, and the pupil generally remains uncovered, the patient may be greatly troubled by double vision. Soon the tumor may be detected by palpation; its situation in the upper outer part of the orbit and its immobility are sufficient to settle the diagnosis. Sometimes the tumor may be seen in the upper fornix of the conjunctiva. The vision of the eye on the affected side ultimately becomes impaired, and may even be totally lost. This is due to the stretching of and the impeded circulation in the optic nerve, leading to œdema of the optic papilla, optic neuritis and subsequent atrophy of the optic nerve.

Such tumors seem to develop mostly after injuries. There is nothing to be done in the way of treatment but to remove the tumor. To accomplish this it is best to make an incision through the upper eye-lid, over the seat of the tumor and parallel with the upper orbital margin. When the tumor has been once reached by careful dissection, it should be separated from the surrounding tissues by means of a blunt instrument, such as the handle of a scalpel, these tumors being, as a rule, soft and easily broken into. It is, of course, best, if possible, to remove the newformation as a whole. The wound usually heals with great rapidity, and the disagreeable symptoms disappear, excepting, of course, such impairment of vision as may be the result of lesions of the optic nerve. Care must be taken not to cut the levator palpebræ superioris muscle, an accident which would, of course, lead to ptosis of the upper eye-lid.

Some surgeons prefer to attack the tumors of the lachrymal gland through the upper fornix of the conjunctiva, after having first made canthotomy.

The nature of these growths is, it appears, but rarely malignant, and local relapses are seldom observed.

In rare cases a cystic distension of the lachrymal gland has been observed; the affection has been called *dakryops*. The cystic character of the tumor may possibly be detected by palpation through the skin. To get rid of it, the whole cyst-wall should be removed, or shrinkage may be induced by injections into the cyst, or by laying a thread through it.

We come now to the diseases of the drainage apparatus.

Eversion of the lower punctum lachrymale causes the tears to run down over the cheek. This condition is called *epiphora**, and may be brought on by conjunctivitis or blepharitis, or it may be due to paresis or paralysis of the orbicularis palpebrarum muscle. It, of course, accompanies all forms of ectropium of the lower eye-lid, and may be due to various other causes.

Simply slitting the canaliculus, the punctum of which is

---

*The term epiphora was formerly used for an increase in the secretion of tears in contradistinction to stillicidium lachrymarum, an overflow of tears, caused by an obstruction in the drainage apparatus. At present these two terms are used promiscuously.

everted, suffices usually to do away with epiphora, when it is not due to paralysis or to excessive ectropium.

Injuries, especially burns, sometimes produce closure of one or both puncta, or the same result may follow chronic inflammation of the lid-margin; cases of congenital obstruction of the puncta are also occasionally met with. Spasmodic contraction of *Horner's* muscle around the base of the lachrymal papilla may sometimes give rise to an obstruction of a canaliculus. In other cases the presence of a foreign body may cause such an obstruction. A small calculus, an eye-lash caught in a punctum, *leptothrix* (a vegetable parasite), and various other foreign bodies have been found in such cases. Sometimes a small polypus has been found growing from the mucous membrane of the canaliculus and plugging it. The symptoms caused by the obstruction of a canaliculus (it is usually a lower one), by a foreign body, are slight pain, swelling and epiphora. Slitting the canaliculus and removing the foreign body will give immediate relief. If only the punctum is contracted, it may be sufficient to dilate it by means of a large pin.

Like the puncta, one or both canaliculi, or the single canal formed after their union before entering the lachrymal sack, may become closed in consequence of injuries or burns. It is then usually impossible to re-establish the canaliculus.

The mucous membrane of the lachrymal sack and nasal duct is frequently the seat of inflammatory processes. These are often caused by inflammations of the mucous membrane of the nose, but they may also originate in the lachrymal sack or nasal duct.

The most frequent form is the catarrhal inflammation, *dakryocystitis catarrhalis*. This is attended with hyperæmia, swelling and hyper-secretion of mucus, so that the entrance into the nasal duct becomes blocked up, and the tears cannot pass down into the nose. In this way the lachrymal sack becomes gradually filled with fluid and slightly distended. Lachrymation follows, and the eye seems to be standing in water nearly all the time. Then the lachrymal caruncle and the conjunctiva become inflamed, and sometimes blepharitis ciliaris is developed.

The distended lachrymal sack can be seen as a small swelling just below the ligamentum palpebrale internum. If the distension progresses, this swelling may reach a considerable size, and cause the skin above it to become atrophic. This condition has been called *mucocele*. Even the adjacent bones may yield to a certain extent to the continued pressure of the distended lachrymal sack.

By pressing upon the swelling in an upward direction, it is sometimes possible to squeeze the contents of the distended lachrymal sack into the conjunctival sack, and the mucus will then be seen oozing out through one or both of the lachrymal puncta as a viscid, grayish or clear fluid. More frequently it is possible to empty the lachrymal sack into the nose by pressing upon it in a downward direction.

Dakryo-cystitis catarrhalis may go over into a *dakryo-cystitis purulenta* as the inflammatory process increases, or the latter form may occur as a primary affection. Both forms of inflammation of the lachrymal sack may, furthermore, be due primarily to inflammation and consequent obstruction of the nasal duct.

In dakryo-cystitis purulenta the contents of the sack are of a yellow or brownish or greenish color, and are often very fœtid. The other symptoms noticed in the catarrhal dakryo-cystitis are present in an aggravated form; there is often considerable pain. Purulent dakryo-cystitis is generally a chronic affection.

In the severe forms a free opening of both canaliculi and of the conjunctival wall of the lachrymal sack (*Agnew*) should be made, and thus its contents be evacuated. If there is no obstruction in the nasal duct, the treatment of the mucous membrane of the lachrymal sack by injections of zincum sulfuricum in a one per cent solution, or similar remedies, may restore the normal condition.

Sometimes the catarrhal form, more frequently, however, the purulent form of dakryo-cystitis gives rise to a phlegmonous inflammation of the subcutaneous tissue in front of the lachrymal sack. There is then great swelling, heat and redness, combined with severe pain, and the eye-lids, and the surrounding tissues may become so much swollen, that the condition very much resembles an attack of erysipelas. It is then impossible to squeeze out the contents of the lachrymal sack, and the swelling of the eye-lids makes it, moreover, impossible to slit the canaliculi. It is therefore best in such a case to make an incision through the skin and lachrymal sack down to the bone. If this is done at an early stage, great suffering will be prevented. If the abscess is allowed to open by itself, a *lachrymal fistula* may probably result. Hot fomentations and the careful removal of all further discharge should follow the incision. Although this mode of operating leaves no disfiguring scar and is not likely to be followed by the formation of a lachrymal fistula, it is better to empty the lachrymal sack by slitting the canaliculi, whenever this is possible. In most cases, however, the swelling of the eye-lids will prevent this.

Dakryo-cystitis may, through the formation of scar-tissue, give rise to lasting folds or impassible strictures in the lachrymal sack or nasal duct, which may prevent the tears from flowing down in the normal way. If a free opening of the lachrymal canaliculi and treatment by astringent injections do not bring the mucous membrane back to its normal condition, we must sometimes be content to advise the patient to squeeze out the contents of the lachrymal sack as often as it becomes filled, if possible, into the nose, if not, into the conjunctival sack.

As the pus coming from the suppurating lachrymal sack is very apt to cause ulceration of the cornea, especially when the latter is in the least abraded, perfect cleanliness must be insisted upon. Bathing the inflamed eye with a lotion containing salicylic acid and applying compresses dipped in the same solution is sometimes very beneficial.

Although dakryo-cystitis may be a primary affection, it is as a rule caused by strictures in the nasal duct and consequent confinement and decomposition of the fluids in the lachrymal sack. The treatment of dakryo-cystitis must, therefore, in most cases be conjoined with the exploration and dilatation of the nasal duct.

If the symptoms of such a secondary dakryo-cystitis are not very severe, it will suffice to slit one canaliculus and preferably the upper one. As soon as this is done, it is well to enter the sack with a probe and explore, whether the entrance into the nasal duct is free. If not, it is best to wait a few days, until, under the use of cold compresses, and perhaps astringent solutions, the inflammatory symptoms have subsided. Then a careful exploration of the lachrymal sack and the nasal duct should be made with a medium sized probe of the kind devised by *Bowman* and which bear his name (See figure 20). This is done in the following way. Direct the patient to look downwards and push the probe gently through the slit canaliculus, into the lachrymal sack until it reaches the opposite (bony) wall. That the wall is reached, may be judged by the feeling of solid resistance, and by the fact, that movements of the probe in a horizontal direction, do not cause the skin of the upper eye-lid to become wrinkled. During this first step of the little maneuvre, it is well to draw the eye-lid towards the temple. As soon as it is certain that the probe has reached the opposite wall of the lachrymal sack this traction

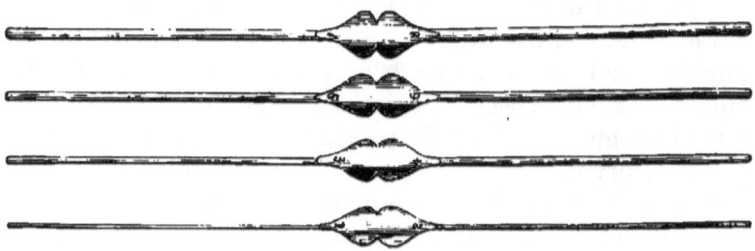

FIG. 20. Bowman's Probes for Exploring and Dilating the Nasal Lachrymal Duct.

of the eye-lid must be released. Now sliding the point of the probe along this wall of the sack the probe is brought into a nearly vertical position, slanting slightly towards the centre of the forehead. It will now be in the position to be slipped down into the nasal duct. This last step is the most difficult, and ought not to be attempted by an inexperienced hand, as a slight pressure in the wrong direction may cause the formation of a false passage, which will not only not accomplish the wished for result but will cause great pain, and sometimes profuse hemorrhage. If the point of the probe has once entered the nasal duct it must be gently pushed down, until it has reached its nasal orifice. We must make sure of this latter point, as obstructions just here are occasionally met with. While the probe is passing down the nasal duct the feeling of resistance will give us an exact idea where a stricture is situated. The treatment then consists in the gradual or forcible distention of such stricture or strictures. The gradual distention is in most cases the preferable method. After a probe of a certain diameter has been introduced, it is generally allowed to remain in the duct for ten or fifteen minutes and then gently withdrawn. When this probe can be easily introduced, a little larger one should be used, and again, when this can easily be passed down through the stricture, the next larger one is employed. The probing should be done at first daily, but when large sized probes pass easily through the duct, the intervals between the probing should be increased. If the patient has pain after the probing, although no false passage has been made, cold compresses or bathing will give relief, and the pain need not interfere with the treatment; yet it indicates sometimes that too large a probe has been used, and that it would be better to go back to a smaller size. While in children and young people a perfect recovery is generally to be expected, adults and older people are less apt to be perfectly cured, and have generally to be probed again from time to time.

Forcible distention by the introduction of a large probe at the first sitting, does not seem to yield as good and lasting results as does the gradual distention ; it is, moreover, very painful.

When the obstruction of the nasal duct is not due to a stricture in the mucous membrane, but to an affection of the surrounding bone, chiefly caused by syphilis or scrophulosis, successful probing and dilatation of the duct, is but rarely possible.

If there is a fistula of the lachrymal sack, this will heal without any special treatment, as soon as we have succeeded in restoring the caliber of the duct, so as to allow the tears to flow down through it.

Although it would seem scarcely possible to break off a probe in the nasal duct, I must give warning against this accident, as I once had occasion to remove such a broken probe, left in the duct by the operator.

In a certain percentage of cases the tears will, in spite of successful probing and enlarging of the formerly closed duct, refuse to be drained off. In such cases, and in others also, in which for any reason a re-establishment of the drainage from the lachrymal sack downwards is impossible nothing can be done, but to obliterate the lachrymal sack. This may be done by a free incision into it and followed by the destruction of the mucous membrane, by actual or galvano-cautery, or by the use of caustics. Care must always be taken, to destroy all of the mucous membrane, and not to omit cauterizing well up in the cupola of the lachrymal sack. The healing by granulation takes place in from two to three weeks. The scar is but slightly disfiguring, and, although the epiphora remains, the patients are greatly benefitted by the operation. The whole lachrymal sack may also be cut out, instead of destroying its mucous membrane.

Instead of obliterating the lachrymal sack, *Laurence* advised the removal of the lachrymal gland, but he seems to have had few or no followers.

The lachrymal caruncle is sometimes the seat of a malignant tumor. The most frequent form is *melano-sarcoma*. It must be removed early; the operation is easily performed.

## CHAPTER V.

### DISEASES OF THE ORBIT.

Periostitis. — Hemorrhage. — Cellulitis Orbitae. — Inflammation of Tenon's Capsule. — Neoplasms.

The diseases of the orbit are either diseases of its bony walls and periosteum, or they concern chiefly its contents. In all these affections the eye-ball, its muscles, and the optic nerve suffer only secondarily.

If the disease of the orbit causes the volume of its contents to become increased, the eye-ball will be pressed out of its normal position, and, as it cannot escape in any other direction, it will be pushed out of the orbit. This condition is called exophthalmus, and may, furthermore, be due to diseases of the neighboring cavities, encroaching upon the orbital cavity, or to tumors of the eye-ball itself or of its appendages. The exophthalmus will, in a general sense, be always in a direction opposite to the swelling in the orbit upon which it depends and the movements of the eye-ball will be restricted in the direction towards this swelling.

*Periostitis of the walls of the orbit* is usually confined to a part of the orbital margin and it seems to be more frequently observed in the upper and outer part, than at any other point. In the beginning the patients complain of spontaneous pain, and soon at the seat of this pain a slight immoveable swelling appears, which is very sensitive on pressure. Gradually the swelling increases, the eye-ball is slightly pushed forwards and towards the opposite side, and its movements in the direction of the swelling become restricted and painful. The localized swelling and pain are the most important symptoms for the diagnosis.

In the acute form of periostitis fluctuation will be soon felt and on incision, or spontaneously, pus will be evacuated.

If the acute form goes over into the chronic form, caries or necrosis of the bone will result, and fistulous openings through the skin will allow of their detection with a probe. The probing ought to be done very carefully, as an acute inflammation of the orbital tissue might follow.

In acute periostitis of the orbital margin, when seen at a very early stage, ice compresses and leeches may sometimes suffice to effect a cure. If not, an incision should be made so as to give a free opening for the escape of the pus.

If the case is already a chronic one, matters will be more complicated. After an incision has been made down to the diseased portion, the necrosed bone must be removed or the carious parts well scraped out. In these chronic cases this operation must often be followed by a plastic one, as the formation of scars bound down to the bone often causes ectropium.

Orbital periostitis is most frequently the result of an injury. In other cases it is due to a strumous or syphilitic diathesis, and in the treatment we must, of course, take these points into consideration.

Injuries and heavy falls may cause *hemorrhages* into the orbital tissues. Such hemorrhages cause sometimes considerable exophthalmus conjoined with paretic symptoms in the muscles of the eye-ball. The blood can usually be seen, as it genererally infiltrates the ocular conjunctiva, and in some cases raises it so as to form a dark red, shining, ring-shaped elevation around the cornea-scleral margin. Such a hemorrhage may, of course, be due to the rupture of blood-vessels alone, or it may be complicated by fracture of the bony wall of the orbit. It may, therefore, be a comparatively simple affection, and its alarming symptoms may disappear after a short time without leaving any trace behind. In the other case it may give rise to rather serious affections, and especially, as the fracture often concerns the the walls of the optic canal, to atrophy of the optic nerve and consequent blindness.

*Cellulitis orbitæ*, phlegmonous inflammation of the orbital tissue, may be a primary affection, or it may be due to an injury with or without the subsequent presence of a foreign body; it may be caused also by orbital caries or necrosis, especially when its seat is far back in the orbit.

Pain in the orbit, restriction of the movements of the eyeball and exophthalums are the first symptoms complained of, and are usually attended with fever. The exophthalums is mostly in a forward direction, and the restriction of the movements of the eye-ball is then general, and not particularly pronounced in any one direction. Gradually the eye-lids begin to swell, and the conjunctiva becomes œdematous. The upper eye-lid usually swells so considerably that it is impossible for the patient to raise it.

The pressure and traction on the optic nerve may cause œdema of the optic papilla or optic neuritis, with attendant amblyopia. In other cases sight is apparently not at all impaired.

Gradually pus is formed, and the abscess may point either in the eye-lid or in the conjunctiva, and thus a spontaneous cure may take place.

In rare cases the pus may break through the lamina papyracea of the os ethmoidei into the nasal cavity or downwards, into the antrum of Highmore, or even upwards into the cranial cavity. The inflammation may, moreover, extend to the eye-ball, and cause its destruction by purulent irido-choroiditis and subsequent shrinking of the eye-ball. In other cases the cornea may slough away in consequence of the impaired nutrition and exposure due to the exophthalmus.

The formation of pus in the inflamed tissue is occasionally very slow, and yet, the impairment of sight due to it may be comparatively small. I once had occasion to see a case of orbital cellulitis five weeks after the first symptoms had set in, and evacuated the pus by an incision. The recovery was rapid, and only a partial atrophy of the optic nerve remained behind.

In rare cases no pus is formed, and the inflammatory symptoms subside again after a short period of existence. The etiology of orbital cellulitis, when it is not due to an injury or to caries, is, as yet, unknown.

With regard to the treatment, first of all, perfect rest and warm applications should be insisted on. If after a few days the symptoms continue unabated, an incision should be made, whether fluctuation can be felt or not. If pus is already found, it will escape through the incision, and the eye-ball will gradually recede to its normal position in the orbit. If no pus is there, or even if the knife has not reached it, the bleeding and subsequent oozing of serous fluid will reduce the tension of the tissue, and thus give relief. The wound must, of course, be kept open until all symptoms have disappeared, and the warm applications must also be kept up.

The incision into the orbital tissue is best made through the conjunctiva. If this is impossible, it may be done through the lid. A narrow knife should be used and great care be taken not to wound the eye-ball or the optic nerve. It is sometimes very difficult to reach the pus-cavity, and it is then preferable to make further exploration with a blunt instrument. The wound heals very readily, and if the optic nerve and eye-ball have remained intact, a perfect recovery is obtained in the course of a few days.

It is well to know that symptoms which resemble very much those of orbital cellulitis may be due to thrombosis of an ophthalmic vein, or, which is more frequent, to thrombosis of the cavernous or longitudinal sinus. In the latter cases, however, the affection usually concerns both orbits and their contents, and, moreover, the cerebral symptoms will help to make the diagnosis clear.

After tenotomy of one of the external muscles of the eye-ball for strabismus an *inflammation of Tenon's capsule* is some times observed. Although the pain and swelling, and the visible inflammatory symptoms are somewhat like those of an orbital cellulitis, a mistake is hardly possible, since the inflammation of Tenon's capsule (*Tenonitis*, as it is inappropriately called), causes only a comparatively slight protrusion of the eye-ball.

A small, red swelling is in these cases at first observed near the incision made in the tenotomy. It is immoveable, but may be fluctuating, and is covered by hyperæmic and œdematous conjunctiva. This swelling may increase in size and gradually extend around the whole of the periphery of the cornea. The movements of the eye-ball are painful and somewhat restricted, but only in consequence of the pain, for the eye-ball may be moved in all directions. The upper eye-lid is usually slightly œdematous. The fluctuation is due to serous fluid within Tenon's space.

(The same condition is observed as a complication in cases of panophthalmitis).

The application of iced compresses and rest are usually sufficient in the treatment of these rare cases.

*Emphysema* of the orbital tissue (and eye-lids) is sometimes observed in consequence of a fracture of the lamina papyracea of the os ethmoidei ; also occasionally, in consequence of injuries of the lachrymal bone, or of the bony walls of the nasal duct from forced dilatation of this passage for the cure of an obstruction.

The orbit is not infrequently the seat of *neoplasms*, which may be either benign or malignant.

*Cystoid formations*, when met with in the orbit, usually lie under the upper eye-lid near to and above the outer angle of the palpebral fissure, and outside of the funnel formed by the external muscles of the eye-ball. These cysts contain an oil-like fatty, or mucoid fluid, of an amber or brownish tint. Their walls may become firmly adherent to the periosteum of the orbit or even to the eye-ball itself, and are often very vascular. They grow slowly and may bring about a partial atrophy of the eye-lid by their continued pressure. They, moreover, displace the eye-ball and may cause a noticeable exophthalmus with attendant double-vision, and with the other symptoms which depend upon continued stretching and impaired nutrition of the optic nerve.

True dermoid cysts, and echinococcus cysts have also been observed in this locality.

Such cysts must be removed, and, of course, if possible enucleated in toto. In doing so care must be taken not to injure the eye-ball or its exterior muscles.

A number of primary *epithelial cancers* of the orbital tissue have been described, yet it seems that the tumors of this tissue are, as a rule, not of an epithelial, but on the contrary of the connective-tissue type. Thus we find *round and spindle-cell sarcoma, melano-sarcoma, fibro-sarcoma, myxo-sarcoma, cysto-sarcoma and cylindroma* of the orbital tissue.

The symptoms of all these different forms of orbital tumors are similar, and the most prominent one is always the exophthalmus. To this may be added intercurrent inflammatory symptoms, and, again, all the symptoms referable to the optic nerve and to the cornea, as we observe them in cases of exophthalmus due to a newformation in the lachrymal gland or to orbital cellulitis.

The tumor may frequently be detected by palpation and does not, of course, move when the eye-ball is moved.

Such a newformation must be removed, as soon as detected. As long as it does not interfere with a clean removal, an attempt should be made to preserve the eye-ball. If this is impracticable, the eye-ball must be sacrificed, and in some cases the whole of the orbital tissues will have to be cleaned out in order to save the patient's life.

In case the eye-ball has been removed with the tumor, a suggestion made by *Green* is very valuable, indeed. It is, to further remove the lid-margin, the palpebral conjunctiva and tarsal tissue to, and sew the eye-lids together. The eye-lids heal promptly together and thus form a permanent cover, which protects the deeper tissues from injurious influences.

I had once occasion to examine a large orbital tumor, removed from a negro woman, with preservation of the eye-ball, by the late *Dr. Darby*, of New York. It proved to be a *leiomyoma*, and consisted almost wholly of organic muscular fibres. No similar case has been anywhere reported, and I suppose the tumor originated from the organic muscular fibres lying in the orbital tissue.

Another class of orbital tumors spring from its bony walls. We thus find simple *osteoma and periosteal sarcoma* of the orbit.

The contents of the orbit may, moreover, be invaded by tumors originating in the neighboring cavities, especially the nasal cavity and the antrum of Highmore ; the symptoms will be much the same as in cases of primary orbital tumors.

Pulsating exophthalmus, as well as exophthalmic goitre (*Basedow's, Graves' disease*) will be spoken of in Chapter XXIII.

# CHAPTER VI.

## MINOR MANIPULATIONS IN THE TREATMENT OF EYE DISEASES.

COLD AND WARM APPLICATIONS.—LEECHING.—REMOVING DISCHARGES.-INSTILLATION OF MEDICATED FLUIDS. — APPLICATION OF ASTRINGENT SOLUTIONS. — APPLICATION OF CAUSTIC SOLUTIONS. — APPLICATION OF REMEDIES IN SUBSTANCE.— OINTMENTS. — INSPERGATION OF POWDERS. — ISOLATION. — REMOVAL OF WILD HAIRS.—REMOVAL OF SMALL FOREIGN BODIES.—INSERTION OF LID RETRACTORS. ARTIFICIAL EYES. — BANDAGING. -- HINTS FOR ASSISTANCE IN EYE-OPERATIONS.

Continued *cold applications* to an eye are best made by means of a piece of light linen, which after having been cooled either in cold water, or ice water, or directly on ice, is laid upon the closed eye. This linen should be folded several times, because it will then keep its temperature for a longer time, and a second one ought always to be kept cooling while the first one is lying on the eye. As soon as the linen on the eye no longer causes a cooling sensation, it should be changed. The time in which this will have to be done, will, of course, depend on various circumstances. With children it may be necessary to fasten the linen with a simple bandage.

Care must always be taken to wring the linen dry before applying it, and not to allow any cold water to trickle down and enter the ear. This may be the better guarded against by putting some oiled cotton into the ears.

Instead of the linen a very small ice-bag may sometimes be used. Yet its weight must be so small as not to be felt disagreeably.

When cold bathing only is required from time to time, this is best done by gently pressing a cooled sponge or linen rag against the closed eye. This may, however, be replaced with great advantage by an eye-douche. A quart or more of cold water may thus be allowed to flow against the eye from a moderate hight through a very fine rose.

Opening the eyes under water should be avoided.

In cases of plyctænular keratitis, with great dread of light and spasmodic entropium, it is often of great value to apply a sudden cold bath to the whole face. This is best done by plunging the child's face into a basin of cold water and by holding it there until it struggles for breath.

This procedure may be varied by holding the child over a basin and directing a moderately strong stream of cold water full in his face through a rather coarse rose.

Continued warm applications are best made in the same way as cold ones, or they may be made in the form of poultices. The best material for the latter is a mixture of ground linseed and shorts. To keep these poultices warm the one not in use should lie in a sieve on top of a vessel with water, which is kept gently steaming.

Dry heat may sometimes be indicated, and may be applied by means of little bags containing a light material, such as bran, which will retain the heat for sometime.

*Leeches* must never be applied either to the eye-ball itself or to the eye-lids. The best place for the application of leeches in eye affections is the temple, or, more accurately, the space between the outer angle of the palpebral fissue and the line, where the hair begins to grow.

This is also the best place for the application of *Hœurteloup's* artificial leech.

Any *discharge* from the palpebral conjunctiva should be gently and carefully removed. What sticks to the eye-lashes and the lachrymal caruncle, when semi-fluid, can be easily wiped away by the use of a soft, moist sponge or linen rag. When the discharge is dried up and hard, it must first be well soaked by bathing with warm water. It can then be removed by brushing the eye-lashes back and forth in a horizontal direction with a sponge, or still better with a dry towel. After the eye-lashes and lid-margins have thus been cleansed, the conjunctival sack must be inspected and every film of coagulated discharge be removed. This may be done by gently wiping it off with a very soft sponge or linen rag, or with a moistened camel's hair brush. If the conjunctiva tends to bleed, when even but slightly touched, a gentle stream of salt water should be allowed to flow over the eye and thus wash the discharge away. It is better not to employ forceps for the removal of coagulated discharge, but, if used, great care must be taken, not to grasp the underlying tissue. How to evert the eye-lids for examination of the palpebral conjunctiva and fornix, has been described in chapter II.

For the *instillation* of medicated fluids into the conjunctival sack, it is best to use a dropping tube. (See figure 21). Where this cannot be procured a goose-quill or even a teaspoon may answer the purpose. A somewhat simpler way, with which, however, the patients usually are not successful, is to replace the

FIG. 21. Dropping tube. Pressure on the rubber expells the air from the tube. Releasing the pressure, while the tube is dipped into the solution, to be used, allows the fluid to mount in the tube. When the tube is thus charged, slight pressure upon the rubber will expell the fluid in the shape of drops, and in a quantity which can be easily regulated.

cork of the bottle with the index-finger of the hand, which holds the bottle, and to allow the fluid to escape in drops by the side of the finger. If this does not work, a small notch may be cut in the cork along its side so as to form a channel through which the fluid can slowly escape, when the bottle is tilted. In order to instill the fluid into the conjunctival sack, the eye-lids should be held apart with the other hand and the lower eye-lid be drawn down sufficiently to allow the drop to enter, while the patient is directed to look upward. Medicated fluids, which have no astringent or caustic quality, and whose effect is to be reached by absorption, such as solutions of a mydriatic or myotic drug, should, if possible be allowed to drop directly upon the cornea, as they are thus absorbed more readily. The drop must not fall from any appreciable height, should not be cold, and must not be allowed to be washed out at once by the tears. Whenever, therefore, it is difficult to make such instillations, it is best to direct the patient to lie on his back and to hold his eye-lids apart for some time after the instillation has been made.

*Astringent solutions* should be applied by means of a moderately large camel's hair brush, dipped into the fluid and then drawn across the conjunctival surface of the everted eye-lid. It usually suffices to apply them to the lower eye-lid. If pain and irritation are very annoying after such an application, the patient should be directed to bathe the eyes for some time with cold water.

The application of *caustic solutions* should always be made by the surgeon himself. When making such an application the cornea must never be left unguarded. It is therefore best to treat each diseased eye-lid separately with a brush. While the caustic solution is brushed upon the inner surface of the everted upper eye-lid, the patient looking down, the lower eye-lid is gently drawn upward, so as to cover the cornea perfectly. By a similar manœuvre the upper eye-lid is made to protect the cornea while the lower one is treated. As soon as the application is made, the brush should be dipped into a bowl of water, held by the patient under his chin, and the superfluous caustic washed off with it. It is, of course, impossible to neutralize the primary effect of the caustic by washing, so there need be no hesitation in using plenty of water. The application of caustic fluids should not be repeated until the superficial eschar caused by the last application is cast off, which takes place in from 20 to 24 hours. It is therefore best to use these remedies only once in 24 hours and to make the application at about the same hour every day, preferably in the fore-part of the day or at least not in the evening.

By quick, intelligent manipulation with the brush the effect of the caustic application can be nicely graded, and even to a certain extent localized.

Sulphate of copper, in substance, the sovereign remedy in trachoma, should also be applied by the surgeon himself. For this purpose a large crystal should be trimmed thin and perfectly smooth and mounted in a crayon holder to make its handling easier. No sharp edges or roughness must be allowed to remain before the application, and the surgeon should therefore examine the crystal every time before using it, and dry it well after the treatment of every eye-lid. The application to the conjunctiva should be made very gently by simply drawing the crystal once across the part to be treated, and the conjunctiva should then be washed off at once with a brush dipped in water. All rubbing and prolonged contact, producing a caustic effect, is to be avoided. What is wished for is only irritation and stimulation, and not the "burning off" of the granules. As the seat of the granules is mostly in the fornix, the surgeon must be careful to apply the copper crayon to this part especially.

In treating the fornix of the upper eye-lid, it is necessary therefore to go high up under the everted eye-lid, and in doing so to lay the crystal against the lower eye-lid, so as to drag it along and protect the cornea while the copper is shifted upwards. Treating the fornix of the lower eye-lid is, of course, very much easier, since it can be fully exposed. All these little manipulations must be performed with great delicacy and care in order to obtain the best possible result. In this point lies the secret of the different results obtained by different physicians with the sulphate of copper in substance.

*Alum* in substance may be used in the same way as the sulphate of copper. Nitrate of silver in substance or in the form of the mitigated stick is best altogether avoided.

Some remedies are best applied to the eye in the form of *ointments*. The common advice to simply smear a little of the ointment into the eye or on the inner surface of the lower eye-lid, is not sufficient, as only very little of the ointment will reach the part it is chiefly intended for, namely, the cornea.

The best method of applying an ointment, if it is not fluid enough to be brushed upon the inner surface of the upper eye-lid, is to take a little on the end of a blunt probe, to bring it between the separated eye-lids, and then to close the lids quickly while the carrier is withdrawn. If this does not succeed the upper eye-lid must be everted and the probe with the ointment be brought upwards between it and the eye-ball. Then the probe is withdrawn, and the eye-lid returning to its normal position wipes off the ointment.

It is then well to gently rub the ointment with the eye-lids all over the eye-ball in circular and radiating movements, exerting all the time a slight pressure. These movements have the value of massage, and are especially to be recommended in corneal affections.

For the *inspergation* of medicinal *powders*, as calomel or iodoform, into the conjunctival sack, it is best to make use of a small, dry camel's hair brush. This is lightly dipped into the powder, the eye-lids are separated with the fingers of the other hand, and the powder is snapped off the brush into the conjunctival sack.

As the discharge in most forms of inflammation of the conjunctiva is contagious, a great many efforts have been made to perfectly *isolate* a healthy eye, so long as its fellow continues diseased. Yet most of these contrivances are very annoying and after all useless, as perfect isolation is almost impossible. Absolute cleanliness in the fullest sense of the word, which involves a free use of plenty of fresh water, is, according to my experience, at least as good a preventive as any appliance for isolating a

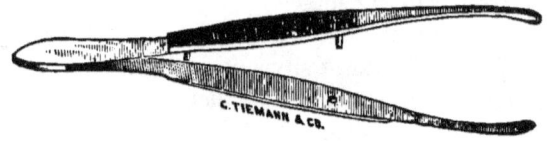

Fig. 22. Cilia Forceps.

healthy eye, especially when the patient remains in such a position that no discharge from the diseased eye can run across the bridge of the nose into the healthy one.

To isolate, however, a child suffering from one of the serious forms of conjunctivitis (purulent, gonorrhœal, diphtheritic or trachomatous conjunctivitis) from other children, is highly to be recommended, nor should such a child ever be allowed to go to school. This is often allowed when children suffer from trachoma or from chronic purulent conjunctivitis, but is to be absolutely condemned as bad practice.

*Wild hairs*, ingrowing eye-lashes, are easily pulled out, when they are large and well pigmented, with appropriate forceps. (See figure. 22). But often the most annoying ones are very thin and fine, and almost unpigmented. To detect these is then sometimes rather difficult, and is best done by placing the patient sideways to the light, and then looking along the lid-margin, which should be slightly drawn away from the eye. Alternately applying the lid-margin to the eye-ball and lifting it off will help greatly in the detection of such eye-lashes, since they will raise the tear-fluid somewhat before being drawn away by the eversion of the lid-margin. Great care must be taken to extract the cilia with the root and not to break them off.

The whole procedure is, however, of but little value, and, to afford a temporary relief, must be repeated again and again. The patients should therefore be persuaded to have an operation for trichiasis performed. (See Chap. III).

The removal of *small foreign bodies* from the conjunctival sack is, as a rule, a very simple affair, as the foreign bodies lie

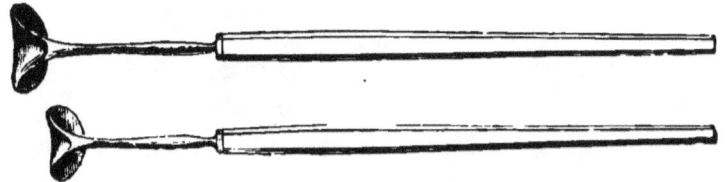

FIG. 23. Desmarres' Lid-retractors.

for the most part loosely on the conjunctiva. They may be removed from the everted eye-lid by means of a moist camel's hair brush or a piece of soft linen. In the lower conjunctival sack they are usually found lying in the fornix. In the upper conjunctival sack they lie most frequently in the small depression just above the inner edge of the lid-margin. When one small foreign body has been thus removed, the surgeon should scan the whole conjunctival sack once more, and, if necessary, sweep the upper conjunctival sack as high up as possible with a moist camel's hair brush. When the foreign body is not easily detected by its color, it is well to draw the finger gently over the surface of the palpebral conjunctiva and thus to satisfy ourselves that nothing has been left behind.

For a careful inspection of the eyes of children, it is often necessary to separate the eye-lids by means of *Desmarres' lid retractors*. (See figure 23). During their use great care must be taken not to exert nor to let the patient exert any pressure on the eye-ball. It is therefore best to insert the retractor for the upper eye-lid first. This is done by everting the lid-margin slightly by dragging the skin upwards with the index finger of one hand and slipping the retractor under the eye-lid with the other hand, all the time pulling the eye-lid slightly away from the eye-ball. The insertion of the retractor for the lower eye-lid is much easier, but must be done in the same manner.

To insert and remove a *wire-speculum* (See figure 24), to hold the eye-lids apart during an operation on the eye-ball, requires the same delicacy. The branch for the upper eye-lid must always be inserted first, while the branches are held tightly together,

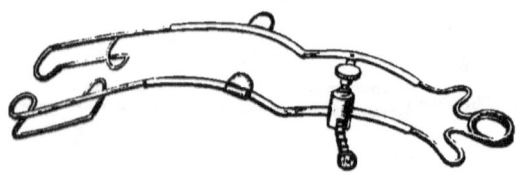

FIG. 24. Wire-speculum to force and hold the eye-lids apart during an operation on the eye.

and the same precautions are to be observed as in inserting the lid-retractor. While this is being done the patient is directed to look downwards. Then, while the patient looks upwards, the branch for the lower eye-lid is inserted, and the two branches are allowed to separate. When the speculum is removed, the branch for the lower eye-lid is first taken out, while the branches are pressed together, and then the one for the upper eye-lid. In doing this the eye-lids are gently pulled away from the eye-ball with the speculum, so as to avoid the exertion of any pressure upon it.

The insertion of a wire speculum is, of course, necessary, or at least of great advantage, in all important operations on the eye-ball, yet the general practioner should also be familiar with it, as he is frequently called upon to remove small foreign bodies from the cornea. Such patients are often utterly unable to counteract the reflex-action of the orbicularis palpebrarum muscle and then a speculum has to be inserted to hold the eye-lids apart.

After the speculum has been properly adjusted, the conjunctiva must be grasped with the fixation-forceps (See figure 25) near the cornea, and best near the lower corneo-scleral margin, as the

FIG. 25. Sharp-toothed Fixation Forceps.

eye-ball will instinctively fly upwards to avoid the instrument used for the removal of the foreign body. The latter should not be a sharp instrument, especially in the hands of the unpracticed operator. A bent needle, or a somewhat blunt minute spud or gouge, is the most appropriate instrument. (See figures 26 and 27).

Care must be taken not to injure the neighboring parts of the corneal tissue, and to attack, as far as possible, the foreign body only. The unexperienced operator, however, had better keep his hands from this apparently trifling, but sometimes rather difficult, little operation.

FIG. 26. Bent needle for the removal of small foreign bodies from the cornea or conjunctiva.

FIG. 27. Spud or gouge for the removal of small foreign bodies.

When inserting an *artificial eye*, it is best to follow the rule for inserting the speculum, that is to insert it first under the upper eye-lid, and again, when removing it, to lift it first out of the lower conjunctival sack while the patient looks upwards. The patient should be directed to bend his head over a bed or pillow, when removing the artificial eye, until he has acquired sufficient skill in the manipulation to accomplish it without fear of letting the artificial eye fall.

For *bandaging* eyes the surgeon should have on hand a number of rolled flannel bandages from one and one-half inches to two inches wide and from two to three yards long. Pad the eye nicely with picked lint or absorbent cotton, or common cotton dipped in water, and, while the patient holds the pad against the lower orbital margin, begin to unroll the bandage over the ear and on the same side as the affected eye. Wind the bandage first around the head, merely covering the upper edge of the pad with it, then come around the back of the head in such a way that the bandage runs across the eye from below upwards, thus making

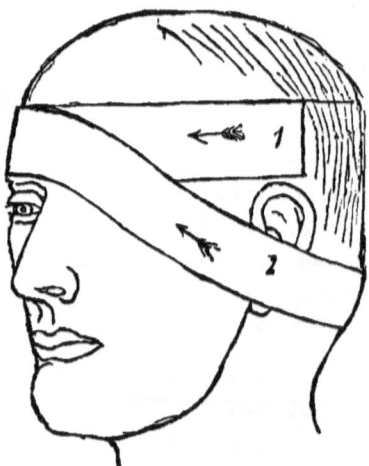

FIG. 28. Diagram showing the method of bandaging one eye with a flannel roller-bandage (monoculus). 1—is the end of the bandage first applied. In the drawing it lies too near the forehead. 2—is the second turn, covering the eye.

any degree of pressure, that is required with this turn of the bandage. Then unwind the rest of the bandage around the head, and fasten it with pins. Put the pins in a vertical direction, point downwards. (See figure 28).

If both eyes are to be bandaged, go around the head with the bandage, after the first eye is covered in the way just described, and then go across the second eye from above downwards and towards the ear, and again unroll the remainder of the bandage around the head. (See figure 29).

This bandage has great advantages, but also the disadvantage, that it is very warm, especially in summer. In hot weather a lighter material, such as bunting, may be substituted. Linen bandages lack elasticity, and are therefore not to be recommended.

When the patient is bandaged, see to it that the bandage is neither too tight nor too loose. If it is too tight, relief may sometimes be given by pulling in a forward direction, near the ear, on the piece coming across the eye. If this relief is insufficient, or if the pressure is felt again to be too great after a few minutes, it is best to remove the bandage altogether, and to apply it anew. If it is too loose, it should always be reapplied.

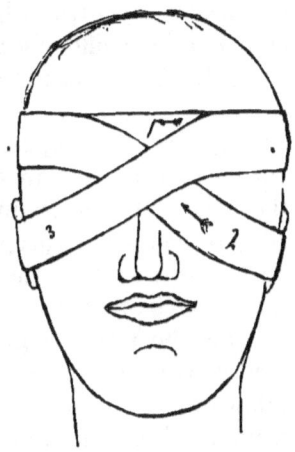

FIG. 29. Diagram showing the method of bandaging both eyes (binoculus). 1—is the first turn around the head. 2—is the second turn, covering the eye operated upon, or injured. 3—is the third turn covering the fellow-eye.

It is sometimes wise further to secure the bandage by means of a strip of flannel extending transversely across the head, especially in children.

This is probably the best place to give a few hints for the use of general practitioners who are asked to *assist* in an eye-operation. The tenderness and delicacy of movements required in the operator should also be possessed by the assistant. The observance of a few simple special rules by the assistant will make his services valuable, while no assistant would be preferable to one, not observing these rules.

As good light is absolutely and especially required in every eye-operation, the first rule for the assistant is, to keep out of the light, and, as perfect freedom of movement is necessary for the operator, the second, and no less important rule, is to keep out of his way. Both rules are usually best followed, if the assistant stands on the side of the patient opposite to the operator. As the operator will, as a rule, be ambidexter, the assistant ought to be so too. If, for instance, the assistant is required to hold the eye steady during a certain stage of an operation, he should hold it with the right hand when the operator uses his left, and vice versa, at least when they stand on opposite sides of the patient. To have the eye steadied by a trusty hand is of such great assistance to the operator, that he would not be likely to do without it, when it is to be had. Yet, a hand that is not trusty, is worse than none.

In order to steady the eye-ball the conjunctiva is grasped with the fixation forceps near the cornea-scleral margin, and as directly as possible opposite the field of the operation, and the teeth of the forceps are inserted into the tissue as deeply as possible. The forceps should always be held so that the thumb can at any moment press on its spring-catch and open it without any further movement. No traction and no pressure must be exerted. If the globe must be turned downwards by the assistant, this is not to be done by pulling downwards on the fixation forceps, but by rotating the eye-ball around its horizontal axis, by slightly raising the hand that holds the forceps and lowering the part attached to the globe gently towards the lower fornix. This little manipulation, if awkwardly done, may ruin an eye. Therefore, remember: no pulling, no pressure, but steadiness.

It is sometimes necessary for the removal of a small foreign body from the cornea, or the division of the lens-capsule, etc., to have the field of operation well illuminated by artificial light. To do this we use a large magnifying lens, which, of course, must be held by the assistant. It seems an easy matter to throw sufficient light with such a lens upon the field of operation, yet, it requires careful attention on the part of the assistant to do it satisfactorily, as the position of the lens must be changed with almost every movement of the eye-ball or head of the patient. The assistant should therefore not divide his attention between this and anything else of interest during the operation, or it may happen that the operator will find himself suddenly with a dark field of operation before him.

When the operation is a bloody one, as, for instance, an operation on the eye-lids, or a strabismus operation, or the enucleation of an eye-ball, the assistant should be prompt in wiping away the blood. For this purpose the sponges must be well squeezed out, and a careful assistant will, by wiping quickly after every cut that draws blood, enable the operator to work rapidly and never in the dark.

It is always best to wipe the blood away, not to soak it up, as is frequently done, by pressing the sponge on the bleeding surface. On the contrary, all pressure should be carefully avoided, especially in operations upon the eye-ball itself.

When, after the operation, the bandage is applied, the assistant can be of great help also. This is especially the case when the patient is under the influence of an anæsthetic. The assistant should then support the patient's head with one hand, and with one finger of the other hold the end of the bandage tightly against the head, so as to prevent it from slipping while the first two turns are taken around the head.

# CHAPTER VII.

### DISEASES OF THE CONJUNCTIVA.

HYPERÆMIA.—CATARRHAL CONJUNCTIVITIS.—PURULENT CONJUNCTIVITIS.—CROUPOUS CONJUNCTIVITIS.—DIPHTHERITIC CONJUNCTIVITIS.—GRANULAR CONJUNCTIVITIS.—PHLYCTÆNULAR CONJUNCTIVITIS.—SUBCONJUNCTIVAL ECCHYMOSIS.—INJURIES.—BURNS.—SYMBLEPHARON.—PINGUECULA.—PTERYGIUM.—NEOPLASM.

*Hyperæmia* of the conjunctival blood-vessels is frequently observed, especially in the conjunctiva of the eye-lids. It may be more pronounced in one part than in another, but it always shows least in the fornix. The color of the hyperæmic parts is a bright red, almost scarlet. In hyperæmia of the eye-ball we have seen (see Chapter II.), that it is necessary to distinguish between hyperæmia of the ocular conjunctiva, and that which lies more deeply and has its seat in the sclerotic.

When hyperæmia of the conjunctiva has existed for some time, the fornix, and later on the ocular conjunctiva, show a slightly œdematous condition. Later the papillæ of the conjunctiva become enlarged, and protrude slightly above the general surface of the conjunctiva, especially near the fornix.

Hyperæmia of the conjunctiva may be due to some irritation, and especially to the presence of small foreign bodies in the conjunctival sack, it accompanies coryza, and it may even originate in the strain incident to an error of refraction. It can, furthermore, be symptomatic both in certain more serious forms of eye-diseases, and in other disorders.

Patients suffering from hyperæmia of the conjunctiva complain of a dry, heated feeling, especially in the evening. Their eyes get easily tired, and there is slight photophobia and lachrymation.

When idiopathic, the affection usually yields readily to treatment. If due to the presence of a foreign body or to an error of refraction, the removal of the one or the correction of the other will be sufficient. In other cases when the hyperæmic condition has become chronic, weak astringent solutions of alum, sulphate of zinc or biborate of soda are useful. The effect of these remedies will be greatly enhanced by systematic cold bathing of the eyes, or, by the use of the eye-douche. In some cases bathing with warm water is more agreeable to the patient.

When the hyperæmia of the conjunctival blood-vessels is combined with an increased and abnormal secretion of the conjunctival glands, we have to deal with *conjunctivitis*.

The discharge from an eye suffering from any form of conjunctivitis (except the phlyctænular) is contagious. The physician must, therefore, never forget to guard the family of such a patient against conveying any of the discharge to their own eyes by means of towels, handkerchiefs, etc. Constant and careful removal of any discharge, and absolute cleanliness must be insisted upon. Eyes suffering from conjunctivitis should, therefore, never be bandaged.

In the lightest form, the *catarrhal conjunctivitis*, when in the acute stage, we find hyperæmia and œdematous swelling of the palpebral and ocular conjunctiva, and sometimes small subconjunctival ecchymoses. Gradually the papillæ of the conjunctiva become enlarged and give it a velvety appearance. The eye-lids, especially the upper one, swell, and the papebral fissure appears therefore smaller. Photophobia and lachrymation are but seldom absent and pain or great discomfort is a prominent symptom. The patients often locate the latter in the outer or inner angle of the palpebral fissure and insist that they have a foreign body in the eye.

The secretion in catarrhal conjunctivitis is mucoid or muco-purulent. It is not secreted in large quantity, and it coagulates easily. It will be found in yellowish flocks within the conjunctival sack, especially in the lower and upper fornix and upon the lachrymal caruncle. Some of it usually adheres to the eye-lashes. During sleep the eye-lashes of the two eye-lids are glued together and the patient is unable to open his eyes on waking in the morning. This often gives rise to excoriations along the lid-margins and near the outer angle of the palpebral fissure.

Catarrhal conjunctivitis may be caused by innumerable irritating influences, and is usually attributed to a "cold."

Light forms of this affection may get well without interference. When the symptoms are severer cold water applications or ice-water compresses should be used continuously to cool the inflamed tissues. If the discharge is profuse, a one per cent solution of nitrate of silver should be applied once a day by the physician. When the continued use of iced compresses is no longer required, but the photophobia is as yet marked, colored glasses should be worn.

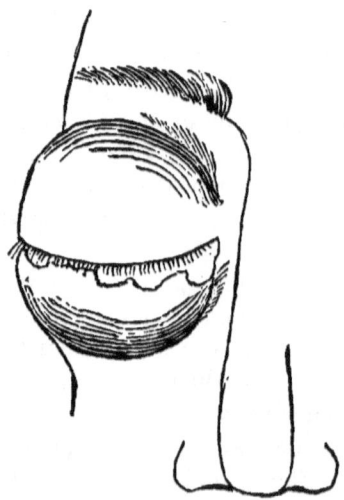

FIG. 30. Purulent conjunctivitis; showing especially the immense swelling of the eyelids in this affection.

Acute catarrhal conjunctivitis may pass over into the chronic form. In the latter the symptoms are all considerably ameliorated, and the patients are able to attend to their duty although continually annoyed by the affection. During sleep some discharge collects at the inner angle of the palpebral fissure or adheres to the eye-lashes, and often the eye-lashes of the two eyelids are found stuck together in the morning. The eyes become easily tired and complaint is often made of a feeling, as if dust or sand were in the eye.

These symptoms usually yield promptly to cold bathing conjoined with the daily application of an astringent solution. Sulphate of zinc, tannic acid and others, are all very useful in a one per cent solution. In some mild cases a few drops of a one per cent solution of boracic acid dropped once or twice daily into the conjunctival sack may suffice to mitigate the symptoms.

*Purulent conjunctivitis* is really an exagerated catarrhal conjunctivitis and the one may pass over into the other. An acute purulent conjunctivitis shows, therefore, all the symptoms of an acute catarrhal conjunctivitis, only much intensified and with a different character of secretion.

The whole conjunctiva is intensely and uniformly red, the papillæ are greatly swollen, and deep fissures are seen between them. The ocular conjunctiva and the eye-lids are œdematous, the latter so much so that the patient is often unable to open his eyes. (See figure 30). The feeling of heat and pain in the eyes is very distressing. The discharge is at first scant, a serous fluid containing flocks of yellowish mucus. Then it becomes thicker, a cream-like pus, which dries up easily and thus frequently gives rise to excoriations of the skin. With the profuse secretion the epithelial surface of the conjunctiva is cast off and the blood-vessels are apt to be wounded in turning the eye-lids. The swollen ocular conjunctiva forms an elevated ring around the corneoscleral margin (chemosis).

The impaired nutrition of the cornea, as well as the direct infection from the pus, in which it is continually bathed, frequently cause corneal affections. These are usually infiltrations and ulcers, which are especially destructive when occurring during a purulent conjunctivitis. The ulcers begin for the most part near the corneo-scleral margin, and may travel around the whole periphery of the cornea (ring-shaped ulcer). If the disease is not brought promptly under control, the ulceration leads to perforation of the cornea, prolapse of the iris, and eventually to the total destruction of the eye-ball.

The etiology of purulent conjunctivitis is in most cases absolutely clear. The irritating poison comes directly by contact, or indirectly through the air, from another purulent eye or from a patient suffering from gonorrhoea (gonorrhoeal conjunctivitis).

Even a slightly morbid discharge from urethra or vagina brought into the conjunctival sack, may set up a purulent conjunctivitis. This is the way in which the purulent conjunctivitis of newly born children is brought about.

Purulent conjunctivitis caused by a gonorrhœa is especially dangerous, and is greatly to be dreaded on account of its very rapid and destructive course.

With regard to the treatment of the affection under consideration, the rule usually laid down is, to make continued ice applications alone, as long as the discharge is scant and serous or blood-stained. When the discharge becomes purulent and abundant, caustic treatment is to be commenced. The latter consists in the daily application of a two, and later of a one per cent solution of nitrate of silver to the diseased conjunctiva. Corneal affections are no contra-indication to this treatment, but they call for increased carefulness in confining the application of the caustic solution to the conjunctiva and also for the instillation of either sulphate of atropia or sulphate of eserine. (1 per cent).

To this caustic treatment may be added other anti-phlogistic measures besides the ice applications. These are the application of leeches to the temple, or, what is of greater value, scarification of the conjunctiva. The patient should, furthermore, be kept in bed and in a moderately darkened room.

In some cases the pressure from the swollen lids is very great, and relief may be given by canthotomy.

Some surgeons have of late divided the upper eye-lid into two halves by a vertical section through its whole thickness, in order to reduce the pressure on the eye-ball, and to be able the better to remove the discharge.

From the fact that certain micrococci are found in the gonorrhœal discharge, which can be killed by corrosive sublimate in extremely weak solutions, such a solution had been recommended for the cure of gonorrhœal conjunctivitis, but it has not proven successful.

Whether the so-called prophylactic instillations of a solution of nitrate of silver, or of salicylic or carbolic acid into the conjunctival sack of new-born infants are of as great a value in preventing purulent conjunctivitis, as is at present claimed, time will show.

Acute purulent conjunctivitis may pass over into a chronic form, or the affection may, so to speak, be chronic from the beginning. In such a case all the symptoms are much milder. The swelling of the eye-lids and of the ocular conjunctiva is but little marked, yet the fornix is much swollen, its surface is velvet-like from the swelling of the papillæ, and the discharge is a thin, fluid pus.

The treatment is, in the main, the same as in the acute form of the disease. Sometimes during the course of a chronic purulent conjunctivitis the appearance of granules is observed. I then prefer to treat it with the sulphate of copper in substance. In the chronic form of the disease the cornea is less apt to become secondarily affected.

*Croupous or membranous conjunctivitis* is as well marked and distinct a form of inflammation as is the similar affection of the mucous membrane of the larynx. Its characteristic feature is the formation of a grayish white membrane on the surface of the conjunctiva, combined with slight swelling of the eye-lids and a scant mucus or muco-purulent discharge. This croupous membrane may involve a part only, or it may cover the whole area of the palpebral conjunctiva. It is, however, never observed to form on the ocular conjunctiva. Small patches of such a membrane are often seen accompanying purulent conjunctivitis.

At first the croupous membrane adheres rather firmly to the conjunctiva, and can be removed with difficulty. When the affection has lasted a few days, however, it may be easily removed by rolling it up with a sponge or linen rag, but only to be rapidly reformed. The conjunctiva beneath it is very succulent, its papillæ are enlarged, and it has a bluish-red tint. The removal of the croupous membrane often causes a slight bleeding. As the affection progresses the papillary swelling increases.

The cornea during a croupous conjunctivitis is but rarely affected, although it may be partially or totally destroyed by ulceration. Still the cases, in which the croupous conjunctivitis leads to serious results are very rare.

When the croupous patches are small, continued ice-water applications and daily caustic treatment are indicated, just as in a case of purulent conjunctivitis. When the membranes cover the whole inner surface of one or both eye-lids, and can only with difficulty be removed, it is best to confine the treatment to cold applications and careful cleansing. Only, when the membrane becomes loose and can easily be removed, is caustic treatment advisable.

The conjunctiva is, furthermore, sometimes the seat of a *diphtheritic inflammation*. This affection is less frequent in America than it is, for instance, in Germany, yet it is met with from time to time, and in hospital practice it sometimes occurs epidemically.

Its appearance is so characteristic that the physician who has once seen a case of diphtheritic conjunctivitis, can hardly confound it with anything else.

In diphtheritic conjunctivitis the eye-lids are swollen, stiff and very hard, so that they can hardly be everted, or only with the greatest difficulty. The pain is extreme, and is aggravated by the slightest pressure. While the exudation in croupous conjunctivitis lies on the surface of the conjunctiva, in diphtheritic conjunctivitis it fills also the whole tissue of the conjunctiva. The latter, therefore, although greatly swollen, is whitish in color and anæmic from the pressure of the exudition on the blood-vessels; moreover, the diphtheritic membrane cannot be removed. The ocular conjunctiva is greatly swollen and the secretion is watery and small in quantity. An attack of diphtheritic conjunctivitis is usually attended with high fever.

During this affection the cornea very rarely remains intact, and oftener is totally destroyed. The eye-lids also may suffer extensively, or may even slough off altogether.

After the active stage of the disease is past, the exudation is slowly dissolved, leaving an ulcerated conjunctiva in a state of purulent inflammation. This ulceration may heal without causing any deformity, or it may leave a considerable amount of scar-tissue behind.

Diphtheritic conjunctivitis is mostly found to be from the start, and to remain during its course a localized affection; a fact which has an important bearing upon the question of diphtheria in general. It sometimes extends from a diphtheritic process in the throat and nose, but this is very rare.

Diphtheritic exudation may also appear in small patches on the conjunctiva, and this is more frequently the case during the course of a purulent conjunctivitis.

The treatment consists simply in continued ice applications, until the exudation begins to dissolve; afterwards caustic treatment as in purulent conjunctivitis is indicated. Any corneal affection must, of course, be especially cared for.

*Trachoma, granular conjunctivitis, granulated eye-lids,* is that form of inflammation of the conjunctiva in which in addition to swelling of the eye-lids, œdema and swelling of the papillæ of the conjunctiva, and an abnormal secretion, there is also a formation of granules. These latter are round, grayish, translucent, sago-like bodies, slightly elevated above the surrounding conjunctival surface, but embedded in the conjunctival tissue. They are aggregations of lymphoid cells and resemble the lymph-follicles of the intestinal tract. Their usual seat in the beginning of the affection is the fornix of the conjunctiva, but they may spread over the whole inner surface of the eye-lids, and even to the ocular conjunctiva and corneo-scleral margin. Later on these granules undergo characteristic changes, and give rise to characteristic affections of the cornea, of the subconjunctival tissue, and of the eye-lids. The presence of the granules is the characteristic feature of trachoma, although they may be partially hidden, in the beginning, by the swollen papillæ, and thus may for a time escape detection. On the other hand the characteristic results produced by this form of conjunctivitis in the conjunctiva, cornea and eye-lids enable us to make the correct diagnosis of trachoma having existed, even when the granules have entirely disappeared.

The granules are not arranged in any regular way, but are usually irregularly grouped. They vary in size, yet are always larger than a swollen conjunctival papilla. After having existed for a certain time the granules become organized, and are transformed into connective tissue, so that in the end their former seat is marked by scars in the conjunctival tissue.

During the progress of the disease the papillæ of the conjunctiva are also swollen, and the subconjunctival tissue is often greatly infiltrated; later on this infiltration becomes organized and the newly formed connective tissue contracts, causing shrinkage of the conjunctival sack and atrophy of the mucous glands. The tarsal tissue undergoes fatty degeneration, and by the contraction of the new-formed scar-tissue its curvature becomes gradually changed. Thus the margins of the eye-lids are more and more turned inward, and the eye-lashes begin to scratch the cornea (entropium).

By the trachoma of the conjunctiva itself, and by the ensuing entropium and trichiasis, a constant irritation of the cornea is kept up and an inflammatory reaction takes place in its tissue. This latter may progress but slowly and may lead only to the destruction of the superficial layers, or it may progress rapidly, and lead to destructive ulceration or even to sloughing of the cornea.

In the former case the superficial layers of the cornea at its upper part become dim and infiltrated, the epithelial coat loses its luster, small superficial ulcerations may appear, and gradually blood-vessels are seen to grow into the infiltrated tissue from the corneo-scleral margin. This condition is called *pannus*, and may extend downwards over the area of the pupil, and thus render the patient virtually blind.

In the second case we have to deal with larger ulcers, and the formation of abscesses in the corneal tissue. These may then lead to perforation of the cornea with prolapse of the iris, and subsequently to shrinkage of the globe or to the formation of a staphyloma.

Iritis is often observed in connection with corneal affections dependent on trachoma, and is a very serious complication.

Finally the shrinking of the conjunctival sack may attain such a degree, as to render it nearly impossible for the patient to open his eyes. The mucous glands may then become so wasted as to leave the conjunctiva and cornea almost perfectly dry. This latter condition is called *xerophthalmus*.

The symptoms here described are in the main those of the *chronic form of trachoma*, which is the most frequent one.

In rarer cases we may have occasion to observe an *acute trachoma*, either as a primary affection or as an exacerbation during the progress of chronic trachoma.

Acute trachoma causes great irritation of the eye, lachrymation and swelling of the eye-lids and conjunctiva (the latter, however, to a lesser degree than chronic trachoma), and, of course, the formation of granules. There is a little watery discharge, or perhaps no discharge to speak of. If the acute trachoma appears during the progress of the chronic disease, its symptoms are, of course, more or less modified by the pre-existing condition. The intercurrent acute attacks are, moreover, very apt to affect the cornea. Acute trachoma may end in recovery or it may go over into the chronic form.

In the acute, as well as in the chronic type of trachoma, the subjective symptoms are chiefly the feeling as of dust or sand in the conjunctival sack, and of heat in the eye-lids. These symptoms are particularly noticeable in the morning. The discharge sometimes glues the eye-lashes together, but not always. The eyes refuse all application to close work.

Trachoma but rarely occurs in one eye only. It usually affects both eyes from the beginning, or one soon after the other. In chronic trachoma the subjective symptoms may for a long time be very mild, so that the patient is not even aware of his disease, until, perhaps, the eyes begin to tire when used at night, or to feel uncomfortable in the morning, or until an intercurrent acute attack brings him to the physician.

The affection is a very tedious one, and even with the best treatment and care, it will take many months to cure it; in some cases no cure seems possible. Frequently when we think we have won the battle a relapse occurs, which may cause the patient to lose confidence in the physician, and possibly drive him into the hands of quacks, until, perhaps, blinded altogether, he returns begging for the help which it is no longer possible to give.

Trachoma is one of the most frequent of eye-diseases, and, although oftener observed among the poor, it is found in all classes of society. Its appearance seems to be dependent largely on terrestrial influences, as it is very rare in higher altitudes, and very common in low, moist regions. In Illinois and Missouri and farther West, where malaria is prevalent, trachoma seems to be frequent also, and I have even heard it stated that trachoma is so intimately related to malaria that it will yield to anti-malarial treatment to the exclusion of local applications. It is almost needless to say that the latter idea is an erroneous one, although the conditions which favor malarial diseases are very much the same as those which favor the appearance of trachoma. Although anti-malarial treatment has no direct value in the treatment of trachoma, still the general debility, caused by malarial fever, may, like any other constitutional affection, render the system less able to resist disease, and for this reason only, an anti-malarial treatment may have a place in the treatment of trachoma.

The frequency of trachoma, and the difficulty of curing it, has for many years led to all sorts of trials in search of an ideal remedy. Thus far such researches have been but little successful, and therefore quackery has always had a fruitful field in trachoma.

In the acute inflammatory stage it is best to simply apply continued cold, and only when the patient cannot bear cold, to try warm applications. If the cornea is affected, we instill sulphate of atropia. As soon as the acute stage is past, stimulant treatment of the conjunctiva should be resorted to. The remedy most to be depended on in trachoma is most decidedly the sulphate of copper in substance, used in the way already described. Nitrate of silver, yellow oxide of mercury, acetate of lead, and whatever else has been and is used, do not yield as a rule the comparatively good and quick results attainable by the judicious use of sulphate of copper. Besides applying the copper once in twenty-four hours, which must always be done by the surgeon himself, the patient may be directed to bathe his eyes two or three times a day with cold water, or to use an eye-douche as often. Affections of the cornea are, as a rule, no contra-indication to the use of the copper, unless, indeed, they are attended with very great irritation. As the continual discharge from the eyes soon gives rise to erosions of the skin of the lower lids and the outer angles of the palpebral fissure, it is well to advise the patient to protect the lid-margins by the application of fresh lard, or better, of vaseline before retiring.

This treatment may be kept up unchanged for a very long period, and the copper does not seem to lose its effect by continued use.

If the palpebral fissure has become contracted so as to interfere with the raising of the upper eye-lid, canthotomy is very useful.

When the granules have disappeared under this treatment, as they will in comparatively recent cases in from 2 to 6 months, the patient should be treated from time to time for some months longer to assure against a relapse. Besides this he should use an astringent solution himself.

Excision of the granules, their destruction by actual or galvanic cautery, etc., have never given me the satisfaction which in most cases I have derived from the careful use of the sulphate of copper.

In some cases, as has been stated, no remedy seems to be of any lasting value, the eyes alternately improving and getting worse, even while under treatment. In these cases, especially when there is considerable pannus, the inoculation of pus from an eye suffering from purulent conjunctivitis has formerly been practiced, and sometimes with apparently great success. At other times, however, the result has been a very disastrous one, as the eyes have been destroyed. Very recently *von Wecker* has introduced a new agent for producing purulent conjunctivitis in such trachomatous eyes, which appears to be sometimes successful. The artificial disease is brought about by bathing the eyes in a 2 to 5 per cent infusion of the shelled and crushed seeds of *abrus precatorius*, a leguminous plant growing in the tropics. The inflammation which is set up by these infusions is, however, often very violent, and cases have recently been reported which show that their indiscriminate employment may be followed by disastrous consequences.

The treatment of the corneal affections dependent on trachoma will be spoken of in Chapter VIII.

The operative treatment of the affections of the eye-lids caused by the same disease has already been detailed in Chapter III.

Another form of inflammation to which the conjunctiva is subject, especially in childhood, is the *phlyctænular* (so-called *strumous*) *conjunctivitis*. It affects primarily the ocular conjunctiva, and especially the limbus conjunctivæ. On the injected and infiltrated conjunctiva a small papula or vesicle is formed, or sometimes several at the same time. This vesicle contains in most cases only a serous fluid and a few round cells, in others it is filled with pus (*pustular conjunctivitis*). The inflammation may remain confined to the neighborhood of the vesicle or it may spread over the entire ocular conjunctiva, and later on even to the conjunctiva of the eye-lids. Frequently we find the same formation of vesicles also on the cornea (phlyctænular keratitis). By and by the vesicle bursts, its contents escape, and a small ulcer remains in its place. The ulcer may now gradually heal, or the morbid process may be confined by the successive appearance of new vesicles.

In some cases the general irritation is but slight; in many cases, however, it is very great. The eye-lids are ædematous and hot; there is continued lachrymation, and such a dread of light that a child suffering from this affection will not only hide his face in the day time, whenever this is possible, but even bury it deeply in the pillow at night.

As a consequence of this habit the skin becomes irritated, and in warm weather the whole face may present a continuous surface in a state of eczematous inflammation.

The disease belongs essentially to childhood, and is but seldom seen in the adult. The severer cases, and especially such as show a tendency to frequent relapses, are generally accompanied by marked signs of scrophulosis. Phlyctænular conjunctivitis is not, like the other forms of conjunctivitis, a contagious affection. It leads but seldom to serious consequences, and may even get well without medical interference. Yet, as the primary cause is not easily removed, relapses are frequent, or are even the rule.

Besides the general treatment, which is directed against the constitutional disorder, this affection calls for vigorous local treatment. This consists in cold applications and in the daily inspergation of calomel or iodoform, or the use of an ointment containing from 1 to 4 per cent of yellow oxide of mercury. When there is a great deal of photophobia and spasm of the eye-lids, it is well to open the eyes forcibly and hold them open for some time. Another old and reliable method is by dipping the child's face into cold water. The success of the treatment will be especially promoted by giving the little patients plenty of fresh air and by forcing them to bear moderate light. To bandage such eyes, or to allow the children to exclude the light from them, and especially to sleep on their faces, is the worst thing that can be done. Sometimes the photophobia will cease when the pupil is well dilated by sulphate of atropia. The latter must, of course, be used whenever the cornea is implicated in the disease.

*Subconjunctival ecchymosis* is frequently observed as a result of contusions; also after a fit of violent coughing, as in whooping cough, etc. It is harmless, and calls for no treatment; in fact, treatment is wholly unavailing to hasten the absorption of the extravasated blood, which will disappear of itself in from two to four weeks, according to circumstances.

Among the *wounds and injuries* of the conjunctiva none are of great importance, or require special treatment except burns.

Burns with gun-powder, if they concern the conjunctiva only, are usually of little importance. Yet if a great many grains of powder are embedded in the conjunctiva, it is best to remove them by cutting them out, by lifting up a minute fold of conjunctiva with fine forceps and snipping it off with scissors.

Burns by acids or alkalies, especially by lime or by melted metals and glass, may give rise to the most disagreeable affections, through the destruction of the tissues. Lime even infiltrates the tissues to a considerable depth, and thus sticks fast to them. If an eye burnt with lime is seen immediately, a careful washing out of the conjunctival sack with acidulated water (vinegar will do) may in some measure limit the destructive action, but unfortunately we seldom see such cases early enough to do much in this way.

In all cases of burns of the conjunctiva the first thing to be done is to cleanse the conjunctival sack carefully of all foreign substances which can be easily removed. This done, atropine should at once be instilled and, ice applications be made.

If the destruction extends to the subepithelial tissue of the ocular and palpebral conjunctiva, and perhaps to the cornea, the ulcerated surfaces, lying continually closely applied to each other, may grow together, thus forming a *symblepharon*. (See figure 31). In mild cases we may sometimes succeed in preventing its formation by keeping the eye-lid everted as much as possible, but as a rule symblepharon will occur in spite of all our efforts. Instillations of oil into the conjunctival sack are usually resorted to, but are of little value. I have seen better results in two cases where the melted metal could not at once be removed from the lower conjunctival sack, and where by its presence it subsequently successfully opposed the formation of a symblepharon. I am therefore inclined to think, that where the burn of the conjunctiva is caused by melted metal, which is unirritating in its nature, and is usually flattened out smoothly, its presence in the conjunctival sack might be allowed for some time under careful watching. We must, of course, be on our

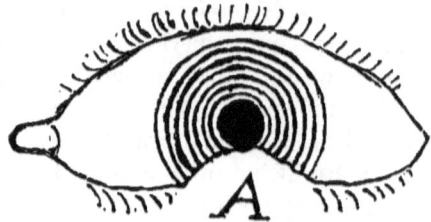

FIG. 31. A. Symblepharon.—The lower eye-lid is firmly adherent to the eye-ball.

guard against possible danger to the cornea, which, however, is not very likely to result from the presence of a smooth, indifferent foreign body lying in the lower cul-de-sac.

When the palpebral and ocular conjunctiva near the corneoscleral margin, or the palpebral conjunctiva and the cornea are grown together in the shape of a bridge, the condition is called symblepharon anterius. When the union has taken place farther back in the conjunctival sack and reaches to the very fornix of the conjunctiva, it is called a symblepharon posterius. It is clear that any such attachment between the eye-lid and eye-ball must impede the movements of the latter. When the whole, or at least the largest part of the conjunctival sack is thus obliterated by the union of the palpebral with the ocular conjunctiva, and, perhaps, the cornea, we speak of *anchyloble-*

## DISEASES OF THE CONJUNCTIVA.

*pharon*. In this condition the movements of the eye-ball are, of course, almost totally abolished; the eye also is generally so far damaged, as to be worthless as an organ of vision.

In symblepharon anterius, in which the fornix is not involved and in which the adhesion forms a bridge-like band, connecting the eye-ball with the eye-lid, the simple division of this bridge is generally sufficient; but in cases of more extensive symblephara division of the bands is unavailing, unless some means can be devised to fill the gap resulting from the destruction of the ocular or palpebral conjunctiva. This may be effected by covering the ocular wound-surface by conjunctival flaps from the same eye, by transplantation of flaps from other (even rabbits) eyes, or by covering the defect on the inner surface of the eye-lid by a cutaneous flap tilted over the lid-margin or even drawn through a cut through the lid and fastened to the inside.

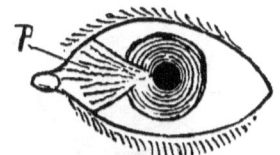

Fig. 32. P. Pterygium internum.

In cases of symblepharon of the lower eye-lid it has also been recommended to keep the eye-lid permanently everted after the dissection, until the wounds are healed by means of a needle run through a fold of skin.

The conjunctiva, especially the ocular conjunctiva, is sometimes the seat of *newformations*, which may be either benign or malignant.

*Pinguecula*, a small yellowish elevation near the cornea-scleral margin on the medial or lateral side of the cornea and in the line of the palpebral fissure, is perfectly harmless. Its name would imply that it is of a fatty nature, which, however, is not the case. It is simply condensed subconjunctival tissue and its formation probably due to the movements of the eye-lids. If it tends to become irritated and thus gives rise to annoyance, besides being in some measure disfiguring, it may be removed by a clip of the scissors.

Pinguecula has been accused also of being the starting point of the development of *pterygium*. (See figure 32).

This growth consists of a triangular fold of the conjunctiva, widest near one angle of the palpebral fissure or the fornix and more or less pointed towards its insertion on the corneo-scleral margin or on the cornea. It is oftenest found on the nasal side more rarely on the temporal side of the eye-ball, occasionally in the direction of one of the other recti muscles. It may for a long time remain stationary; when inflamed, however, it is apt to grow farther towards the centre of the cornea, and thus may in time interfere with vision. It is frequently a cause of chronic conjunctivitis.

With regard to the etiology of pterygium, it seems to be, as a rule, the result of a marginal ulcer of the cornea, to which an

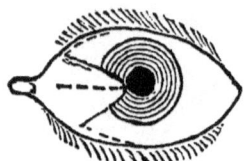

FIG. 33. Shows the incision in Knapp's method of transplanting pterygium into the fornix of the conjunctiva.

overlapping fold of the nearest part of the ocular conjunctiva has become adherent. We find, therefore, in transverse sections a layer of conjunctival epithelium, incarcerated between it and the cornea or sclerotic, undergoing retrogressive metamorphosis. In a case, which I saw in the practice of my friend Dr. J. Green, this colloid metamorphosis of the incarcerated epithelial cells had caused the formation of a cyst under the pterygium, which on being punctured discharged a small amount of a viscid, colloid material.

Pterygium should be removed as soon as it begins to encroach on the cornea or causes continued irritation. When the pterygium is small, this is best done by the excision of a rhomboid piece with subsequent union of the wound-lips by a suture.

# DISEASES OF THE CONJUNCTIVA.

When it is large, it should first be dissected off the cornea and sclerotic, and then by a longitudal cut be divided into an upper and a lower half (*Knapp*) one of which is to be stitched into the lower and the other in the upper fornix. (See figure 33.) Although this method is good and insures against a relapse, I find another method simpler and just as reliable; it consists in first dissecting up the pterygium, then undermining the tissue at its base and lastly doubling the pterygium on itself and stitching the two raw surfaces together by a single suture carried through the apex of the pterygium and the conjunctiva (Galezowsky). The elevation which is at first caused by this operation, gradually disappears.

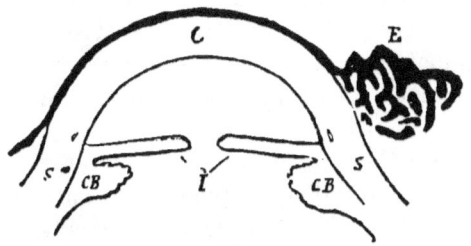

FIG. 34. Meridional section through the anterior third of an eye-ball affected by epithelioma of the conjunctiva.   E. Epithelioma.   C. Cornea.   S. Sclerotic.   I. Iris.   CB. Ciliary body.

Cysts, fatty tumors and granulomata (polypi) are sometimes found in the conjunctiva sack and are to be simply excised. If the wound is large its lips may be stitched together.

*Epithelioma* (See figure 34), *melanosarcoma* and *leukosarcoma* of the ocular conjunctiva are not very rare. They always start near the corneo-scleral margin, and when seen early should be carefully removed. These tumors later on extend to the cornea, yet before entering its tissue they spread between its epithelium and Bowman's layer, so that even then, if they have not extended too far, there is yet a chance for a successful removal. Later on the eye-ball must be removed altogether.

# CHAPTER VIII.

### DISEASES OF THE CORNEA.

PHLYCTAENULAR KERATITIS.—PARENCHYMATOUS KERATITIS.—SYPHILITIC KERATITIS.—ABSCESS OF THE CORNEA.—HYPOPYUM.—ULCERS OF THE CORNEA.—MALARIAL KERATITIS.—NEURO-PARALYTIC KERATITIS.—SCARS IN THE CORNEA.—TATOOING.—ARCUS SENILIS.—STAPHYLOMA OF THE CORNEA.—CONICAL CORNEA.—INJURIES, BURNS.—NEOPLASMS.

All forms of inflammation of the cornea, *keratitis*, cause a transient or lasting dimness of a part or the whole area of the corneal tissue. This dimness may lie deeply or superficially, or it may involve the whole thickness of the cornea. Keratitis is always accompanied by a symptomatic conjunctivitis, and is frequently complicated by iritis. It is often followed by the new-formation of blood-vessels within the corneal tissue, which spring from the terminal loops, at the corneo-scleral margin, (see Chapter I). These blood-vessels may disappear again, or they may remain persistent. Keratitis mostly attacks but one eye, although, some forms nearly always affect both eyes.

In every case of keratitis atropine should at once be instilled to guard against the accidents which may result from an intercurrent iritis. This treatment should be persisted in, until the pupil is dilated as widely as possible. Sulphate of eserine, a myotic drug which has of late been highly recommended in some corneal troubles, is according to my experience of no greater usefulness in these affections than the sulphate of atropia, and has besides the very grave disadvantage of specially disposing to the development of iritis.

Its greatest usefulness with, perhaps, some advantage over atropine, I have noticed in cases of abscess of the cornea.

*Phlyctaenular keratitis* is essentially the same affection, as phlyctaenular conjunctivitis, and as has been stated under that head, the one is very often seen, associated with the other. The treatment is exactly the same, and need not be again insisted on. The affection often leaves no trace behind, but in other cases a slight superficial scar is formed, which appears as a small gray spot (*macula*). In other cases in which a leash of blood-vessels extends from the periphery towards the seat of the phlyctaenula (*fascicular keratitis*), these may remain for some time after the healing of the phlyctaenula. They usually disappear later on, but often leave a dimness of the cornea in their place.

*Parenchymatous keratitis* consists of an infiltration of the corneal tissue proper. After the eye has been in an irritated condition for some time, a gray spot begins to show at the periphery of the cornea, which very soon grows and slowly spreads over the whole cornea. While this infiltration concerns usually the middle layers of the corneal tissue, the epithelium is also implicated and loses its lustre, and it appears rough or steamy.

Sometimes the infiltration is first seen in the center of the cornea, and may extend, leaving a small band of corneal tissue at the periphery perfectly clear. The spreading of the inflammation over the cornea usually takes several weeks, but it may even take months. Soon after or, perhaps, even before the progress of the infiltration has ceased, blood-vessels are seen to grow from the periphery into the cornea. Sometimes but a single large vessel is seen; in other cases the vascularity and dimness of the corneal tissue are such, as to make it appear almost like raw flesh. In most cases of parenchymatous keratitis the iris does not become affected, yet there are many exceptions to this rule.

Sometimes the patients suffering from parenchymatous keratitis complain of no subjective symptoms, beyond the loss of vision; more frequently, however, there is great photophobia, lachrymation, and pain.

By and by the corneal tissue begins to clear up from the periphery toward the center and the infiltration may be absorbed so perfectly that no trace remains. The blood-vessels then become atrophied and disappear with the dimness of the corneal tissue. In other cases part of the infiltration may lead to the formation of scar-tissue, and then one or more translucent, grayish spots may remain in the otherwise transparent cornea. Even these spots may afterwards shrink and partially disappear. If they lie just in front of the pupil or just below it, they will materially interfere with vision.

Parenchymatous keratitis is always slow in its course, although the time over which it extends may be shortened by intelligent treatment. If the cases come under treatment at the beginning, from 2 to 3 months are usually required for the disease to run its course, but a much longer time may be consumed in old cases.

The English writers, influenced by *Hutchinson's* statements, call this form of keratitis *syphilitic keratitis*. No doubt it is often the case that patients suffering from parenchymatous keratitis exhibit signs of inherited syphilis, yet the affection is also seen in patients who show absolutely no such specific taint. They suffer, however, nearly always from a noticeably weak or anæmic condition of the whole system, although marked signs even of that may be wanting. The affection is most frequent in childhood, and is but seldom seen in the adult. It appears as a rule in both eyes, in one a little later than in the other, and occasionally recurs.

The prognosis with regard to the absorption of the infiltration seems the better, the greater the vascularisation of the cornea. Our treatment, therefore, consists chiefly in the use of such remedies, as tend to stimulate the newformation of bloodvessels in the corneal tissue. This is most effectively done by the application of moist heat. Warm bathing, therefore, 3 or 4 times a day for an hour ought to be ordered. Furthermore, an ointment of yellow oxide of mercury (2 to 4 per cent) should be daily applied to the cornea, and its application be combined with massage. Of late I have used inspergations of iodoform and touching of the cornea with copper in this affection, and think I can recommend them both. Calomel inspergations may also be used. Instillations of atropia are, of course, as necessary in this as in all other corneal affections.

To this local treatment constitutional treatment must be added, where it is called for, and it may be well in all cases to give some tonic or iodide of potassium.

In some slow cases paracentesis of the cornea or iridectomy have been resorted to in order to shorten the process. I have not yet seen a case in which operative interference was necessary.

When an infiltration of the cornea produces a local necrosis and formation of pus within the corneal tissue we call it an *abscess of the cornea.*

This affection appears always in an acute form. We see in the cornea a dim yellowish spot, which may be near the surface or lie embedded in the deeper layers. It is usually round or semi-lunar, or it may be ring-shaped. Its outlines are, however, never sharply defined, as the surrounding tissue is also in a state of infiltration. If the affection progresses the nearest surrounding parts become also necrosed. When such an abscess has reached a certain size, pus cells will wander from it into the anterior chamber and there fall to the lowest point, and form what is called *hypopyum*. In the formation of this hypopyum the iris and ciliary body, which frequently become also inflamed, may take a part. The aqueous humor becomes generally turbid. The abscess may, furthermore, increase so as to break through the anterior surface, and thus form an ulcer. Sometimes it breaks through into the anterior chamber. The pus may also become absorbed with or without the newformation of blood-vessels. The cavity of the abscess is then filled with newformed connective tissue and a gray spot will be left to mark its former location. In very rare cases the pus is absorbed without leading to the newformation of tissue, or at least not enough to fill the cavity. On the other hand the abscess may cause perforation of the whole thickness of the cornea and lead to anterior synechia, loss of the crystalline lens and vitreous body, staphyloma, or total loss of the eye.

Abscess of the cornea is a very painful affection, the pain being apparently greatest at night and keeping the patient from sleeping. There is great irritation, photophobia and lachrymation. The disease appears, as a rule, in one eye only. It is seen more frequently in old and debilitated individuals than in young persons, and is frequently caused by slight injuries to the cornea, especially when there is a pre-existing affection of the tear-passages.

The prognosis is always doubtful, as we cannot predict how far the process will extend. As a rule, however, its progress stops when the abscess has perforated the surface. If there is a great quantity of pus in the anterior chamber, the prognosis is, of course, more doubtful than if there is little or none.

The treatment consists in hot moist applications to the closed eye, as hot as the patient can bear them. This sometimes relieves the pain very rapidly. Instead of the instillations of atropine, eserine has of late been used frequently, but seems to have only a slight advantage over the atropine and only in some cases. If the bowels are constipated, they ought to be freely opened.

If, under this treatment, the pain and the process of the affection do not stop, and rupture or absorption do not readily occur, I have seen great and immediate benefit, not from opening the anterior chamber, as many do, but from cutting simply through the layers anteriorly to it into the cavity of the abscess and allowing the pus to escape, just as one would open an abscess elsewhere. Saemisch's method, which is frequently practiced, consists in cutting through the whole thickness of the cornea about in the middle line of the abscess, and letting the aqueous humor and pus escape through this. The incision should begin and end in healthy tissue, and it must be reopened from day to day until the formation of pus ceases. This method is very painful, does not give quick results, and in the end the case often does no better than it would have done with less interference; anterior synechia moreover follows very frequently. The simple opening of the abscess is more rational and fully as effective.

If there is a lachrymal trouble present it must, of course, be attended to.

*Ulcers of the cornea* are either caused by a previous abscess in the way just described, or the infiltration is at first superficial, leading presently to necrosis of the epithelium and most superficial layers of the cornea.

Such ulcers may be caused by an injury, or they may appear without a known cause. They may lie centrally or peripherally, or they may even travel gradually around the whole circumference of the cornea.

Ulcers, like abscesses of the cornea, cause a great deal of

pain, as a rule, and give rise to photophobia and lachrymation.

As long as the ulcer (See figure 35) is progressing, its walls and fundus, as well as the surrounding parts, are grayish or yellow from infiltration. The pus cells may also invade the anterior chamber and form a hypopyum. Iritis is also a frequent complication. When the ulcer heals, its walls and fundus first become clear, and then, with or without the formation of blood-vessels in the cornea the process of repair begins. The ulcer is gradually filled up with new-formed translucent connective tissue, which becomes covered by epithelium, thus leaving behind it a gray spot. Often the progress of the ulcer does not

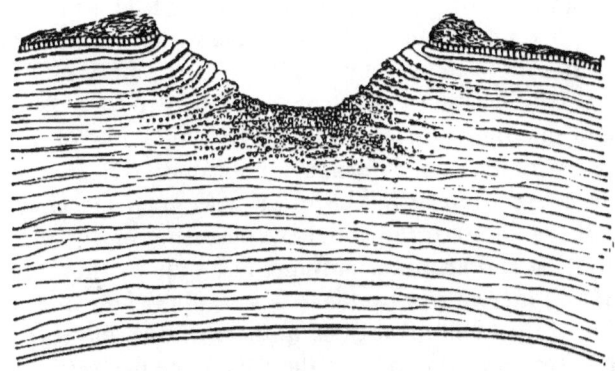

FIG. 35. Ulcer of the Cornea. The ground and walls of the ulcer are infiltrated with round cells. The epithelial cells around the ulcer are proliferating. (From Lectures on the Human Eye, by A. Alt. G. P. Putnam's Sons: 1880).

stop until it has eaten through the whole thickness of the cornea and caused a perforation. The aqueous humor then escapes, the iris prolapses into the corneal wound, and the ulcer may heal with anterior synechia. In other cases these accidents may lead to the loss of the crystalline lens, and even of the vitreous body, to the formation of a staphyloma, or to total loss of the eye through shrinkage.

The occurrence of ulcers of the cornea is not particularly confined to any period of life. They frequently appear, as has already been stated, during conjunctival affections. Corneal phlyctaenula and ulcers occur also in connection with malarial fever, and a particular form of ulcer has been described as *malarial keratitis* by *Kipp* and others.

The prognosis depends, of course, on the size and locality of the ulcer.

The treatment of corneal ulcers, when not too large, and when there is no hypopyum, consists of instillations of sulphate of atropia (or perhaps sulphate of eserine), hot bathing, and the application of a compressive bandage. The bandage not only excludes light, but steadies the eye-ball, and thus prevents the pain caused by moving it. It is therefore important to bandage both eyes.

Too much care can scarcely be urged in consideration of the use of lotions and eye-drops containing acetate of lead, a practice still far too common and leading to most disastrous results through the formation of lead-incrustations in the corneal tissue.

When the healing does not seem to progress favorably, the use of an ointment containing yellow oxide of mercury or the inspergation of iodoform are indicated. Some surgeons apply the actual cautery to the ulcer with good success. When these methods do not bring about the cleansing of the ulcer, but the infiltration and necrosis continue, and hypopyum is formed, the operation introduced by *Saemisch* is applicable and is here of greater utility than in cases of abscess of the cornea. Care must be taken to begin and end the cut in the healthy tissue, as far as this may yet be possible.

In other cases simple paracentesis of the cornea will be sufficient, or an iridectomy may be called for, as the intra-ocular pressure is sometimes increased (*secondary glaucoma*).

In paralysis of the trigeminus ulcerations (sometimes abscesses) of the cornea are often observed. These cases are easily recognized from the fact that the sensibility of the cornea is greatly reduced or totally abolished. Usually the secretion of tears and of mucus is also diminished with consequent dryness of the corneal epithelium. The reduced sensibility makes it possible for small foreign bodies to wound the cornea or even remain in it, without apparently causing discomfort. The reduced secretion of tears in itself gives rise to superficial excoriations.

If the paralysis cannot be cured, the only way to keep the

# DISEASES OF THE CORNEA.

cornea from inflammation, is by protecting the eye with a bandage, or by shortening the palpebral fissure by the operation of tarsoraphy (See Chapter III.).

As has already been stated, any process in the cornea which is attended with destruction of tissue and which necessitates repair by means of newly-formed connective tissue, must result in a *scar*. Scars in contrast with the normal, transparent corneal tissue, are only translucent, and therefore appear as more or less dense grayish, or even white spots which, according to their situation, may or may not interfere with vision; when large and centrally placed they may render the eye partially or even practically blind by their density, or they may give rise to irregular astigmatism, by altering the curvature of the cornea.

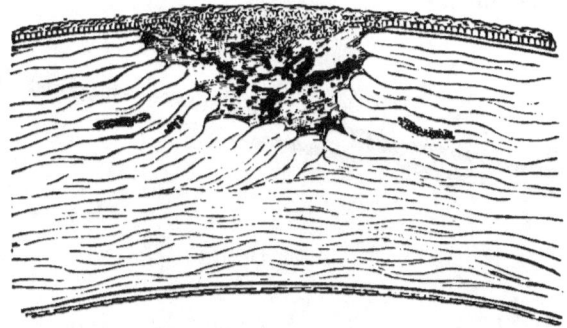

FIG. 36. A Healed Ulcer of the Cornea. The loss of substance is filled with newly formed connective tissue (scar), into which the epithelial layer dips in the shape of papillæ-like offsets. (From Lectures on the Human Eye, by A. Alt).

These scars (See figure 36) may sometimes be influenced by treatment and may clear up to some degree. The use of an ointment containing yellow oxide of mercury, the instillation of tincture of opium diluted with water, and spraying the eye with solutions of sulphate of copper or of tannic acid have been recommended and are in some cases beneficial.

In certain cases patients suffer from very annoying dazzling from light, which is irregularly refracted in passing through such a translucent scar, especially if it covers only a part of the pupillary area. In such cases it is sometimes advisable to tatoo the scar with India ink so as to render it impermeable to light. Tatooing may also be used for a simple cosmetic effect, when a scar of the cornea is very disfiguring. (See figure 37.)

When the scar lies in front of the whole pupillary area, and renders the patient virtually blind, an iridectomy may often restore useful vision. This should be made preferably in a place where the upper eye-lid is not likely to cover it, but the direction of the iridectomy is usually determined by the position of the clearest and best part of the remaining cornea, and thus may have to be made where the surgeon would least desire, were he left free in his choice. An iridectomy for this purpose should be made as small as possible, as the patient will see better through a small pupil, which does not allow many irregularly refracted rays to enter the eye-ball, than through a larger one which admits them.

FIG. 37. Tatooing Needle.

The grayish zone seen in the periphery of the cornea, usually in people of an advanced age, is called the *arcus senilis*. It is of no importance and the result of a fatty degeneration of the corneal tissue and cells.

As has been before stated, an abscess and ulcer of the cornea, which leads to perforation, may result in the formation of a *staphyloma*. The staphyloma consists in a partial or total bulging of the remains of the cornea (See figure 38) and the iris, which in these cases always adheres to it. If left alone, the bulging process may go on until the eye-lids can no longer be closed over the eye-ball. Such eyes are seldom free from irritation, and they are liable to be attacked by various forms of inflammation; sometimes a secondary glaucoma results.

In the beginning of a partial staphyloma the use of eserine, and frequent puncturing of the bulging tissue may be successfully resorted to. The latter procedure causes more and more scar tissue to be found, which by its shrinking often brings about a flattening of the protruding parts. Sometimes an iridectomy or sclerotomy has proved successful in these cases, combined with the application of a compressive bandage. In some cases when the staphyloma is very small it may be best to cut a part of it away.

In total staphyloma of the cornea an abscision of the whole cornea may be made, combined with the removal of the crystalline lens, if it is still present. The margin of the opening thus left in the sclerotic will generally heal together, and a good stump on which an artificial eye can be worn is the result. Still,

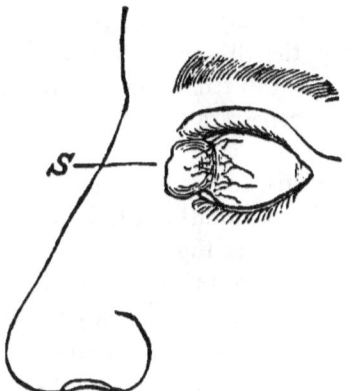

FIG. 38. S. Total Staphyloma of the Cornea after Ulceration.

as such a stump may become inflamed, and cause sympathetic inflammation of the good eye, it is better, as a rule, to remove every eye with total staphyloma of the cornea, whenever the case cannot be kept under continued observation.

A great many experiments have been made, having for their object the transplantation of a piece of transparent corneal tissue on staphylomatous eyes. The results have been thus far discouraging in the extreme, as the implanted cornea, after having remained clear for a short time, has become dim, and in the end nothing has been gained.

*Conical cornea* may be a congenital affection, or may be the result of a centrally located ulcer. The production of a retracting scar by cauterizing the cone at its apex, or the excision of the apex, has sometimes had a beneficial effect on the sight of eyes so affected.

*Injuries to the cornea* are of frequent occurence. Very frequently they are complicated by injuries to the deeper parts of the eye-ball. When the cornea alone is injured the conditions are comparatively simple.

Injuries may be inflicted by blunt or by cutting instruments, by heat, or by chemicals.

Abrations of the corneal epithelium are often seen. They are painful and cause lachrymation, especially when the eyeball is moved. Instillations of atropine and cold or warm applications with rest, which may be brought about by a compressive bandage, will allay the disagreeable symptoms, and the defect will generally be healed in from one to two days.

Cuts that do not penetrate the whole thickness of the cornea heal very readily.

When the corneal tissue is perforated by the injuring body, just as in the case of a perforating ulcer or abscess, the aqueous humor will escape, and, as the posterior parts are thus moved forward by the intra-ocular pressure, the iris may be caught between the wound-lips, or it may even prolapse through them, and be held in that position. As prolapse of the iris increases the danger to the eye, and may even be the means of exciting inflammation of the uveal tract or the formation of staphyloma, the iris should, if possible, be set free. If it is impossible to cause its retraction by slightly rubbing the cornea with the eye-lids, by the instillation of the sulphate of atropia or of eserine, or by instrumental help, the last resort is to cut off the protruding part and thus permit the remainder of the iris to retract within the eye. *Burns* of the cornea by hot foreign bodies, or by chemicals, especially lime, cause a more or less superficial necrosis of the corneal tissue with subsequent ulceration. When the cornea alone is injured the treatment will be the same as in the case of a cut of the cornea, except when the burn resulted from lime. In this case every particle of lime should, if possible be removed and the remainder neutralized by acidulated water (vinegar). It sometimes happens that we find a shell of lime lying on the cornea after all inflammatory symptoms have passed off. This can be readily removed and the patient's sight often greatly improved.

When the burning material has at the same time injured the conjunctiva there is danger of the formation of a symblepharon, which must, if possible, be prevented. This point has already received the necessary attention. (See Chapter VIII).

The tumors of the cornea take their origin from the adjacent conjunctival tissue, and therefore only secondarily invade the corneal tissue. They have been spoken of in Chapter VII.

# CHAPTER IX.

## DISEASES OF THE SCLEROTIC.

EPISCLERITIS AND SCLERITIS.— SCLERAL STAPHLYOMA.— NEOPLASMS.— INJURIES.

The sclerotic proper is not very apt to become inflamed, and such inflammatory symptoms as sometimes occur in it take their origin probably in the episcleral tissue.

*Episcleritis* or *scleritis acuta* is usually a localized inflammation. Near the limbus of the cornea and beneath the highly hyperæmic conjunctiva, a purple elevation is seen, which is often painful and tender on pressure. The deeper the seat of the inflammation the deeper is the purple color. Although beginning as a small localized tumor, the swelling often wanders around the whole periphery of the cornea. Episcleritis may run its course without further complication, or it may be complicated with affections of the cornea, iris, choroid and even of the retina. It is a tedious disease, and often resists treatment for a long period. It is also very apt to recur.

The reason for these peculiarities lies in the fact that its occurrence is generally due to some general diathesis, rheumatism, gout, or syphilis being present in the majority of cases. Another class of cases occur in females at the climacteric period, or when suffering from some trouble of the sexual organs. Episcleritis is also occasionally due to an injury, in which case it yields more readily to treatment than when it is of constitutional origin. The direct cause of the non-traumatic cases of episcleritis is, as *Mooren* states, probably a pathological condition of the bloodvessels brought about by the diathesis.

The treatment which appears to be most successful, consists in hot bathing, instillations of atropine and the use of an ointment of yellow oxide of mercury, combined with massage. At the same time it is well to keep the bowels open. The treatment of any existing diathesis must, of course, be attended to. In a few cases that have come under my observation at a very early stage, the use of the muriate of pilocarpine, either hypodermically or instilled into the eye, has been followed by remarkably rapid recovery. It has been recommended also to cut through the swollen part down to the healthy sclerotic, or even to scrape the whole swelling off with a sharp curette.

There is a chronic form of scleritis conjoined with inflammation of the uveal tract, which is for the most part noticed by its results only, namely, the formation of a *scleral staphyloma*. This forms a bluish elevation which begins at one of the weaker parts of the sclerotic, where it is pierced by blood-vessels, and may

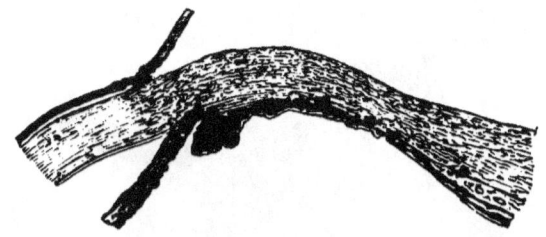

FIG. 39. Staphyloma of the Sclerotic in the Ciliary Region. The atrophied ciliary body adheres to the sclerotic. (From Lectures on the Human Eye, by A. Alt.)

gradually grow to a considerable size. (See figure 39). The seat of the staphyloma is oftenest in the equatorial, or the ciliary region of the eye-ball. In some cases the whole sclerotic may become staphylomatous (total staphyloma).

At the seat of the staphyloma the sclerotic and uveal tract are firmly adherent to each other, and become together more and more attenuated and stretched. Although the disease may at first interfere comparatively little with vision, it leads gradually to further alterations in the tissues of the eye-ball, and frequently gives rise to secondary glacoma, or perhaps, ultimately, to sympathetic inflammation of the fellow-eye. Scleral staphyloma is sometimes caused by an injury, but in most cases the etiology is obscure.

With regard to treatment, it is generally best to leave such an eye alone, but to keep it under observation. If this is for any reason impracticable, and the case is an aggravated one, the best thing is to remove the whole eye-ball. The abscision of a small staphyloma may be tried, however, under certain circumstances. The patient must be well watched, moreover, as this operation may be followed by bad results, sometimes even by the speedy development of sympathetic symptoms in the fellow-eye.

Another form of scleral staphyloma is the *posterior staphyloma*, an attenuation and stretching of the sclerotic adjoining the optic nerve entrance and generally in the direction of the macular lutea. As in this form of staphyloma there is always elongation of the anterior posterior axis of the eye-ball, myopia, short-sightedness, (See figure 40) is always present.

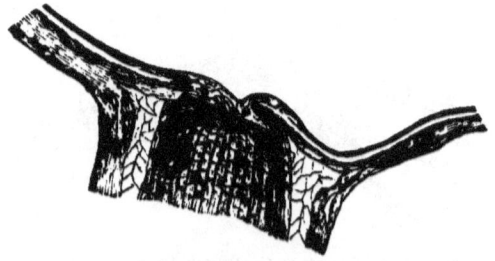

FIG. 40. Posterior Scleral Staphyloma from a Myopic Eye. Choroid and sclerotic adhere to each other, and are atrophied. (From Lectures on the Human Eye, by A. Alt).

*Tumors* of the sclerotic are, as a rule, of conjunctival origin ; the sclerotic proper is seldom, if ever, the primary seat of a new-formation.

*Wounds* of the sclerotic, if uncomplicated, may heal by first intention. It is often well to close them by sutures. I have even seen extensive complicated wounds of the sclerotic with prolapse of the choroid, retina and vitreous body, heal well and apparently give no further trouble. Yet, as a rule, such complicated wounds must be looked upon as something very dangerous, both for the wounded eye-ball itself and for its fellow, especially when the ciliary region is involved. The physician should, therefore, be extremely guarded in giving a prognosis in such cases, or a bad result may bring him into discredit.

## DISEASES OF THE SCLEROTIC. 107

If there are inflammatory symptoms, the continued application of cold is called for, together with absolute rest in a dark room. If the cold is not borne well, we may try warm applications. If the patient comes under observation early, instillations of atropine and a compressive bandage are often the best therapeutic measure.

If the wound is followed immediately or within a short time by severe inflammatory symptoms, it may become necessary to remove the eye-ball.

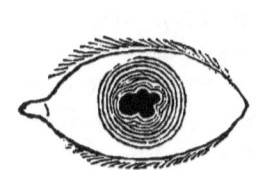

FIG. 41. Posterior Synechiæ from Iritis. The pupil is dilated, as far as possible, by Sulphate of atropia.

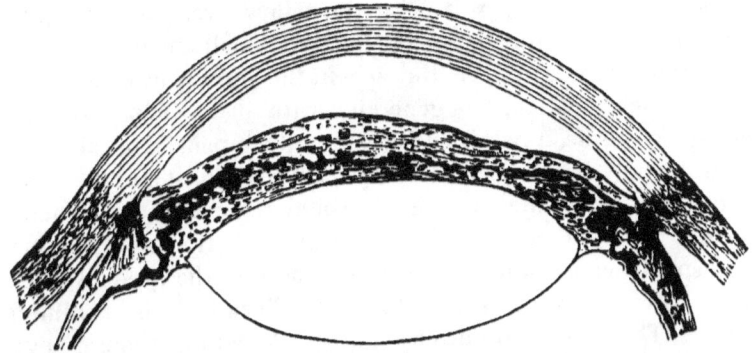

FIG. 42. Newly Formed Connective Tissue, the result of a fibrino-plastic iritis, unites the iris with the anterior lens-capsule. (From Lectures on the Human Eye, by A. Alt.)

These two cuts, erroneously placed here, ought to have been on page 109.

# CHAPTER X.

## DISEASES OF THE IRIS.

PLASTIC IRITIS.—SEROUS IRITIS.—PURULENT IRITIS.—GUMMATOUS IRITIS.—POISONING BY ATROPIA.—INJURIES.—TRAUMATIC COLOBOMA.—IRIDODIALYSIS.—NEOPLASMS.—CYSTS.—SARCOMA.—MYDRIASIS.—MYOSIS.

Inflammation of the iris is a rather frequent affection, and is easily recognized in its severer forms or later stages. It is chiefly in its beginning that it is frequently confounded with catarrhal conjunctivitis. It may be well, therefore, to make it a rule to dilate the pupil by instillations of a 1-per cent solution of sulphate of atropia in all doubtful cases.

The different forms of iritis are chiefly recognized by their products, and we have four typical forms, namely : plastic, serous, purulent and gummatous iritis.

Every form of iritis is characterized by hyperaemia of the episcleral blood-vessels, and secondarily of the superficial vessels of the ocular conjunctiva.

The iris loses its luster and is changed more or less in color, a change which is most easily recognized, when only one eye is affected, by comparing it with the fellow eye. Excepting in certain cases of serous iritis, the pupil is small and immoveable.

Every attempt to open the eye in the light is attended with profuse lachrymation, and generally with sharp pain. Iritis is, as a general rule, a painful affection, and the pain is usually constant. It may be confined to the eye-ball itself, or it may irradiate into the supra-orbital and infra-orbital regions ; it is usually severer at night, and is often extremely distressing. Besides this spontaneous pain we generally find that the eye-ball is tender on pressure, which shows that the ciliary body is also implicated. The eye-lids are often slightly œdematous, though never to a very high degree, except in purulent iritis.

## DISEASES OF THE IRIS.

Iritis generally appears in one eye at a time, but very often the fellow eye is attacked while the disease is still active within the first eye.

If iritis is not properly treated in time, it always leads to attachments between the iris and the anterior lens-capsule (*posterior synechiæ*). These are easily detected by the instillation of atropia, under whose action the pupil will assume a very irregular shape, according to the number and extent of the synechiæ. (See figure 41*). When there is a circular attachment between the pupillary margin of the iris and the anterior lens-capsule, the pupil will remain absolutely unchanged (*circular synechia*).

Vision is always impaired in iritis, although in a varying degree, dependent on the size of the pupil, and the quantity and quality of the inflammatory products in the anterior chamber, and on the anterior lens-capsule. Moreover, as the ciliary body and choroid are hardly ever free from inflammatory action in iritis, exudations from these into the vitreous body help also to impair vision. The latter exudations are frequently observed after the other symptoms of iritis have entirely disappeared. Some forms of iritis are very apt to recur, especially when it has been impossible to break all the synechiæ.

In *plastic iritis*, which is the most frequent form, the exudation from the iris is of a fibrinous nature. This is deposited first at the pupillary edge of the iris, then on its posterior surface, and sometimes also on the anterior surface. It glues the iris to the anterior capsule of the crystalline lens, and thus renders it partially, or totally immoveable. If the disease goes on, a perfect membrane may be formed in the pupillary space, into which blood-vessels may grow from the adjacent iris. By the formation of such a pupillary membrane or of a circular synchia, or by both together, the anterior chamber may be shut off from the parts of the eye-ball lying behind the iris, and thus the slow current of the fluids within the eye-ball, which goes from behind forwards, is seriously obstructed. (See figure 42*). This causes an increase of tension in the posterior parts of the eyeball, and the periphery of the iris, if not also glued down to the lens, may be pushed forward so as almost to touch the cornea. That such a condition cannot exist long without seriously endan-

*See page 107.

gering the function of the eye, is obvious. Most frequently the inflammation spreads backwards upon the ciliary body and choroid and leads to perfect destruction of the eye-ball by a chronic iridochoroiditis. In other cases the eye is destroyed by secondary glaucoma. In these stages of the disease the formation of cataract is a frequent complication.

From the serious results which such a plastic iritis may bring about, it is easily understood, how important it must be for the general practitioner to recognize the disease early and treat it accordingly. It may, therefore, be well to enumerate again the symptoms of iritis, as contrasted with those of conjunctivitis. In conjunctivitis the hyperæmia of the blood-vessels is confined to the mucous membrane of the eye-ball and eye-lids; in iritis, although there may too be a considerable hyperæmia of the conjunctival vessels, there is, in addition, hyperæmia of the episcleral (ciliary) blood-vessels, which shows as a bluish-red zone around the corneo-scleral margin, over which the hyperæmic conjunctiva can be moved. In conjunctivitis the appearance of the iris is unchanged, and the pupil dilates promptly when the eye is shaded; in iritis the appearance of the iris is materially altered, and it is inactive. In conjunctivitis, if there is pain, it is usually located in the eye-lids; in iritis there is nearly always pain, and it usually irradiates into the regions surrounding the orbit. In conjunctivitis, vision is only momentarily impaired (by mucus lying on the cornea, which can be wiped off with the eye-lid); in iritis sight is considerably, often greatly, impaired. Finally, in conjunctivitis there is mucoid or muco-purulent discharge, in iritis there is no discharge, except of tears.

If, in a case of iritis, the physician has made a wrong diagnosis, the symptoms will remain unchanged, or, more probably, become worse, so long as he treats the patient for conjunctivitis; if he persists in the wrong treatment, permanent injury to the eye, or even loss of vision may be expected.

Plastic iritis is mostly an acute disease, and may in some cases get well without proper treatment; but very seldom, without leaving its traces behind in the shape of posterior synechiæ.

In some cases of plastic iritis, which seem to be characterized by hemorrhages into the tissue proper of the iris, a special form of exudation into the anterior chamber occurs, which has been called a spongy exudation. It can be recognized, probably only after having been partly dissolved, as a grayish, lens-like body in the anterior chamber, which in the course of a week may be totally dissolved. This spongy exudation is not frequently observed, and might possibly be mistaken for a dislocated crystalline lens. A few days' observation will, however, suffice to show its true character.

The average duration of a plastic iritis, even under treatment, varies from three to six weeks. Cases that come under treatment at the very beginning may, however, recover much more rapidly.

*Serous iritis* is that form of iritis in which the exudation is

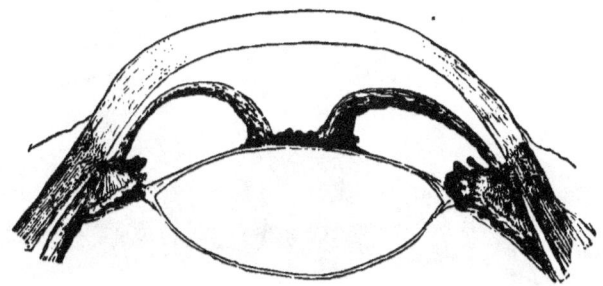

FIG. 43. Crater-shaped Iris. The pupillary edge of the iris adheres to the anterior lens-capsule (circular synechia). The peripheral parts of the iris are protruding into the anterior chamber. (From Lectures on the Human Eye, by A. Alt.)

chiefly of a serous nature. Besides the general symptoms of iritis, which are, for the most part, mild and not clearly defined, we find usually slight increase of tension. The synechiæ formed in serous iritis are usually not very firm, nor is the pupil as apt to be small, as in plastic iritis. During the progress of the affection, the posterior layers of the cornea become involved, and the endothelial cells of the membrane of *Descemet* proliferate so that we see numerous small whitish dots on the posterior surface of the cornea. These dots appear mostly in the lower part of the cornea, and sometimes form a triangle, with its base downwards, and its point upwards in the region of the pupil. From this peculiar arrangement it was formerly thought that the dots were simply deposits of fibrine from the exudation in the aqueous humor, and it is not impossible that such deposits may be the cause of the undoubted proliferation of endothelial cells on *Descemet's* membrane, to which the picture referred to is due.

If the disease progresses, the synechiæ become firmer, and the result may be again a circular synechia of the pupillary edge combined with bulging periphery of the iris. (See figure 43).

This form of iritis is rather chronic in its course, and does not yield readily to treatment, which should be, in the main, the same as in plastic iritis.

The characteristic feature of *purulent iritis* is that pus-cells are exuded into the tissue of the iris and into the anterior chamber. (See figure 44). The iris in this form of inflammation is apt to have a yellowish tint; and the pus exuded into the aqueous

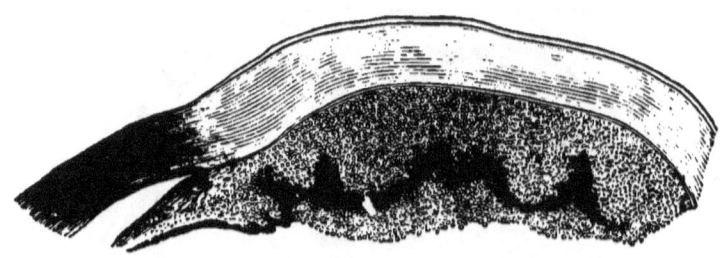

FIG. 44. Purulent Iritis. (From Lectures on the Human Eye, by A. Alt.)

humor falls to the lowest portion and forms what we have already seen in ulceration or abscess of the cornea, a hypopyum. If the affection is not a part of a general purulent inflammation of the eye-ball (panophthalmitis), recovery may take place, but not without leaving its traces behind. The pain accompanying this form of iritis is usually very severe.

Anatomically very similar, though clinically distinct, is the fourth form of iritis, the *gummatous iritis*. In it the infiltration with round cells is more localized, and we see small tumors (*gummata*) forming mostly near the pupillary edge. (See figure 45). Generally we find only one, sometimes several. They gradually increase in size and become yellow. Then they gradually disappear again, and leave usually a scar and synechiæ behind.

In some cases the yellowish mass (which is, however, not fluid pus), may increase enormously in size. I have had a case under treatment, in which it filled the whole anterior chamber, and yet under proper treatment the whole mass disappeared, and only a partial attachment between the pupillary edge of the iris and the anterior lens-capsule remained behind. Gummatous iritis generally occurs in but one eye, more rarely in both at the same time.

The etiology of iritis is not always clear, especially in the plastic and serous forms. In a great many cases a syphilitic complication exists, and the iritis may then appear at the same time with the cutaneous affections, or at a later period. Often, however, it occurs much later and at a time when no other symptoms of syphilis can be any longer detected. Rheumatism and gout predispose also to attacks of iritis. Iritis may also follow

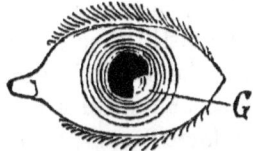

Fig. 45. G. Gummy Tumor of the Iris.

gonorrhœa, especially if this was associated with articular rheumatism. In other cases we are unable to assign any cause. Purulent iritis is almost always due to an injury, and is one of the unfortunate sequelæ of operations on the eye. It may also follow an incarceration of the iris after the extraction of cataract. Gummatous iritis is always a syphilitic affection.

In the treatment of iritis, the main point must always be to prevent the formation of synechiæ or to rupture those that have already been formed. This is accomplished by the forcible dilatation of the pupil by means of mydriatic drugs, among which the sulphate of atropia holds the first place. A 1 per cent solution of this drug is to be instilled into the eye every half hour, or even every quarter hour, if necessary, until the pupil is well dilated (ad maximum, if possible). Those who are not often called upon to use atropia, are, as a rule, afraid to use it strong enough and often enough, and frequently when the pupil is nicely dilated they get frightened, lest it should stay so by going on with the instillations. This is all wrong, and the fact is, that only the persistent use of a strong solution (1 per cent) will accomplish anything. The pupil will resume its normal condition (if there are no synechiæ, of course), about a week after the last instillation has been made.

Most people will bear such instillations for a prolonged period without any disagreeable symptoms; except, perhaps, a dry throat. A small number of patients, however, will be found to be most sensitive to the use of atropia, and show signs of poisoning after a comparatively small number of instillations. The face becomes flushed, the pulse becomes rapid and feeble, the patient is nauseated, has hallucinations and sometimes even becomes delirious. In such a case the use of atropia must be discontinued and extract of belladonna, or duboisine, or hyoscyamine should be tried in its stead. Before, however, changing the remedy, we should try to prevent the instilled solution from running down the tear-duct, by turning the patient's head in the opposite direction and closing the canaliculi for a few minutes after the instillation by pressing a finger against them.

Sometimes atropia proves irritating to the conjunctiva and causes a follicular swelling, which may become very disagreeable. In such a case it may again be well to change the remedy. I am inclined to think that this form of conjunctivitis is due to the fungi that generally form, after a few days, in a solution of atropia. I certainly have never seen it since I have taken the precaution not to allow the solution to be used after the fungi have appeared, unless after repeated filtering.

The next point to be considered is the relief of the often almost maddening pain, which does not always yield, even when we have succeeded in fully dilating the pupil. An old and undoubtedly good remedy for this in many cases is the application of from 3 to 6 leeches to the temple. I have also often seen immediate relief following the use of cold compresses or even of a small ice-bag; in some cases bathing with warm water has been more successful in abating the pain. If none of these remedies are effective, the use of narcotics is indicated.

# DISEASES OF THE IRIS.

Where there is the least idea of a specific origin in a case of iritis, it will be best to at once give mercury in some form or other. Inunctions rapidly pushed, calomel in small and frequent doses, and protiodide of mercury, or corrosive sublimate may be used. If the syphilitic infection has taken place many years before the appearance of the iritis, the use of iodide of potassium is very effective. Even in cases where a syphilitic origin cannot be traced, mercury has often a very beneficial influence.

Salicylate of soda (which of late has been highly recommended against iritis, especially when of a rheumatic origin) has not yielded any good results in my hand.

With all this the patient should be kept in bed, or at least in a darkened room, and his bowels should be kept open.

*Injuries* to the iris are in most cases complicated by injuries of the cornea or sclerotic, and often of the crystalline lens or even of the deeper parts of the eye. The conditions and the

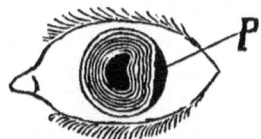

FIG. 46. Iridodialysis. P is the newly formed pupil, caused by the rent.

treatment necessarily vary very much in different cases and will be spoken of in Chapter XVII.

A contusion of the eye-ball, however, may result in an injury to the iris without further complication. In such a case we find either a rupture (sometimes several) of the circular fibres at the pupillary edge of the iris, resulting in small colobomata, or a detachment of the iris at its periphery. The former injury is comparatively rare and is usually of little importance. In the latter there is considerable hemorrhage into the anterior chamber, and after the blood is absorbed we find at the seat of the rent, at the periphery of the iris, a new, abnormal pupil which may be larger or smaller according to the extent of the detachment. Through this second peripheral pupil rays of light enter the eye-ball, as well as through the normal pupil, giving rise occasionally to some confusion of vision. When the rent is very large, so that the loosened iris floats about with the movements of the eye-ball, it might be of use to catch the iris in the corneoscleral tissue by drawing it between the lips of a small incision made in this region. Otherwise nothing is to be done. This condition has been named *iridodialysis*. (See figure 46).

The iris is sometimes the seat of *newformations*. They are either cysts, sarcomata or, in rare cases, tubercles.

The *cysts* are the result of an injury and may be of a serous nature, in which case they are usually caused by the adhesion of a fold of iris-tissue to the posterior surface of the cornea. In other cases they are atheromatous in nature, and originate from cells or cilia, which have been forcibly driven into the anterior chamber, and have become grafted into the iris-tissue. Both kinds of cysts may grow to a considerable size before they come under our observation. The only remedy is their total removal from the eye by iridectomy.

*Sarcoma* of the iris may be pigmented, or unpigmented. The diagnosis is rather difficult. Yet, when we find a small solid tumor in the iris which is steadily growing, and perhaps causes pain and increase of tension, the diagnosis of a sarcomatous newformation will probably be correct. In a very early stage such a tumor may, possibly, be removed by iridectomy with reasonable hope of saving the patient's eye as well as his life.

As functional disorders of the iris we have to mention *mydriasis*, a condition in which the pupil has lost its contractility and remains in a state of maximum dilatation; and *myosis*, in which the pupil is strongly contracted, but may contract still more in the acts of accommodation and convergence.

Mydriasis (when not caused by a drug) is, as a rule, only a symptom of further disorders, and especially of disorders in the nervous apparatus.

Myosis, if not caused by the action of a drug, is almost always a pathognomonic symptom of affections of the spinal cord.

Mydrasis may be caused by the use of the following drugs, viz: belladonna, or its alkaloid atropine; hyoscyamus, or hyoscyamine, duboisia or duboisine; datura or daturine; and homatropine. Myosis is brought about by the use of eserine, pilocarpine, opium, aconite, etc. The use of any of these drugs must, of course, have been disproved, before we can look upon mydriasis or myosis in any given case, as a pathological condition.

## CHAPTER XI.

### DISEASES OF THE CILIARY BODY.

PLASTIC CYCLITIS.—SEROUS CYCLITIS.—PURULENT CYCLITIS.—GUMMATOUS CYCLITIS.—NEOPLASMS.—SARCOMA.—INJURIES.

The close anatomical relation which exists between the parts of the uveal tract, makes it impossible for an inflammation to exist for some time in the ciliary body without involving the iris or, later on, the choroid. The forms of inflammation which are observed in the ciliary body are, therefore, also essentially the same, as those which occur in the tissue of the iris.

The symptoms of cyclitis are mainly those of iritis. There is hyperæmia of the conjunctival and episcleral (ciliary) blood-vessels, impairment of sight, photophobia, lachrymation and severe pain, either spontaneous or on the slightest pressure on the ciliary region. The way, in which a patient will rapidly withdraw his head upon such pressure, is almost characteristic of cyclitis.

*Plastic cyclitis*, the most frequent form of inflammation of the ciliary body, may be acute, but it is usually a chronic affection. It is characterised by the exudation of fibrinous or plastic material into the posterior chamber (See Chapter I.) and the anterior portion of the vitreous body. After some time this fibrinous substance becomes organized, connective tissue is formed, and cells and blood-vessels grow from the ciliary body into this newly formed, cyclitic membrane. As this membrane shrinks, the crystalline lens is pushed forwards, and finally the posterior part of the ciliary body, with the adjacent choroid and retina, becomes detached from the sclerotic. During this process the iris and the crystalline lens become glued together, and the eye-ball is destroyed by shrinkage. (See figure. 47).

In *serous cyclitis* the exudation is mainly serous in character.

This form of cyclitis is never recognized, without a co-existing serous iritis. There is increase of intra-ocular tension and all the symptoms of serous iritis are observed.

*Purulent cyclitis* is usually seen in cases of panophthalmitis. It is almost always due to an injury. In some cases the yellow

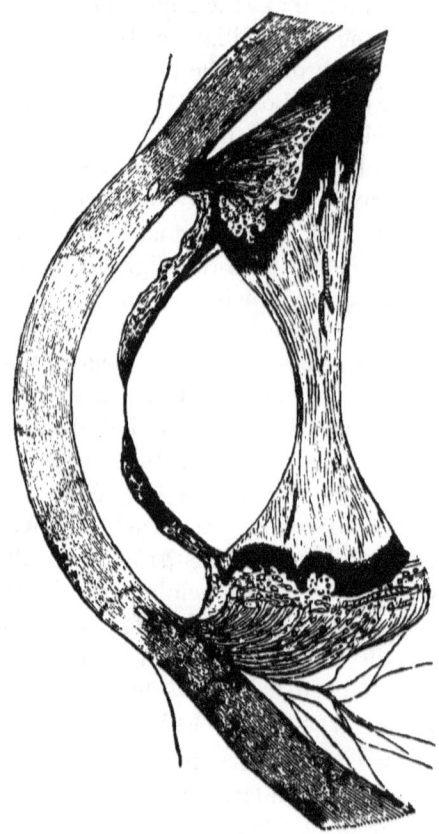

FIG. 47. The Results of Fibrino-Plastic Cyclitis. A cyclitic membrane lies upon the posterior surface of the crystalline lens. The posterior chamber is obliterated. The iris and the crystalline lens are pressed forward by the contraction of the newly formed connective tissue. The ciliary body is detached from the sclerotic. (From Lectures on the Human Eye, by A. Alt.)

pus exuded from the ciliary body may be seen in the anterior portion of the vitreous, when the other membranes of the eyeball have only as yet began to inflame.

# DISEASES OF THE CILIARY BODY.

*Gummatous cyclitis* is but seldom recognized, although it surely is not of very infrequent occurrence. It may remain a localized affection of the ciliary body, without doing further damage; the gumma may break outwards through the sclerotic, or it may be absorbed.

The treatment of cyclitis is in no way different from that of iritis.

Cyclitis in all its forms is but rarely a genuine primary disease; it is generally due to an injury, or to syphilis. Experience has shown, that an eye, which has been destroyed by

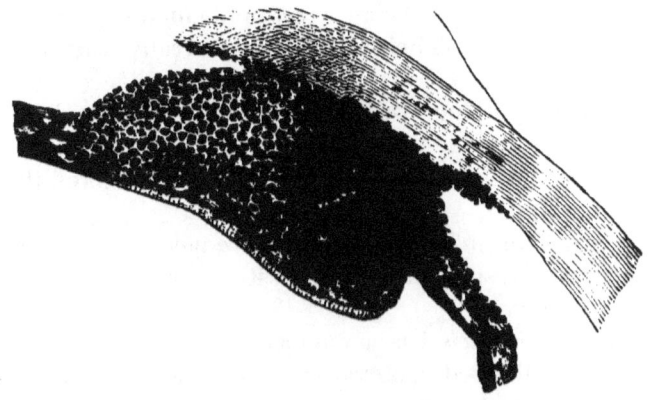

FIG. 48. Primary Melanosarcoma of the Ciliary Body. (From Lectures on the Human Eye, by A. Alt.)

cyclitis is a most dangerous companion to its fellow. Sympathetic ophthalmia is very frequently the result of this affection. It is therefore, best, as a rule, to remove such an eye in time by enucleation, unless the patient is so situated that he can be kept continually under observation.

*Newformations* start, it seems, but rarely from the ciliary body. They are *sarcomata* and chiefly *melano-sarcomata*. (See figure 48).

*Injuries* of the ciliary body, are, as has been already stated, of a very serious nature. They will be further discussed in Chapter XVIII.

# CHAPTER XII.

## DISEASES OF THE CHOROID.

PLASTIC CHOROIDITIS. — SEROUS CHOROIDITIS. — PURULENT CHOROIDITIS.— NEOPLASMS.—GUMMA.—TUBERCLE.—SARCOMA.—ISOLATED RUPTURE OF THE CHOROID. HEMORRHAGE.

The diseases of the choroid, like those of other structures which make up the posterior portion of the eye-ball, can only be correctly diagnosticated by the use of the ophthalmoscope. Without its aid the old by-word still holds good, that in diseases of the back-ground of the eye, the patient can see nothing, nor the physician either. It is not to be expected that every physician should be able to make a correct ophthalmoscopic diagnosis, nor can the use of the ophthalmoscope be really learned from a book.

The chief symptom usually complained of in the diseases of the back-ground of the eye-ball is a partial or total loss of sight. We shall in the following give a short description of these affections.

The forms of inflammation which we meet with in the choroidal tissue, correspond very much with those, found in the iris, and ciliary body.

*Plastic choroiditis* has a number of clinical names, which, however, are all based upon varieties of one and the same pathological process; thus we speak of atrophic, disseminate, and areolar choroiditis, and central choroido-retinitis.

In all of these forms we find the exudation of fibrino-plastic material into the tissue of the choroid and the adjacent retina. This exudation is preceded by hyperæmia of the choroid, and is combined with cloudiness of the vitreous body and congestion of the blood-vessels of the optic papilla and retina. The cloudiness

## DISEASES OF THE CHOROID.

of the vitreous body may be diffuse, or separate smaller and larger flocks of a fibrinous substance may be seen floating about in it.

The fibrino-plastic material exuded into the choroid and retina may be absorbed again, but in most cases it becomes organized, and when retraction of the newly formed connective tissue takes place, an atrophic spot in the retina and choroid results, which is devoid of blood-vessels and pigment, and through which the whitish sclerotic can be seen. The pigment, which has been set free by the destruction of the pigmented cells of the choroidal tissue, and of the cells of the pigmentary epithelium, is collected at the periphery of the atrophic spot in such a manner as to give it a darkly pigmented, irregular outline. (See figure 49).

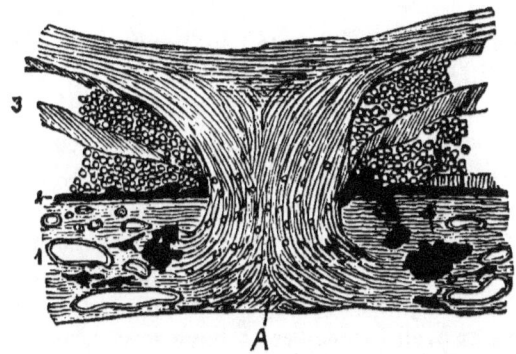

FIG. 49. Transverse Section through an Atrophic Spot in the Choroid and Adjacent Retina, the result of plastic choroiditis. A. Atrophic spot. 1. Choroid. 2. Pigmentary epithelium. 3. Retina.

At least one, in most cases several, of these spots is formed during an attack of plastic choroiditis, and frequently both eyes are affected at the same time, or one soon after the other.

In the most frequent form of plastic choroiditis, the atrophic spots lie, as a rule, toward the periphery of the choroid and retina, and therefore peripheral vision is chiefly disturbed.

In central choroido-retinitis the exudation takes place in the macula lutea (yellow spot) itself or its immediate neighborhood. In the beginning of this form of choroiditis central vision is indistinct, and objects are seen distorted and often apparently smaller or larger than when seen with the healthy eye (*metamor-*

*phopsia*), straight lines appear bent or notched, etc. Finally central vision is totally abolished.

In both these forms of plastic choroiditis hemorrhages into the choroidal tissue may also occur.

Plastic choroiditis is very apt to recur, and thus to render vision more and more defective. Yet from the fact that it always appears in patches, which leave healthy tissue between them, it is not apt to cause total blindness.

Syphilis, rheumatism and gout are often the basis on which such a plastic choroiditis is developed. It happens also, comparatively often, in women at the climacteric period. It is, however, seen most frequently in short-sighted eyes, and the short-sightedness, as such, must therefore predispose to such inflammations.

If plastic choroiditis is treated in its first beginning, especially in syphilitic cases, it may yield perfectly to treatment. This consists in rest in a darkened room, local depletion and the use of iodide of potassium or of some form of mercury. Quite recently, subcutaneous injections of muriate of pilocarpine have been used. In older cases corrosive sublimate, taken in small doses and for a prolonged period, seems to have a very beneficial action. In some cases in which exudation into the vitreous body has been the predominant symptom, and in which other treatment has proved ineffective, I have seen very good results from the use of electricity in the form of the continuous current.

*Serous choroiditis*, when not combined with serous iritis and cyclitis, is seldom, if ever, recognized, unless it causes glaucomatous symptoms (increase of the intra-ocular tension). Its chief result is synchisis (liquefaction) of the vitreous body, either wholly or in part. The vitreous body, which is of a jelly-like consistency in the normal state, becomes in this affection liquid, like water. Serous choroiditis may also give rise to detachment of the vitreous body from the retina, or of the retina from the choroid.

*Purulent choroiditis* is characterized by the infiltration of the choroidal tissue and the vitreous body with pus-cells. It is usually a very acute affection, and thus produces symptoms which

## DISEASES OF THE CHOROID.

are plainly visible without the aid of the ophthalmoscope. The inflammatory process hardly ever remains confined to the uveal tract, but soon spreads over nearly all parts of the eye-ball, and extends to *Tenon's* capsule. It then causes œdema and swelling of the eye-lids and ocular conjunctiva (chemosis), and swelling of the orbital tissue with consequent exophthalmus. (See figure 50). The disease, almost without exception, leads to total destruction and shrinking of the eye-ball.

It is, as a rule, very painful; in some cases, however, the pain is but slight. In the acute form, the pus may break through the sclerotic or the cornea, and thus escape. The chronic forms, to which the acute form often leads, are the main cause of the formation of bone within the eye-ball.

In some cases purulent choroiditis is due to septic infection

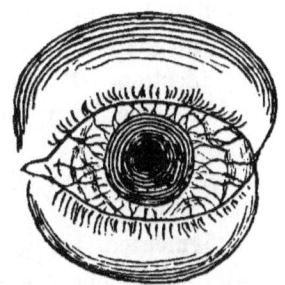

FIG. 50. Shows the appearance of an eye affected with purulent panophthalmitis. The eye-lids are œdematous; the eye-ball protrudes. The hyperæmic conjunctiva is folded and infiltrated. The pupil is irregular in shape.

(*metastatic choroiditis*), especially during puerperal septicæmia. In most cases, however, it owes its origin to an injury with or without the subsequent presence of a foreign body within the eye-ball. It will, therefore, be further spoken of in Chapter XVIII.

Treatment is usually unavailing as regards the cure of this form of choroiditis, and it should therefore be simply addressed to the relief of the more important symptoms. The pain, which is usually unceasing and very distressing, may be sometimes alleviated by cold applications, but, as a rule, the patients prefer warm ones. The latter, furthermore, hasten the progress of the supuration, and as the eye is already doomed, this is usually the best thing which can be done. If the chemosis is very pronounced, so that it prevents the eye-lids from closing over the eye-ball, scarifications of the œdematous conjunctiva are sometimes indicated.

In such cases the question will often arise whether, and if so, at what stage of the disease such an eye-ball should be enucleated. I have often removed eyes as soon as the very worst inflammatory symptoms were over, and without any bad results. The patient's suffering has been thus shortened and all danger of sympathetic ophthalmia in the future has been removed. Some surgeons fear to operate before the shrinkage of the eye-ball has begun.

*Gummata* undoubtedly occur in the choroid, but they are seldom recognized as such.

*Tubercles* are sometimes found in the choroid during the tuberculosis of the lungs. In rare cases the occurrence of tubercles in the choroid is a primary affection. When the diagnosis is of primary tubercular choroiditis, the immediate removal of the eye-ball is indicated.

The malignant tumors of the eye-ball take their origin most frequently from the tissue of the choroid. These tumors are *sarcomata*, and are either pigmented, or, in rarer cases, unpigmented. They may, furthermore, contain newly-formed cartilage or bone-tissue.

The marked clinical symptoms presented in its different stages by such a growth within the eye-ball, ought to be known to every physician. In the first stage the patient is gradually losing sight, although externally the eye shows nothing pathological, except, perhaps, a few dilated blood-vessels in the episcleral tissue. In the second stage, the growing tumor produces inflammatory symptoms, which are plainly visible without the ophthalmoscope. The intra-ocular tension is increased, the crystalline lens and iris are pushed forward, and the general picture of glaucoma (See Chapter XVII) is the result. There is usually considerable pain during this stage. As it may yet be possible in this glaucomatous stage of an intra-ocular tumor, to save the patient's life by the removal of the eye-ball, the physician should be well posted on

# DISEASES OF THE CHOROID.

this symptom. Finally, in the third stage, the tumor breaks through the sclerotic, or possibly the cornea, and grows either into the orbital-tissue or through the anterior portion of the eyeball, out of the orbit; it may also grow along the course of the optic nerve.

In this last stage, as a rule, metastatic tumors have already begun to be formed in the brain, the lungs, the liver or some other distant organ of vital importance, and the patient is irrevocably lost.

There is no treatment for such tumors. The only thing to be done is to remove the affected eye-ball at the earliest possible period. Anything else is useless, and delay only enhances the

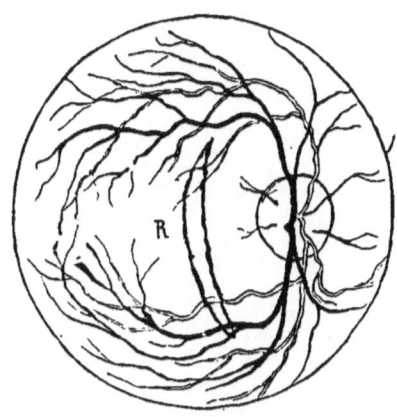

FIG. 51. Isolated Rupture of the Choroid (after Knapp). R. Rent in the choroid, over which the retinal blood-vessels are seen to pass.

danger to the patient's life. Yet, as there are but few people who are intelligent enough to submit at once to the inevitable, the family physician will generally be applied to for advice, and he will often have the disagreeable duty involving on him, to endorse the statement of the oculist, and to impress the patient in the most earnest manner with the danger of his condition. The early removal of such an eye-ball almost always saves the patient's life.

*Injuries* to the eye-ball with a blunt instrument may cause an isolated *rupture of the choroid*. After such an injury the fundus of the eye is usually at first obscured by blood, and no details can be seen. When the blood is absorbed, the patients usually notice an impairment of sight, and sometimes complain of metamorphopsia, just as in a case of central choroido-retinitis. We find then, on ophthalmoscopic examination, a slit in the choroid, forming a crescent, generally concentric with and at some distance from the mucula lutea. (See figure 51).

*Hemorrhages* are but seldom seen in the choroidal tissue, except after injuries, and during some forms of choroiditis.

## CHAPTER XIII.

### DISEASES OF THE RETINA.

HYPERÆMIA.— ANÆMIA.— EMBOLISM OF THE CENTRAL RETINAL ARTERY.—THROMBOSIS OF THE CENTRAL RETINAL VEIN.— DETACHMENT OF THE RETINA.— PIGMENTARY RETINITIS.—SYPHILITIC RETINITIS.—ALBUMINURIC RETINITIS.—HEMORRHAGE.—GLIOMA.

*Hyperæmia* of the retinal blood-vessels is but seldom seen without being caused by some other eye-affection. It is always combined with hyperæmia of the optic papilla. When retinal hyperæmia is the primary affection, it produces no pathological changes in the structure of the retina. It is usually caused by over-work, especially in bad light. Rest, and the moderate exclusion of light will usually suffice to do away with its symptoms, which consist chiefly in the weakness of sight. Sometimes an error of refraction is the predisposing cause, and its correction by glasses may be followed by a return to the normal condition.

*Anæmia* or *Ischæmia* of the retinal blood-vessels, without accompanying pathological changes in the tissue of the retina, is sometimes seen as a sequel of a severe, prostrating illness, especially when the heart's action is considerably enfeebled. Such an ischæmia of the retina causes partial or total blindness, which may be momentarily relieved by puncture of the anterior chamber; the weakened heart may then suffice to overcome the reduced intra-ocular pressure, and to force the blood again into the small retinal blood-vessels.

A similar condition may be caused by very large doses of quinine, and I have once seen it occur after a very severe fright. In this case the normal condition was restored after a very few days. The amblyopia, caused by anæmia dependent on prostrating disease, usually yields as the patient recovers strength and health.

A partial or total anæmia of the blood-vessels of the retina, with subsequent anatomical changes in the retinal tissue, is, furthermore, observed in consequence of *embolism* of the *central retinal artery* or of one of its retinal branches, or in consequence of *thrombosis* of the *central retinal vein*.

In these cases the partial or total blindness occurs suddenly. In embolism of the central retinal artery the ophthalmoscope reveals a perfect anæmia of the retinal arteries; the retinal veins are attenuated, but contain here and there broken columns of blood. Near the optic papilla and around the macula lutea, the retina appears obscured by a whitish infiltration, and the fovea centralis is seen as a small cherry-red spot. This pronounced color

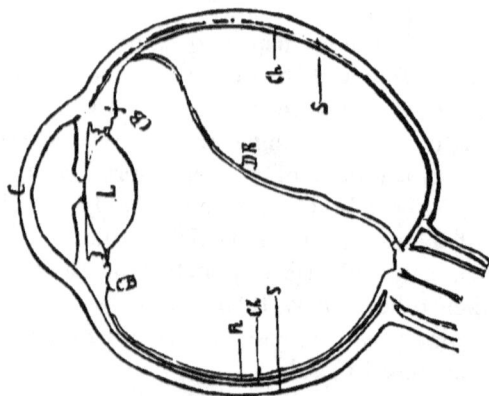

FIG. 52. Diagram showing Detachment of the Retina from the Choroid in a Short-sighted Eye. C. Cornea. CB. Ciliary body. L. Crystalline lens. S. Sclerotic. Ch. Choroid. R. Retina. DR. Detached retina. O. Optic nerve.

of the fovea centralis is probably due to contrast. After some time the infiltration in the retinal tissue disappears, and later on the retina and optic nerve become atrophic.

In embolism of a single branch of the central retinal artery these symptoms are confined to the part of the retina which it supplies.

In thrombosis of the central retinal vein the arteries appear also very thin, but the veins are usually greatly enlarged, and a number of hemorrhages are seen in the retinal tissue.

No treatment is of any value in these affections.

Another form of more or less sudden. blindness owes its origin to the *detachment of the retina* from the choroid. (See figure 52.) This is due to an effusion of a serous fluid between the two membranes, and is most apt to occur in eyes suffering from a high degree of myopia.

Patients attacked by detachment of the retina usually state that a cloud seemed gradually to spread over the sight until it allowed them to see only a part of the object looked at, and this only as if through a mist; at a later stage sight is reduced to virtually nothing. It may have taken a few hours, or days, or even months to develop all these symptoms.

When a large portion of the retina is detached, and especially when the detachment involves the peripheric parts of the retina, the detached bladder-like membrane may sometimes be seen with the naked eye floating behind the crystalline lens.

By the examination of the field of vision the extent of the detachment may readily be judged; examination with the ophthalmoscope will enable us to make the diagnosis sure.

Sometimes we see small rents in the detached parts of the retina, caused evidently by the pressure of the fluid exuded behind it. The vitreous body is usually liquified, and the tension of the eye-ball is less than normal.

The diagnosis is, as a rule, easily made. The only affection with which detachment of the retina might easily be confounded is sarcoma of the choroid, in which, moreover, retinal detachment is often actually present as a complication.

The prognosis is unfavorable. Although we may sometimes succeed in perfectly curing a recent detachent of the retina, relapses are almost sure to occur, and getting less and less tractable, they finally leave the eye in a useless condition.

The treatment now most practiced, consists in repeated hypodermic injections of a solution of the muriate of pilocarpine, and the results, especially in recent cases, are often for the time very satisfactory. Whether the cures are any more permanent than they were by the old method of treatment, remains as yet to be proved. But this new method of treatment, when successful, requires less time, and is less disagreeable to the patient.

The older method of treatment requires a complete rest for

weeks. This is accomplished by ordering the patient to lie in bed, and even as much as possible on his back, by paralyzing his accommodation with sulphate of atropia, and by keeping the eye-ball under slight, continued pressure with a compressive bandage.

Depletion of the bowels and sometimes leeching at the temple may be useful.

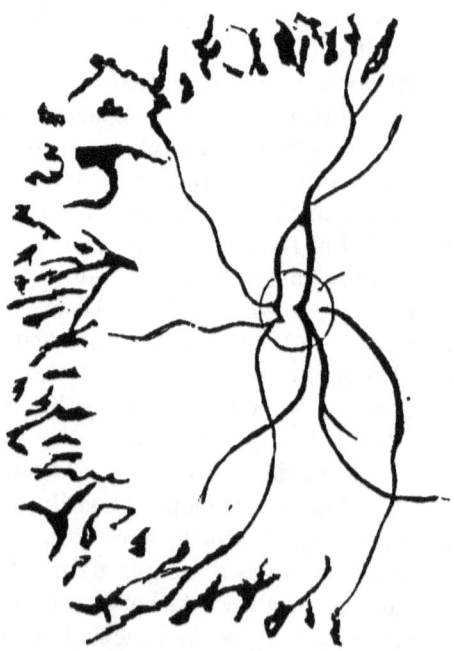

FIG. 53. Pigmentary Retinitis. The optic papilla is anaemic. Of the retinal blood vessels but few are visible and these few are greatly reduced in calibre. Deposits of pigment lie in the periphery of the retina.

Puncture of the detached retina through the sclerotic has been resorted to, but with uncertain and varying success.

Detachment of the retina usually attacks but one eye at the time.

*Pigmentation* of the retina may, as has been stated, be the consequence of plastic choroiditis, and it then, as a rule, remains stationary. There is, however, also a progressive form of pigmentation of the retina, due to proliferation of the pigment which is called *retinitis pigmentosa* (See figure 53). This affection gradually leads to atrophy of the retina, solidification of the blood-vessels by an inflammatory process in their lymph-sheaths and walls, and atrophy of the optic nerve. It terminates in blindness. It takes, however, a great many years before this final result is reached. As the disease begins at the periphery of the retina, and only gradually advances towards its center, the peripheric vision of such patients at first destroyed, and their visual field becomes gradually narrower, until finally their central vision is also lost.

A very characteristic symptom in this affection is the fact that, when night comes on, the patients see much less distinctly. This condition is known as *hemeralopia* or night-blindness.

*Pigmentary retinitis* is always observed in both eyes. Treatment is of no use. With regard to its etiology, consanguinity of the parents has been thought by some writers to be the primary cause.

The retinal tissue is not very apt to become primarily inflamed, and there are only two distinct forms of retinitis, not dependent on choroiditis, namely, syphilitic retinitis and albuminuric retinitis, the latter being actually a neuro-retinitis.

*Syphilitic retinitis* is usually one of the later manifestations of syphilis. The ophthalmoscope shows the retina dull and hazy, particularly in the vicinity of the optic papilla and along the course of the larger retinal blood-vessels. The blood-vessels themselves appear veiled, and sometimes perfectly covered in a part of their course, by the exudation. The retinal veins are broad and somewhat tortuous. The optic papilla usually appears reddish and slightly swollen, and its outlines are not quite distinct. If the disease goes on, it leads to hypertrophy of the connective tissue of the retina, and consequent atrophy of its nervous elements.

The patients complain usually of seeing strange photopsiae; dazzling lights, etc. Then their sight is obscured in such a way, that they need more light than formerly, in order to see distinctly. This impairment of vision is, however, often much less than would be expected from the condition of the retina.

*Syphilitic retinitis* is very prone to relapse, and if not properly treated, it may, as already indicated, lead to blindness.

The treatment consists in vigorous anti-syphilitic measures, combined with perfect rest of the eyes in a dark room, and assisted by the instillation of sulphate of atropia, and by local depletions.

*Albuminuric retinitis* as its name indicates, is chiefly due to albuminuria *i. e.* to nephritis in all its forms, but especially to the shrinking kidney.

In an eye suffering from albuminuric retinitis we find the optic papilla swollen and infiltrated, its normal outlines indistinct, or even perfectly hidden by a whitish exudation, which extends into the neighboring retinal-tissue. The retinal veins are gorged with blood, and very tortuous, almost like corkscrews, their origin in the papilla is invisible, and parts of them within the retina are perfectly covered by the dense whitish exudation. The retina shows, moreover, a number of white, shining spots of various shapes. These appear, especially, around the macula lutea, and are usually arranged in a radial direction around it and thus form a very characteristic stellate picture. Here and there hemorrhages are visible in the retinal tissue. In rare cases detachment of the retina around the optic papilla has been observed. Albuminuric retinitis is due to changes in the blood-vessels of the retina, and belongs to the uræmic stage of nephritis. Yet, in some cases, the ophthalmoscopic diagnosis may reveal nephritis, when its existence has not yet been thought of, because of the absence of other marked symptoms of the disease.

The disturbance of vision is often strangely small, in view of the very conspicuous changes in the structure of the retina; on the other hand patients in later stages, of the disease may sometimes be blind for hours at a time and then regain sight, without any visible changes in the condition of the retinal tissue. This happens during the so-called uræmic attacks.

It is hardly necessary to say, that, as there is no cure for a well established nephritis, there is also none for the albuminuric retinitis.

Similar forms of retinitis are sometimes seen in cases of intra-cranial tumors with subsequent neuro-retinitis. (See Chapter XXII).

*Hemorrhages* into the retinal tissue are observed without being preceded by any inflammatory changes; the old name of *hemorrhagic retinitis*, is therefore, a misnomer. Their cause is undoubtedly a degeneration of the walls of the blood-vessels. They vary in size, shape and number, may attack one eye, or both eyes at the same time, and accordingly interfere with vision to a very varying degree. In some cases the retinal hemorrhages are so numerous, that sight is nearly abolished from the start.

The exuded blood soon undergoes fatty degeneration, and becomes absorbed, leaving an atrophic spot or spots, where the nervous elements of the retina have been destroyed. Sometimes however, the absorption takes place, leaving no trace behind. In other cases a glaucomatous process may be set up leading to the destruction of the eye. Such hemorrhages when they have once occurred in an eye are likely to recur.

The causes of the retinal hemorrhages are heart-disease, athcromatous degeneration of the walls of the arteries, pernicious anaemia, etc., or they may be due to the suppression of the menstrual flow, especially at the period of change of life.

The treatment of retinal hemorrhages must adapt itself in the main to the particular causes which are recognized in the case in hand; at the same time it is well to give the eyes perfect rest, and perhaps, also, to apply leeches to the temple.

The retina is sometimes the seat of a form of malignant tumor, which has been called *glioma*. It is only found in children and in many cases soon after birth.

The affection is usually noticed by the parents through the child's blindness in one or possibly both eyes, together with a characteristic yellowish-gray reflection from the back-ground of the eye-ball, which has given rise to the name of *amaurotic cat's eye*.

The tumor usually grows rather rapidly, and although the eye may show no external sign of anything being wrong within it, so long as the tumor is small, the newformation will at a later period cause exactly the same symptoms which we have described as due to the growth of a choroidal tumor. Finally the eye-ball bursts, and the tumor shows itself outwardly. (See figure 54.) At the same time it has usually already extended into the tissue of the optic nerve. It soon causes metastases in the bones of the skull, the brain and other organs.

The affection may attack only one eye or both, although, as a rule, not simultaneously; it leads, if not interfered with, absolutely to death.

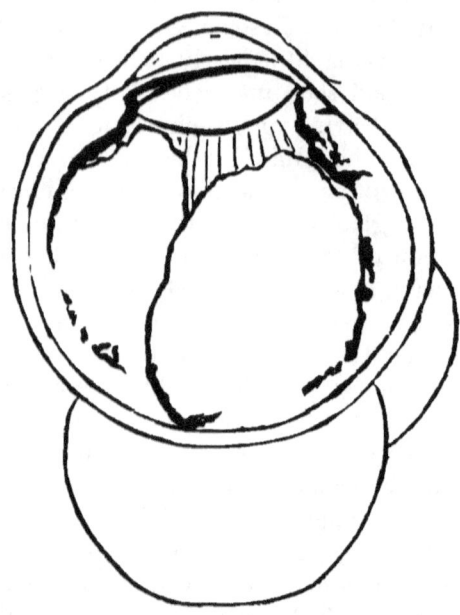

FIG. 54. Diagram showing an Eye-ball affected with Glioma of the Retina. The tumor not only fills the eye-ball, but has already broken through the sclerotic. The pigment lying in the tissue of the glioma is derived from the choroid.

The only remedy is the earliest possible removal of the eye-ball, and when both eyes are affected, the physician may find himself in the very disagreeable dilemma of insisting on the removal of both eye-balls in the hope of possibly saving the child's life, or of letting it die. The latter is usually the result accepted by the parents.

When the eye is removed too late,—and this is unfortunately nearly always the case—relapses will occur within the orbit, leading rapidly to death, although usually with less suffering to the child than when the eye-ball has been allowed to burst and form a huge and repulsive tumor.

In some cases inflammatory deposits in the vitreous body have been mistaken for glioma.

# CHAPTER XIV.

## DISEASES OF THE OPTIC NERVE.

HYPERÆMIA.— NEURITIS OPTICA.—ATROPHY.— COLOR BLINDNESS.— AMBLYOPIA.— AMAUROSIS.—HEMIANOPIA.—INJURIES.—NEOPLASMS.—MYXOMA.

*Hyperæmia of the optic papilla* is almost always accompanied by hyperæmia of the retina, and occurs as a symptom accompanying inflammations of the uveal tract. But we sometimes meet with a genuine hyperæmia of the optic nerve and retina alone, in which case it may be an early stage of a neuritis, or simply a passing pathological condition, brought about by over-work, especially in bad light. The symptoms and the treatment are the same as have been described in connection with hyperæmia of the retina. When the hyperæmia is caused by an uncorrected error of refraction, this should be corrected by properly selected glasses.

*Neuritis optica* appears in two forms: the more frequent one, in which the inflammatory symptoms of the optic papilla are plainly visible (papillitis(!), papillo-retinitis, neuro-retinitis, retinitis ascendens), and a second form, in which the ophthalmoscope may at first reveal hardly any signs of inflammation, but yet the symptoms are such as can only be explained by the supposition, that a neuritis is present in the part of the nerve which lies behind the eye-ball (neuritis descendens).

We sometimes find, preceding neuritis ascendens, an œdematous condition of the optic papilla. This, however, is soon superseded by active inflammatory symptoms.

In most cases the neuritis involves first the interstitial connective tissue of the optic nerve, and the nerve-fibres become only secondarily affected. (See figure 55).

On examination with the ophthalmoscope, we find in early

stages of optic neuritis a hyperæmia of the optic papilla, combined with swelling, and indistinctness of its outlines. The retinal veins are enlarged and tortuous. Later on the optic papilla becomes more and more infiltrated and swollen. Its color is then a whitish gray, its normal outlines become perfectly hidden, and small hemorrhages may appear in its tissue. The main trunks of the retinal blood-vessels in the optic papilla become so covered by the infiltration that they sometimes cannot be recognized. The surrounding retinal tissue appears hazy, and hemorrhages in the retinal tissue are seldom wanting.

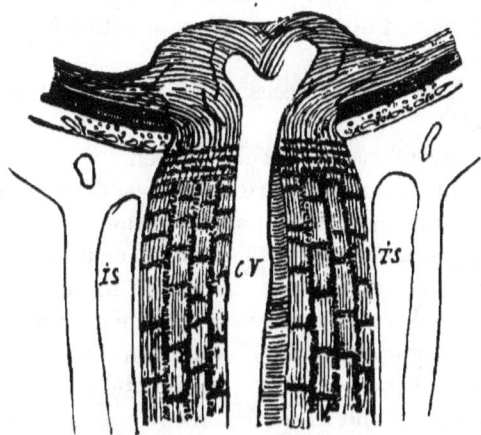

FIG. 55. Longitudinal Section through the Optic Nerve in a Case of Interstitial Optic Neuritis. CV. Central retinal vein greatly dilated. IS. Intravaginal space also dilated. The optic papilla is greatly swollen, and contains a number of newly-formed blood-vessels. The connective tissue is in a state of infiltration.

The more the swelling and infiltration of the optic papilla increase, the more prominent are the symptoms of constriction of the retinal blood-vessels. This fact has given this condition the name of "choked disk." Later on retraction of the newly formed connective tissue and consequent atrophy of the optic nerve and retina take place. In these cases of atrophy after neuritis optica we are often able to diagnosticate the preceding neuritis long after it has occurred by the bluish gray discoloration and irregular outlines of the optic papilla, and from the remaining traces of hemorrhages.

If arrested in its early stages the disease sometimes gets well without impairment of vision.

The patients come generally under observation on account of impaired vision; still, the original causes of a neuritis ascendens may have forced them to seek a physician's advice before the appearance of eye-symptoms, in which case the condition of the the optic nerve may help to diagnosticate the primary disease.

The most frequent primary causes of this form of optic neuritis are intra-cranial affections, and among these especially tumors, then syphilis, lead-poisoning, albuminuria and diabetes. The disease most frequently attacks both eyes.

The treatment of optic neuritis, as of retinitis, is in the main that of its primary cause.

We shall have further occasion to refer to this subject in Chapter XXIII.

Neuritis descendens is but seldom seen.

The affection causes a more or less sudden total or partial blindness of one or both eyes, and with the ophthalmoscope we find at first, perhaps, only a somewhat anæmic optic papilla. This anæmia is caused by pressure upon the arterial blood-vessels. The retinal veins appear fuller, than normal, and there may be also a slight exudation. Later on the optic papilla and retina may show signs of active inflammation.

The disease may end in perfect recovery, or it may lead to a partial atrophy of the optic nerve, and, especially, of those fibres which go to the macula lutea. In this case peripheral vision may be normal, while central vision is abolished (*central scotoma*).

If there is any general cause to be detected, to which the disease of the nerve may be due, treatment must be directed to the removal of this cause. When we are unable to find such a cause, the employment of iodide of potassium, mercury in some form, leeches, diaphoretics and diuretics may be beneficial.

A frequent affection of the optic nerve is *atrophy* without any visible sign of inflammation and due undoubtedly to impaired nutrition and consequent degeneration of the nerve-fibres, conjoined with a slowly increasing newformation of connective-tissue. The atrophy may attack a part only of the optic-nerve fibres, or it may involve the whole nerve.

# DISEASES OF THE OPTIC NERVE.

The optic papilla in such a case appears whitish or grayish, sometimes dotted, in other cases of a uniformly shining white. The retinal blood-vessels are very small, and their peripheral ends and smaller branches are invisible. Later on the optic papilla appears slightly excavated. (See figure 56).

According to the degree of atrophy is the impairment of sight; in the highest grades it is totally abolished. There are often central scotomata, and the color sense is diminished, or color-blindness, especially for red and green, may occur.

The disease usually affects both eyes. A similar condition may come about from any pressure upon and consequent impairment of the nutrition of the optic nerve, as through an ex-

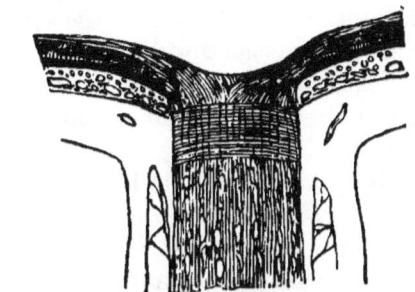

FIG. 56. An Atrophic Excavation of the Optic Papilla.

ostosis, or from exudation in cerebral or cerebro-spinal meningitis.

The most frequent cause of this form of atrophy of the optic nerve is the abuse of tobacco and alcoholic stimulants. Therefore, saloon-keepers are frequently subject to it. The atrophy of the optic nerve following the abuse of tobacco, or of alcohol, or of both together, has a comparatively good prognosis, if the patient has enough moral energy left to abstain totally from the use of these noxious substances. Most patients of this kind, however, will resist the attempt to help them; and here the voice of the family physician will often be of great importance in aid of the efforts of the specialist. I have often heard the existence or even the possibility of such an affection laughed at, or at least doubted; yet, the fact is so absolutely certain, and the disease so perfectly recognizable and recognized, that every physician, who by his doubts aids the patient in evading the necessary restriction, commits a great wrong.

Besides enforcing abstinence, it will be well to give aid to the usually poor appetite, to give iodide of potassium or some other tonic, and to induce sleep by bromide of potassium or hydrate of chloral. In some cases strychnia is of use and in others electricity has proved successful. But all these remedies are of no use unless either total or, if this cannot be obtained at least partial, abstinence from the use of the noxious substances is insured.

When syphilis is the cause of atrophy of the optic nerve anti-syphilitic treatment must be resorted to.

In a number of cases the atrophy of the optic nerve is dependent on tabes dorsalis, or on sclerosis of the spinal cord or medulla and is then always associated with myosis and immobility of the contracted pupils, caused by the loss of reflex-action. The pupil, however, usually becomes still smaller when an effort at accommodation is made.

It has been already mentioned that in cases of atrophy color-blindness may occur.

This acquired color-blindness must, however, not be confounded with the not uncommon congenital color-blindness in which there is no disease, but a lack of perception of certain colors. This congenital color-blindness is usually either a red-green blindness, or a blue-yellow blindness. The general acuteness of vision is usually perfect in this affection, and the color-blindness is incurable. (See Chapter XXIV.)

The terms *amblyopia* and especially *amaurosis* are frequently used by practitioners, and seem to convey to the patients a most fearful idea of their condition. It may, therefore, be well to state, that the term amblyopia means nothing but defective sight, and is, especially, used to designate defective sight from a disease of the back-ground of the eye-ball, and more especially, of the optic nerve. Amaurosis also, is not the name of a disease, but it means simply blindness from disease of the fundus oculi, especially from an affection of the optic nerve.

The term *hemianopia* designates the loss of half of the field of vision. It and its causes will be detailed in Chapter XXII.

*Injuries* to the optic nerve may lead to partial or total atrophy according to their extent. Atrophy of the optic nerve is also observed after injuries to the head and is then in most cases due to a fracture of the walls of the canalis opticus.

The *tumors* of the optic nerve are either *myxomatous, fibromyxomatous* or *endotheliomatous (psammoma)* or *sarcomatous* in nature. They usually spring from the sheaths of the nerve, and destroy sight, by compressing the nerve-tissue.

Besides the gradually increasing blindness which they cause, a gradually increasing exophthalmus is also noticed.

This protrusion of the eye-ball is usually directed straight forward, and, unless the tumor is very large, the mobility of the eye-ball is, perhaps, generally impaired, but not in any especial direction. This is easily understood, since the tumor originates within the hollow cone which the external ocular muscles form within the orbit. For the same reason we find by palpation that the tumor moves with the eye-ball. The ophthalmoscope reveals either optic neuritis, or atrophy of the optic papilla.

The treatment consists in an early removal of the tumor. Formerly the eye-ball was always removed with the newformation, but since *Knapp* first succeeded in removing a tumor of the optic nerve without sacrificing the eye-ball, the operation has been several times repeated, aud should always be attempted.

# CHAPTER XV.

## DISEASES OF THE CRYSTALLINE LENS.

CONGENITAL CATARACT. — ZONULAR CATARACT.— POLAR CATARACT.— TOTAL CATARACT.—ACQUIRED CATARACT.—SOFT CATARACT.—CORTICAL CATARACT.—NUCLEAR CATARACT.—DIABETIC CATARACT.—TRAUMATIC CATARACT.—DISLOCATION OF THE CRYSTALLINE LENS.—ECTOPIA LENTIS.—APHAKIA.

The affections of the crystalline lens, for which patients seek advice, are of two kinds, namely, the formation of a cataract, or the dislocation of the crystalline lens. Both affections may be either congenital or acquired.

FIG. 57. Diagram showing where the Opacities of the Crystalline Lens lie in Cases of Zonular (lamellar) Cataract.

Cataract is the name for every opacity or dimness of the crystalline lens, be it partial or total.

The *congenital* forms of *cataract*, with which we usually count those which are observed soon after birth, are: zonular cataract, polar cataract and total soft cataract.

# DISEASES OF THE CRYSTALLINE LENS. 143

*Zonular (lamellar) cataract* is the name given to a condition in which one or more layers of the crystalline lens, or only parts of one or several layers of its substance, are opaque. (See figure 57.) This is the most common form of congenital cataract. It is usually stationary, seldom progressive, and nearly always affects both eyes. It is often connected with rhachitis or a strumous diathesis; it seems also to be in some cases connected with the fact of consanguinity of the parents.

The affection is usually first noticed by the parents several years after birth, and especially when the children begin to play with small objects.

When the pupil is well dilated in such cases, we see behind the pupil a greyish, circular, often striated, opacity, covered anteriorly by transparent lens-substance, and leaving the periphery of the crystalline lens clear. The opacity generally appears densest in the center, and its outlines are usually well defined.

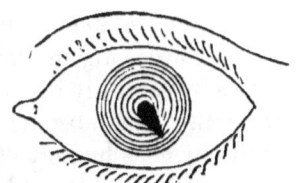

FIG. 58. Shows an Eye operated upon by Iridectomy, on account of Zonular (lamellar) Cataract.

If the outlines of the opacity are indistinct, it may be a sign that the cataract is of a progressive form. By the use of the ophthalmoscope we can see very clearly what parts of the crystalline lens as yet remain clear and available for vision, and, on the other hand, whether some part of the lens is in such a condition that it might, perhaps, be used to better advantage were the pupil more favorably situated. This point is of great importance with regard to the method of operating which is to be chosen. Eyes affected with similar cataract, are often near-sighted, and may, furthermore, show other defects.

Zonular cataract usually prevents children from attending school, and therefore something ought to be done at an early period. The operation, which is most frequently performed, and which is often quite successful, consists in making a small iridectomy in front of the clearest part of the peripheral portion of the crystalline lens. (See figure 58.) An even better visual result may be obtained by allowing the iris to remain entangled in the corneal wound (*iridencleisis*). Thus the pupil will be dislocated toward this side without the enlargement resulting from an iridectomy, and some of the diffuse light, which otherwise would fall into the eye, will be excluded. Although the immediate effect may be thus improved, the procedure of causing an incarceration of the iris in the cornea is of somewhat doubtful advantage, when we consider the future of such an eye-ball. In fact very serious consequences, such as iridocyclitis, glaucoma, and even sympathetic ophthalmia of the other eye, have been occasionally observed as a result of this particular procedure. A simple iridectomy, or, when it can be safely accomplished, a simple iridotomy, is therefore generally to be preferred.

A large proportion of the cases of zonular cataract receive, however, but little benefit, or even none at all, from any of these operations. It is, therefore, necessary in a great number of cases to get rid of the whole lens by carefully incising the anterior lens-capsule and thus allowing the lens-substance to be slowly dissolved by the action of the aqueous humor. This little operation, called discission, must generally be repeated several times, until a clear pupil is obtained. An eye which has been operated upon in this manner is, of course, deficient in refractive power and has also entirely lost the faculty of accommodation, yet with the help of the proper glasses vision is usually comparatively good, and a moveable, round, and central pupil is procured as in the normal eye. I have even performed this operation several times with marked success in eyes which had previously been operated upon by iridectomy with little or no benefit.

*Polar* or *pyramidal cataract* consists in a small densely opaque cone, sitting apparently upon the middle of the anterior surface of the lens-capsule, but really enclosed within it.

What is sometimes called a *posterior polar cataract* is only a deposit upon the posterior lens-capsule, and is, therefore, properly speaking, no cataract at all.

Anterior polar, or pyramidal cataract is frequently combined

# DISEASES OF THE CRYSTALLINE LENS, 145

with other malformations (microcornea, microphthalmus or coloboma of the iris, or of iris and choroid, etc.). (See figure 50.) If no other malformation exists with it, it is not impossible that ulceration with perforation of the cornea and the subsequent adhesion of the anterior lens-capsule to the cornea, during fœtal life or early infancy, may have been the cause of the formation of the opaque cone (*O. Becker*).

In an eye affected with this form of cataract, the light can, of course, only enter the eye peripherally. We may, therefore, be able to improve the sight materially by an iridectomy, or we may have to resort to discission of the lens-capsule, in order to bring about the absorption of the whole crystalline lens.

*Total* congenital *cataract* may be perfectly soft, or it may have a hard nucleus. Sometimes the whole cataract appears

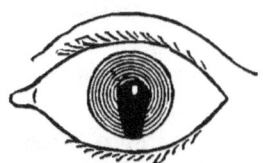

FIG 50. An Eye affected with Congenital Anterior Polar (pyramidal) Cataract and Coloboma of the Iris.

thin and shrunken, in which case it has probably been, in the beginning, a soft cataract, and has lost some of its more fluid parts by exosmosis.

The removal of a total congenital cataract should be effected as early as possible, and the urgency is even greater than in cases of zonular or pyramidal cataract, inasmuch as the latter allow of some sight, while in total cataract there is no vision of objects, but only perception of light. The longer we delay the operation, therefore, the less will be the probability of obtaining good and useful vision. Soft total cataract may be got rid of by discission of the anterior lens-capsule; harder ones have to be extracted, if possible, and this can usually be done, without an iridectomy. Shrunken cataracts may be divided, or may be gently pulled out of the eye through a corneal section with forceps or a sharp hook.

In all three forms of congenital cataract *nystagmus*, i. e., a continued motion of the eye-balls generally in a horizontal direction will develop, if the obstacle to distinct vision is not removed at an early date.

In all forms of *acquired cataract* we can follow up the whole process from beginning to end, and we speak in these forms of an incipient, unripe (immature), ripe (mature) or over-ripe (hypermature) cataract, according to the stage of development. We call a cataract ripe when the lens is opaque throughout. In over-ripe cataract we find the outer or cortical parts fluid or semi-fluid, and we can often see the yellow nucleus lying at the bottom of the lens capsule, and changing its place, according to the law of gravitation.

With regard to the consistency of the cataract, we have a soft or even fluid cataract, a semi-soft cortical cataract, a hard nuclear cataract.

The soft or fluid *cataract* is most frequently found in young people. It appears generally of a white or bluish color, like milk, and the fluid contents seem to bulge the anterior lens-capsule forwards. In later stages deposits of lime or cholesterine may be seen in it, or the cataract may shrink by giving off some of its fluid parts. The anterior lens-capsule, which at an earlier period appeared tense, will then become wrinkled, and it may even happen that, as a result of the shrinkage, a part of the pupil may be uncovered and vision be more or less perfectly re-established.

*Cortical cataract*, the most frequent kind, consists in the loss of transparency of the cortical layers of the crystalline lens. Its nucleus may remain perfectly clear. The formation of this form of cataract usually begins at the equator of the crystalline lens; and, in its incipient stages, it can be diagnosticated only after full dilatation of the pupil. It is then best seen by means of the ophthalmoscope. Gradually the whole cortex of the crystalline lens assumes a striated appearance, and the opalescent striæ are arranged around a center (the anterior pole of the lens) like the spokes of a wheel. As the disease advances these spokes become broader and denser, and appear of a grayish-white or pearl-gray color. Finally, in the stage of ripeness, the whole cortex is involved, and vision reduced to the perception of light. While these changes are going on in the cortex of the lens, the nucleus generally retains nearly the normal degree of transparency and hardness belonging to the age of the patient.

The over-ripe (hypermature) stage we have already described.

*Nuclear*, or *hard cataract*, is the senile cataract proper. In this form of cataract the central hardening of the crystalline lens, which in middle and advanced life results in the formation of the nucleus, goes on to the very periphery of that organ. Such a cataract is hard, and has an amber tint. It does not, as a rule, entirely obscure sight, and it often allows patients to count fingers at some distance, even when it is perfectly ripe. This kind of cataract develops slowly, and the striæ in the cortical substance are but little pronounced.

When these different forms of cataract, which are usually acquired at an advanced period of life, appear in an otherwise apparently healthy eye, they are called *uncomplicated cataracts*. When other affections, or their results, are present in a cataractous eye, they are called *complicated cataracts*. Thus a cataract may be complicated by corneal scars, posterior synechiæ, choroiditis, detachment of the retina, glaucoma, synchisis of the vitreous body, etc. Such complicated cataracts are generally much less favorable for operation than the uncomplicated ones.

When cataract develops in young persons its formation may be, and often is, caused by *diabetes mellitus*.

The development of cataract in youth and in the early years of adult life is, moreover, often dependent on some inherited tendency, and may show itself in several members of the same family.

At a certain stage in the development of a cataract, the crystalline lens becomes swollen, while still tolerably transparent; and in this stage the eyes often become short-sighted, so that a patient who has long used glasses for reading, can read again without glasses, and may even see better at a distance with concave lenses.

For congenital, as well as acquired cataract, there is but one possible way of treatment, namely: to remove the opaque crystalline lens from the eye-ball, or at least from the axis of vision, by means of a surgical operation. The operation of discission, which has been already described in connection with congenital cataract, is applicable also to softer acquired cataracts in persons under about 30 years of age, or the division of the capsule may be followed, after the lapse of a few days, either by the removal of the soft and swollen lens-substance through a simple linear incision made for this purpose in the cornea, or by aspiration by means of a tubular curette. If the cataract is hard or has a hard nucleus, which is ordinarily the case in persons who have reached or passed the middle period of life, the operation known by the name of extraction, and which has for its object the removal of the entire opaque crystalline lens from the eye-ball, is alone applicable. Extraction may again be performed in several different ways, such as varying the form and position of the corneal incision, extracting the lens through the normal pupil, or enlarging the pupil by an iridectomy, opening the lens-capsule and allowing it to remain within the eye-ball after the extraction of the lens-substance, or extracting the cataractous lens in its capsule, etc.

It does not fall within the scope of this book to give more than a bare sketch of such an operation as cataract-extraction, and for this the reader is referred to Chapter XXV.

Every physician ought, however, to have a definite idea as to the best time at which to operate for cataract, and also to know something about the prognosis of such an operation,

Cataract extraction should not be performed until the cataract is ripe, and that is in most cases until vision is reduced to the faculty of differentiating between light and shade. When a ripe cataract is viewed by oblique illumination, the pupillary edge of the iris shows no shadow on the anterior surface of the crystalline lens. With the ophthalmoscope, as a rule, no red reflex can be obtained from the back-ground of the eye. Unripe and over-ripe cataracts give, as a rule, less satisfactory results after an operation than ripe ones. Before advising an operation, the physician must satisfy himself that the eye is in an otherwise healthy condition. It is, therefore, desirable that every physician should be able to examine the eye with regard to its function of vision.

The patient should be able to see a candle-flame in a darkened room across the whole room, and also to point out in what direction it is held. If he cannot do this, the cataract is in some way a complicated one. If there are no visible signs of former inflammation of the cornea or iris, the trouble must be sought for further back. By now examining the field of vision with a lighted candle in a darkened room, as detailed in Chapter II., we first of all confirm or correct the former observation made with the candle; and secondly, we examine whether there may be a well defined portion of the field of vision wanting, in which case the diagnosis of an atrophic choroiditis or a detachment of the retina is to be made, and the prognosis modified accordingly, the latter affection is the most likely to be present if the eye-ball is

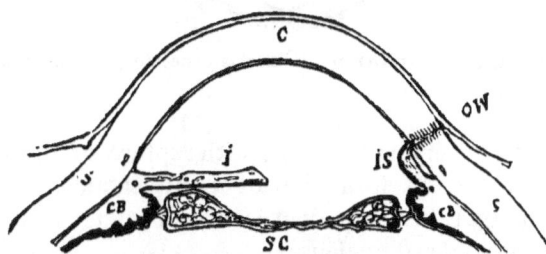

FIG. 60. Secondary (capsular) Cataract after Cataract Extraction. SC. Cataract. C. Cornea. S. Sclerotic. I. Iris. CB. Ciliary body. OW. Corneal incision for the removal of the primary cataract, to the inner opening of which IS, the iris-stump, caused by the iridectomy, is adherent.

also soft. If the pupil dilates but slowly, and then not fully even after the instillation of sulphate of atropia, there is probably something wrong in the uveal tract, and such eyes are especially unfavorable subjects for extraction of the cataract, even when the functional examination reveals no further disturbance.

According to statistics, good operators lose from 6 to 8 per cent. of eyes after operation for uncomplicated cataract.

After cataract extraction has been performed by any of the methods in which the lens-capsule is left in the eye-ball, this membrane may give occasion for a secondary operation through its becoming dim and wrinkled, forming what is called a secondary cataract. (See figure 60). In such a case a simple shifting or tearing apart of the lens-capsule, as soon as may be, after the primary operation, is sufficient. The longer we wait, the tougher the lens-capsule will become, and it may finally become almost impossible to cut it. When there has been an iritis, and perhaps an irido-cyclitis after the operation, the lens-capsule and the newly formed membranes due to the inflammation, become glued together into one continuous membrane. Iridotomy may then be performed with the result of giving the patient some useful sight, especially, if the tension of the eye-ball is not diminished.

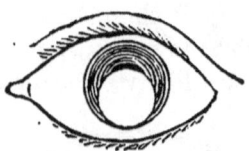

FIG. 61. The Crystalline Lens (reduced in size) is dislocated, and lies in the anterior chamber.

*Injuries* to the crystalline lens, with rupture of the lens-capsule, usually cause the formation of a soft cataract (*traumatic cataract*), at least, if the patient is not of an age at which the lens has already a hard nucleus.

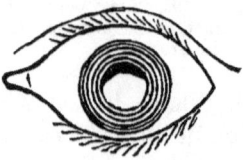

FIG. 62. The dislocated Crystalline Lens lies behind the lower part of the Iris in the vitreous body, and leaves part of the pupillary area free.

From blows upon the eye; or generally from any injury with a blunt instrument, the crystalline lens may be torn from the ligamentum suspensorium (zonule of *Zinn*), or the latter from the ciliary body, and the crystalline lens thus become *dislocated*. The dislocation may take place backwards into the vitreous body. or forwards into the anterior chamber (See figure 61), or the dislocated lens may remain half in the vitreous body and half in the anterior chamber. If the upper part of the zonule of *Zinn* is torn to a small extent only, the crystalline lens may sink behind the iris and a part of the pupil be thus freed from it. (See figure 62). If after such an injury the iris trembles (*iridodonesis*) with the movements of the eye-ball, the diagnosis of a dislocation of the crystalline lens is almost certain ; moreover, the periphery of the lens, as far as it lies in the field of the pupil, may be seen as a black arc, when viewed by diffuse light or with the ophthalmoscope (in consequence of total reflection of the light); but as a shining, yellowish-white arc, when viewed under oblique illumination. When the whole of the crystalline lens is dislocated into the anterior chamber, it may fill the chamber so completely, that there is at first some difficulty in recognizing it, but as it soon becomes dimmer and causes an increase of the intra-ocular tension with all its disagreeable consequences, the diagnosis soon becomes easy.

Dislocation of the crystalline lens may happen spontaneously in consequence of synchisis of the vitreous body. This is the case, as a rule, when dislocation occurs in short-sighted eyes. Dislocation of the crystalline lens may be also a congenital defect, and is known by the name of *ectopia lentis*.

An eye with a dislocated crystalline lens cannot accommodate. In the part of the pupil which is not covered by the lens the eye must necessarily be far-sighted, just as after removal of a cataract; while in the remaining part of the pupil it is usually short-sighted.

Dislocated crystalline lenses gradually become dim, as a rule. Their position may, furthermore, cause irritation and inflammation of the iris, ciliary body, and choroid. A crystalline lens dislocated into the anterior chamber may cause glaucoma, as already stated. A partially dislocated crystalline lens need not be interfered with until it becomes cataractous and until its presence causes further trouble in the eye. The use of eserine or any other myotic agent may, at first, by the contraction of the pupil, be very agreeable to the patient, but its use cannot well be kept up ad infinitum.

A crystalline lens dislocated totally into the anterior chamber should be at once removed by a peripheral section, as in an ordinary cataract extraction.

The absence of the crystalline lens, whether as a result of dislocation or of an operation for cataract, is designated by the name of *aphakia*.

# CHAPTER XVI.

## DISEASES OF THE VITREOUS BODY.

HYALITIS.—MUSCAE VOLITANTES. — LARGER OPACITIES.—SYNCHISIS SCINTILLANS—HEMMORRHAGE.—FOREIGN BODIES.—NEWFORMATION OF CONNECTIVE TISSUE.

Affections of the vitreous body are always secondary affections, and are due to diseases of the membranes surrounding it, in most cases to diseases of the choroid and ciliary body. We distinguish between a *serous hyalitis* (*synchisis corporis vitrei*), a *fibrinous* or *plastic hyalitis*, and a *purulent hyalitis*. Yet, it must be thereby understood, that these forms of inflammation of the vitreous body (hyalitis) are only extensions of inflammatory processes of a corresponding character in the uveal tract, or in the optic nerve and retina. It often happens, however, that the changes in the vitreous body, due to the hyalitis, continue long after the primary affection has run its course, or even permanently.

We find this to be the case especially with the various forms of opacities observed in the vitreous body after a fibrino-plastic exudation into it.

The most common forms of opacities in the vitreous body are the so-called *muscae volitantes*. A patient suffering from such muscae volitantes, when he looks at a bright surface, sees small black and gray dots and threads on or in front of it, which seem to float and to "run away" whenever he tries to "look directly at them." These dots and threads often present the appearance of strings of beads, and also take on other quaint shapes. What the patient really observes, are the shadows cast upon the retina by fibrinous threads or by small aggregations of cellular elements in the vitreous body.

The presence of these minute cellular elements and fine

threads may be demonstrated in the normal eye; therefore, muscæ volitantes are not necessarily to be interpreted as a pathological symptom. When a person has once detected their existence, he is apt to look for them again, and then finds to his dismay that they apparently increase in number, although in fact he simply sees now opacities to which he had previously paid no attention. This discovery may bring him to the physician.

The sudden appearance of muscæ volitantes in an eye, or the actual increase in their number, where they have been present and noticed before, is to be looked upon, especially in shortsighted eyes, as an indication of a disturbance in the uveal tract, and, therefore, as an important symptom.

With this exception, muscæ volitantes, as a rule, call for no treatment, and, if we once succeed in convincing the patient of the fact that, although possibly annoying, they are really of no importance, his anxiety is relieved, and they usually cease to be troublesome.

Opacities in the vitreous body, when they are extensive enough to be detected by the ophthalmoscope, whether as conspicuous films, or flocks, or denser membranes, or as a general diffused muddiness, are of far greater importance.

In such cases the opacities materially interfere with sight, and they are moreover the evidence of the actual or former existence of a fibrino-plastic chorioditis. They are often found in highly myopic eyes. The vitreous body is then usually fluid, and the dense shadows fly about with every movement of the eye-ball.

Even when the choroiditis, which has given rise to the formation of such opacities, is cured, we may try to bring about their absorption. Formerly mercury, decoctum *Zittmannii*, iodide of potassium and the constant current were the chief remedies in such cases; now the muriate of pilocarpine has justly superseded them.

Newformations of large masses of connective tissue within the vitreous body are rare, but when present they seriously interfere with sight. They lie usually near the optic nerve entrance, and are due to inflammation of the optic nerve or retina (*retinitis proliferans*).

## DISEASES OF THE VITREOUS BODY.

*Synchisis scintillans* is the name given to a liquified condition of the vitreous body in which crystals of cholesterine have been formed. When these fly about they sparkle in the light like particles of silver or gold. For this condition we know of no treatment.

*Hemorrhages* into the vitreous body are observed in cases of injuries to the ciliary body, the choroid, or the retina. We shall speak further about them in Chapter XVIII. If the eye in such a case is examined with the ophthalmoscope, it may at first be impossible to get any reflex from the back-ground, or a darker or lighter shade of red may be seen according to the quantity of blood effused into the vitreous body. Such hemorrhages may become perfectly absorbed, or the fibrine may remain and form floating opacities. If the hemorrhage is very extensive, the eyeball will probably become atrophied.

The conditions caused by the presence of a foreign body in the vitreous will be detailed in Chapter XVIII.

# CHAPTER XVII.

### GLAUCOMA.

CHRONIC SIMPLE GLAUCOMA.—CHRONIC INFLAMMATORY GLAUCOMA.—ACUTE GLAUCOMA.—GLAUCOMA ABSOLUTUM—SECONDARY GLAUCOMA.

*Glaucoma* is an affection of the eye, the nature of which is, as yet, not perfectly understood. Its destructiveness, and the insidious slow progress of some of its varieties, make it a disease of grave importance. The general practitioner should be perfectly familiar with its chief symptoms, the more so since they are of such a nature as to bring the patient to seek aid from the physician quite as often as from the oculist.

We shall not give any space here to the discussion of the different theories which have been advanced to explain the nature of this disease, since none, as yet, has been absolutely proven to exist in all cases, and no one of them covers the whole ground. We may, however, state here that the cardinal symptoms of glaucoma may be due to an increase of fluids secreted within the eye-ball, or to an obstacle to the exit of even the normal quantity of fluids.

The name glaucoma is as dark as the disease, and in the present state of our knowledge has little meaning. It used to be said that glaucomatous eyes have a greenish pupil, and for this reason the name has been given to the disease. The greenish pupil is, however, but rarely seen. The name, therefore, is a misnomer.

The cardinal symptoms of glaucoma are, an *increase* of the *intra-ocular tension*, which renders the eye-ball harder than it is in its normal condition, and the loss of vision, which is chiefly, but, as we will see, not solely due to the *excavation* and subsequent atrophy of the optic papilla. (See figure 63). These two cardinal symptoms are usually accompanied or followed by a number of others, which may materially change the picture of the disease.

We will now consider the typical forms of glaucoma.

*Chronic simple glaucoma* is the form in which the disease is oftenest seen. In such cases we find an increase of the intra-ocular tension, and this increase may be slight only, or it may render the eye-ball stone-hard. The eye-ball shows no external sign of inflammation, except, perhaps, a slight tortuousness and enlargement of the few episcleral blood-vessels visible in the direction of the recti muscles. The pupil may be somewhat

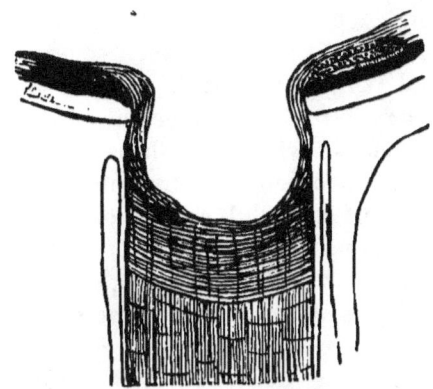

FIG. 63.—Glaucomatous Excavation of the Optic Papilla. The Lamina Cribrosa is forced out of its normal position, and lies behind the Sclerotic. The Optic Nerve is atrophied.

larger than normal, and act but slowly. Examination with the ophthalmoscope reveals an excavation of the optic nerve, with spontaneous or easily excited pulsation of the arteries. Central vision is deteriorated, but at the same time the field of vision gradually contracts, so that the time may come when the patient sees, what little he can see, as if he looked through a tube. The contraction of the visual field begins usually at the nasal side, and the visual field will then be generally found to have an elliptic shape, with the point of fixation in or near one of the foci. The color-sense is, as a rule, perfectly intact. Sometimes the patients notice a slight mist coming before the eye; they see flashes of light or colored rings around the flame of a lamp or candle. Another important symptom is the loss of accommodative power, and as its consequence presbyopia. This presbyopia in a young individual comes on before the normal time and in an already presbyopic individual will cause an abnormally rapid increase of his presbyopia, and necessitate a rapid increase in the strength of his glasses for reading.

In *chronic inflammatory glaucoma* we find again an increase of the intra-ocular pressure and consequent excavation of the optic papilla. Added to these we have externally visible symptoms of inflammation, which may vary in degree from a simple hyperæmia of the episcleral blood-vessels to a participation in the inflammatory process of all the tissues of the anterior portion of the eye-ball. The conjunctiva becomes hyperæmic, the cornea dim, and perhaps ulcerated, the aqueous humor turbid, and the periphery of the iris adherent to the cornea, thus obliterating *Fontana's* cavities. In the latter cases the pupil will appear wide and immoveable, or irregular from posterior synechiæ. The iris itself looks dull and discolored. The light of the ophthalmoscope can usually not penetrate the opacities, and the optic papilla is invisible. There may be intense pain, or it may be but slight. Vision is often reduced to mere perception of light. The cornea loses its sensitiveness to the touch.

The simple and the inflammatory chronic glaucoma often merge into each other, and both lead, when not interfered with, to the perfect abolition of sight.

In *acute glaucoma* the increase of the intra-ocular tension comes in sudden attacks. These may at first cause but little diminution of sight, but generally they leave the eye in a worse and worse condition. In other rare cases one sudden attack destroys the sight in a few hours. These acute attacks of increased intra-ocular tension may also be accompanied by other plainly visible inflammatory symptoms, or they may remain without them. The former is by far the more frequent form.

Attacks of acute glaucoma often come on at night, especially when the eyes have been greatly tired. Pains in and around the eyes rob the patient of his sleep. The patient sees rainbow-colors around a candle light; he shuns the light and sees light-flashes while the lids are closed. There is lachrymation, and there may be œdema of the upper eye-lid ; the conjunctiva is hyperæmic. The cornea appears hazy, the anterior chamber is shallow, the pupil dilated and immoveable, and the iris dull. The intra-ocular tension is increased and the patient usually cannot bear pressure on the eye-ball without pain. Light is generally very much reduced during the attack. The cornea bears touching without quick reflex-action of the eye-lids. Sometimes vomiting is caused by the pain.

In milder attacks these symptoms are less pronounced. Such attacks of acute glaucoma pass off, and although his sight remains impaired, the patient may for a time be quite comfortable again. By and by, however, the attacks come on more frequently, the pain and inflammatory symptoms are more severe, and vision remains worse after every attack, until it is finally extinguished (*glaucoma absolutum*).

An eye that has been lost by glaucoma is, as a rule, not even then at rest, but gradually choroidal, and iritic troubles are developed, the crystalline lens becomes cataractous, the increase of the intra-ocular tension goes on, and may even end in the rupture of the eye-ball. The pain also may continue and make the patient's life miserable.

The etiology of glaucoma is obscure. It occurs almost always in hypermetropic eyes, and the patients are, as a rule, advanced in years. Its prognosis, if the glaucoma is not interfered with, is absolutely bad. By operation the progress of the disease is usually, but not always, arrested, and in a certain number of cases the sight is again improved.

It may be well to state here that when the symptoms complained of by a patient point at all to glaucoma, the physician should not instill sulphate of atropia into the patient's eye, as this is apt to bring about an acute attack. Furthermore, it will be well to tell the patient that operating on one eye when the other is even but slightly or apparently not at all affected with glaucoma, may possibly precipitate an acute attack in this eye too. Yet, of course, this fact cannot be a reason for not operating on the eye first attacked. The operations to be performed are iridectomy, or, perhaps, sclerotomy. Myotics may temporarily relieve slight attacks.

When glaucoma appears in an eye as a consequence of other primary affections, we call it *secondary glaucoma*. These primary affections may be the following, namely:—circular posterior synechia of the iris, all forms of staphyloma and ectatic scars, a dislocated crystalline lens, the rapid swelling of the lens-substance after rupture or division of the lens-capsule, serous iritis, irodochoroiditis, intra-ocular tumors, and sometimes hemorrhages in the retina (*glaucoma hemorrhagicum*). In all of these cases the progress depends, of course, on the possibility or impossibility of removing the primary cause.

# CHAPTER XVIII.

### INJURIES OF THE EYE-BALL AND THEIR CONSEQUENCES.

INJURIES WITHOUT RETENTION OF A FOREIGN BODY.—INJURIES WITH THE RETENTION OF A FOREIGN BODY WITHIN THE EYE-BALL.

Injuries of the eye-ball, especially when the foreign body which has caused the injury remains in the eye, are of the gravest

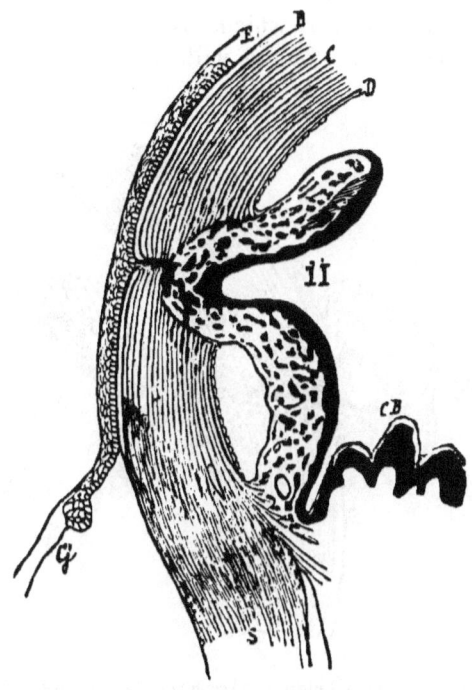

FIG. 64. Incarceration of a Fold of the Iris in a Corneal Wound. II. Incarcerated iris. C. Cornea. D. Descemet's membrane. B. Bowman's layer. E. Epithelial layer. Cj. Conjunctiva. S. Sclerotic. CB. Ciliary body.

importance. We shall, therefore, have to repeat in this chapter some things which have been already mentioned in another connection.

Simple cuts in the cornea, which do not penetrate its whole thickness, heal, as a rule, without trouble and without interference. In rare cases they cause local infiltration, and even the formation of a corneal abscess with all its consequences. Every cut necessarily leaves a scar, which, according to its size and situation, will interfere more or less with sight.

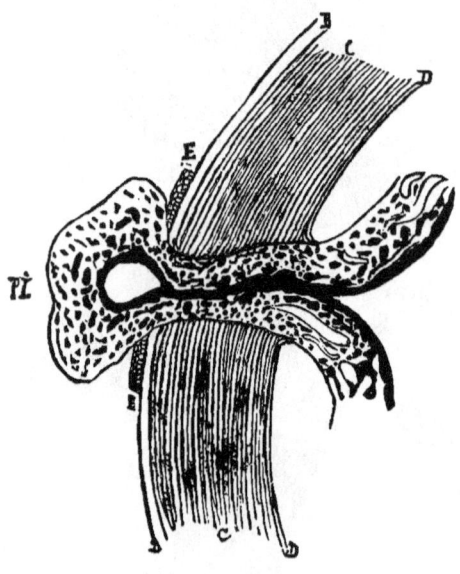

FIG. 65. Prolapse of the Iris. A Fold of the Iris has fallen through a Corneal Wound, and is held in this position. PI. Protruding iris. C. Cornea. D. Descemet's membrane. B. Bowman's layer. E. Epithelial layer.

If a cut has penetrated the whole thickness of the cornea, the aqueous humor escapes and the anterior chamber is emptied. The contents of the posterior part of the eye-ball are then pressed forward, so that the iris comes in contact with the inner opening of the corneal wound, and may thus become caught there (*incarceration*) (See figure 64), or it may actually protrude through the wound and be held in this position (*prolapse*) (See figure 65), thus giving rise to farther troubles. The portion of the iris which lies outside the cornea is, as a rule, gradually cast off, since by the constriction it is deprived of its nutrition. In other cases, when the nutrition is not cut off, it becomes the starting point of a granuloma, and may then grow as far as the eye-lids will allow it. Prolapse, as well as incarceration of the iris, produce what is called anterior synechia of the iris. The pupil in these cases is drawn towards the scar, and every contraction of the sphincter pupillae muscle must pull at this false insertion of the iris. This may give rise to a chronic state of irritation in this membrane, and ultimately to serious disturbances, such as glaucoma and sympathetic ophthalmia. We should, therefore, do what is in our power to restore the iris to its normal position within the eye. Gently rubbing the cornea with the eye-lids, or prying the wound-lips apart with a thin curette, may sometimes suffice to liberate the incarcerated iris; or, if the injury is very recent, the action of a myotic may bring about the desired effect. If the iris is prolapsed, we must cut off the prolapsed part, and thus free the remaining iris, if possible, altogether from the corneal wound. This will virtually amount to making an iridectomy, and can be done even a few days after the prolapse of the iris has occurred.

In some cases, on account of the presence of the iris, the scar does not become strong enough to withstand the normal intra-ocular pressure, so that it begins gradually to bulge (*ectatic scar*), and may, after a time, develop into a *traumatic staphyloma*. In rare cases the incarceration gives rise to the formation of a *cyst* of the iris. The nearer the periphery of the iris the incarceration or the prolapse has taken place, the more serious are the consequences which may follow. The most serious of these are chronic plastic or purulent iritis and cyclitis and sympathetic ophthalmia.

If the cut has penetrated both the cornea and the iris, the conditions will be the same as in simple punctured wounds of the cornea, except that the blood effused into the anterior chamber, may interfere for a time with a careful examination.

If the cut is still deeper and penetrates the capsule of the crystalline lens, the situation is in most cases further complicated by the formation of a total cataract. If the wound in the lens-capsule is large, the pressure from the rapidly swelling lens-substance, giving rise to acute glaucomatous symptoms, may very soon force us to attempt its extraction. In some rare cases (I have seen it twice) the iris, without apparently being cut, may be driven into the crystalline lens, and there remain, held tight by the lips of the wound in the lens-capsule. The ensuing dimness of the lens-substance may then remain confined to the immediate neighborhood of such a traumatic posterior synechia. In some cases the iris, or the iris and crystalline lens, are torn out of the eye-ball altogether by the instrument inflicting the injury (*traumatic irideremia*).

Injuries to the sclerotic can hardly happen without a contemporaneous injury to the ciliary body, or to the choroid and retina. If the wound is not gaping, rest and cold applications may accomplish all that is required; but if the wound gapes widely, and the vitreous body shows itself in the opening, it is best to sew it up. If the vitreous body is prolapsed, and the cut or torn edges of the choroid, and, perhaps, also of the retina, protrude between the lips of the wound in the sclerotic, it is better not to attempt to sew the wound up, but rather to watch the case, and apply only cold compresses. After such an injury the eye-ball is almost always ruined, and it may also become a source of serious danger to the fellow-eye.

If the wound of the sclerotic lies in the ciliary region, and the ciliary body is also wounded, cyclitis is almost sure to follow and the eye will be lost by shrinkage. The injured eye-ball is also especially apt to cause sympathetic inflammation of the other eye. In some cases the injury may involve almost all parts of the eye-ball, and the eye will run out, or after a chronic inflammatory process it will shrink, and may become most dangerous to its fellow.

Injuries to the optic nerve are not often seen. As a rule, they lead to atrophy of the nerve. When atrophy of the optic nerve follows an injury to the head, as from a heavy fall, etc., the atrophy is usually due to a fracture in the walls of the canalis opticus.

If a foreign body perforates the cornea or sclerotic and remains in the eye-ball, the injury is a doubly grave one.

The size of such foreign bodies may vary considerably.

Large pieces of metal, glass or wood will simply destroy the eye-ball by the immediate injury they inflict while entering it. Small foreign bodies may act destructively in a variety of ways. If a foreign body is embedded in the cornea, it is easily removed with a scoop or a needle. If a small foreign body has entered the anterior chamber, it will usually remain entangled in the iris or embedded in the crystalline lens. If it remains in the iris, iridectomy, including the part which contains the foreign body, ought to be made. If it remains in the crystalline lens, it usually causes simply the formation of a cataract, and it may be removed, together with the lens-substance at a later period.

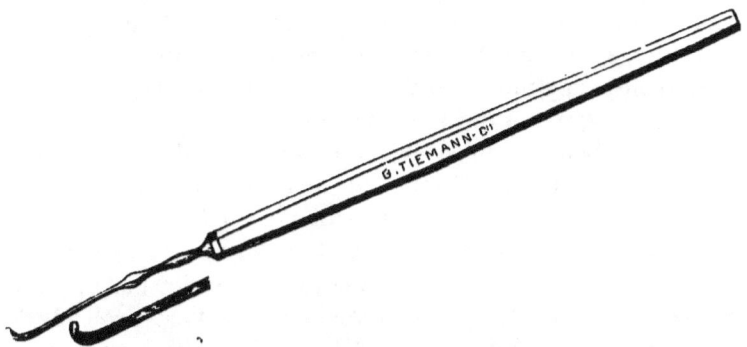

Fig. 66. Knapp's Grooved Hook for the Removal of Foreign Bodies from the Interior of the Eye-Ball.

Sometimes a foreign body, after having struck the iris, will fall into the angle between the iris and the cornea, and its removal from such a position is very troublesome, especially if it is small. In such a case it is well to move the foreign body with a needle into a position on the iris nearer to the pupillary edge, and then to remove it, with a portion of the iris, by iridectomy.

If the removal of a foreign body in the iris or anterior chamber can be accomplished soon after it has entered the eye-ball, the danger is generally averted. We should, therefore, remove such a foreign body as soon as its presence is known. In a few instances the presence of a foreign body in the anterior chamber has been borne without causing any inflammation, but such cases are very rare, and are altogether exceptional.

Small foreign bodies which have entered the vitreous body may be detected with the ophthalmoscope, and can sometimes be removed by its guidance. If the foreign body is a small piece of iron or steel, we may succeed in removing it by the aid of a magnet (*Gruening's*), if it is of a non-magnetic substance, a grooved hook (*Knapp's*) (See figure 66) or forceps may be used. For these purposes the sclerotic must be cut in a meridional direction, as near as possible, to the place where the foreign body is situated. If not removed, foreign bodies in the vitreous body generally give rise to suppurating panophthalmitis, or, perhaps, to a lower type of inflammation, which may endanger the fellow-eye. In a few cases a foreign body in the vitreous body has been observed for years, doing apparently no harm. Even when an eye is already inflamed from the presence of a foreign body in the vitreous, the removal of the offending body may sometimes arrest the progress of the inflammation.

Foreign bodies, which have become lodged in the ciliary body, almost certainly destroy the eye-ball, and are also most frequently the source of the destruction of its fellow.

From the foregoing statements it is easy to understand that an injury to the eye is, in most cases, a very serious affair, as being likely not only to ruin the injured eye, but very probably the fellow-eye also. (See Chapter XIX). The physician should, therefore, be extremely guarded with regard to the prognosis in all such cases, since even an apparently slight injury may turn out to have been a most serious one. We must be especially careful in examining every injured eye-ball, and especially avoid all pressure upon it. If there is blood in the anterior chamber preventing further examination, the injury is probably a grave one. All that can be done, then, is to wait for the absorption of the blood, and meanwhile to prevent, as far as possible, the development of inflammatory symptoms by enjoining strict rest in a dark room, by instilling sulphate of atropia, and by keeping cool or even iced compresses on the eye, day and night. If after a few days no inflammation has taken place and the blood is absorbed, so that the deeper parts can be examined, the eye-ball as such may be considered as safe. If inflammation takes place, in spite of these precautions, the eye-ball will usually be lost by suppuration.

But even when an injured eye-ball is not altogether lost, it is very likely to fall into a condition of irritation or chronic inflammation, which may lead to the destruction of its fellow through sympathetic disease. Such eye-balls must, therefore, be constantly and closely watched to detect the danger in time to arrest it.

It is plain that the subject of injuries to the eye-ball is one of the greatest importance, and especially so for the general practitioner, since he generally sees these cases first, and his counsels generally determine the issue of the case. Unless the injury is an absolutely superficial one, he should not undertake to give more than a doubtful prognosis; but he should do something more. He should at once prepare the patient for what may prove to be his only resource, not only to save him great suffering from the injured eye-ball, but also to avert imminent danger of total blindness from the loss of its fellow, namely: The removal of the injured eye-ball by *enucleation*. The patient will then probably more readily yield to the necessity, or if he does not, and finally becomes blind, the physician has at least done his duty.

The question, whether an injured eye-ball is to be removed or not, depends not only on the nature and extent of the injury, but also on the fact whether a foreign body remains within the eye-ball or not. Of this latter point the patient has usually no means of forming a correct judgment, and the physician should not rely on his statements, unless he can satisfy himself that the instrument which has caused the injury cannot possibly have left a particle within the eye-ball. If there is no doubt remaining as to the necessity of removing the injured eye, the sooner it is done, the better for the patient. The operation affords immediate relief from the often excruciating and continuous pain, and the quiet and speedy healing, which is the rule after enucleation, will enable the patient to resume his work after a very short period.

When in any given case there is well-founded doubt, although still a probability that enucleation will become necessary later on, our action should depend largely on the patient's position in life, and on the possibility of watching the eyes carefully, and doing the necessary thing at the first sign of commencing trouble.

In view of the great frequency and destructive nature of injuries of the eye-ball incident to certain dangerous trades, the use of protective glasses cannot be too strongly urged upon the workmen whose occupation exposes them daily to such perils. Such protective glasses are best made of mica, and in Europe, where they are extensively used, they have been the means of saving many a workman from blindness and many a family from destitution.

# CHAPTER XIX.

## SYMPATHETIC OPHTHALMIA.

SYMPATHETIC IRRITATION.—SYMPATHETIC NEURITIS.—SYMPATHETIC IRITIS.—SYMPATHETIC IRIDO-CYCLITIS. — SYMPATHETIC IRIDO-CHOROIDITIS. — SYMPATHETIC KERATITIS.

Sympathetic ophthalmia is the collective name given to all affections which are brought about in an eye by certain diseases in its fellow, when these, and these alone, are the cause of the affection of the second eye.

If for instance, a patient suffers from idiopathic iritis in one eye, and soon after his other eye is attacked in the same way, we cannot call this a sympathetic iritis, because the second becomes affected through the same constitutional diathesis which has led to the iritis of the first eye.

By far the greater number of cases of sympathetic ophthalmia are due to inflammatory processes induced in the first affected eye by an injury, with or without the continuing presence of a foreign body within the eye-ball. Experience has shown that chronic cyclitis is especially apt to be developed in such an eye, causing often a similar sympathetic trouble in the other eye. From this fact it has been thought that a direct transmission of the inflammatory process takes place along the ciliary nerves. This theory is open to certain serious objections, and we have, moreover, other and more direct channels for the transmission of an inflammation from one eye to the other in the optic nerve with its sheaths and intravaginal space. Pathological anatomy and experiments, as well as clinical observations, point decidedly to these channels as being the most important ones in the transmission of the disease.

The time at which sympathetic affection most frequently occurs is in from 4 to 6 weeks after the injury has been inflicted on the fellow-eye. In a large number of cases, however, such an injury may have preceded the occurrence of the sympathetic affection by many months, and even by years. In rare cases a few days only seem to have intervened between the affections of the two eyes.

As an eye once affected by sympathetic ophthalmia is, as a rule, ruined, and the patient is thus in most cases rendered utterly and hopelessly blind, this subject is one of the most important in ophthalmic practice, and the physician cannot be too deeply impressed with its importance. In most cases the duty will devolve upon him to forestall the fearful results, and to tell the patient what probably will be his only safeguard against utter blindness. If the physician does not recognize his duty but through lack of judgment, or for any other reason encourages the patient to reject the one effective remedy, the enucleation of the injured eye-ball, or of an eye-ball which, for other reasons, is likely to produce sympathetic inflammation, the blame will rightfully fall on his shoulders.

The eyes, which are most apt to give rise to sympathetic troubles are, as just stated, especially injured eyes, and among these again, especially eyes in which the injury has been in the ciliary region, or in which there has been a prolapse of the iris, of the ciliary body, or of the choroid and retina, and those eye-balls within which a foreign body has become lodged. Ectatic corneal scars, staphyloma in all its forms, idiopathic plastic iridocyclitis, and iridochoroiditis, and anterior phthisis of the eye-ball may also cause sympathetic trouble. Furthermore, operations on the eye, and especially cataract-extractions, are sometimes followed by sympathetic inflammation.

The primarily affected eye-ball need not be absolutely destroyed to become a source of danger; it may even be a comparatively useful organ, and yet be so affected as possibly to cause a sympathetic affection in the other eye. In most cases, however, vision in the first affected eye is reduced to the mere perception of light, or is even altogether abolished before the eye becomes dangerous to its fellow.

Sympathetic ophthalmia may appear in very different forms,

which it is especially necessary to recognize in the initial stages.

The lightest form of sympathetic ophthalmia, and usually the forerunner of all other forms, is that which is conventionally termed *sympathetic irritation.*

An eye suffering from sympathetic irritation cannot bear the light well. It tires easily, especially in reading or similar occupations; moving the book farther off may give momentary relief (weakened accommodation). Soon, even, the slightest application of the eye to any work causes lachrymation and redness, and the attendant pain in the surrounding regions makes work utterly impossible. Sight may be at times slightly obscured, or the patient may see fiery spots and flashes of light (*photopsia*).

In this stage of the disease, in which no anatomical lesions have apparently as yet taken place in the tissues of the eye-ball, the enucleation of the eye which is the cause of the trouble, will generally be followed by a speedy recovery. We should, therefore, be very careful to instruct a patient, who is the unlucky possessor of an injured eye, or an eye that may at some time cause sympathetic inflammation, that such symptoms as have been enumerated, however trivial he may consider them, must not be overlooked, but must be promptly reported. He must, in fact, be made so thoroughly aware of the danger to his other eye that he will be startled at even the slightest unusual symptoms in his good eye.

In some cases these functional symptoms of sympathetic inflammation have already attained a higher grade, and *sympathetic neuritis* or *neuro-retinitis* has actually set in when we first examine the eye. Even then, if no further changes have taken place, enucleation of the first affected eye-ball may bring about a perfect cure.

More frequently, however, we observe that the patient is suffering from *sympathetic iritis*, which may be either of a serous or a plastic type. Serous iritis seems to give a comparatively good prognosis, but plastic iritis, which very soon develops into plastic *irido-cyclitis*, as a rule, leaves nothing to be hoped for. In a few reported cases in which enucleation has been performed as soon as the first symptoms of iritis have been detected, a cure has even then been effected, but in most cases it is useless, and it may even be injurious to enucleate at this period.

Gradually the sympathetic iridocyclitis develops into an *irido-choroiditis*, and the contraction of the plastic membranes leads to shrinkage of the whole eye-ball with detachment of the retina and softening of the eye. Every chance of help is gone in this stage.

The process of sympathetic ophthalmia is, as a rule, very gradual; there may be times of apparent freedom from inflammation, or, at best, partial remission of the inflammation; but soon a new exacerbation will take place, and the destructive process goes on. In a few cases the disease stops before the eye is utterly ruined, and then a judicious operation may ultimately give some sight. But no operation on an eye made useless by sympathetic ophthalmia should under any circumstances be attempted, until all signs of inflammation or even of irritability are gone, or better yet, have been gone for some time. If, in such a case, the perception of light and the projection are good, and the intra-ocular tension is but slightly, or not at all reduced, an operation (usually iridectomy, or iridotomy, or one of these combined with extraction of the frequently cataractous crystalline lens), may be undertaken with the hope of restoring some degree of vision. Any attempt at operation at an earlier period will be punished by a new exacerbation of the disease, or at best will prove useless, as even large openings made in the iris and the pathological newformations will be in a very short time closed again by inflammatory products.

While the inflammation is in progress, mercurial inunctions, or mercury given internally, may prove of value; perhaps, also, pilocarpine may be of service. Untiring efforts are sometimes even at such a period crowned with a partial success.

Obstinate keratitis or scleritis has in some cases been caused by the presence of an injured or shrunken eye-ball, and has been cured only after the enucleation of the offending organ.

It has been recommended to substitute for enucleation the operation of division of the ciliary nerves and the optic nerve close to the posterior surface of the eye-ball (optico-ciliary neurotomy). It has also been proposed to remove a piece of these nerves (optico-ciliary neurectomy). The results of these operations have, however, not been encouraging, and thus far timely enucleation remains the only trustworthy remedy, and, when it is performed in time and before any sign of sympathetic ophthalmia has appeared, the only safe prophylactic measure.

The wearing of an artificial eye will, in a great measure, do away with the disfigurement caused by the enucleation.

# CHAPTER XX.

## ERRORS OF REFRACTION AND ACCOMMODATION.

EMMETROPIA.—AMETROPIA.—HYPERMETROPIA.—MYOPIA. — ASTIGMATISM. — ACCOMMODATION.—PRESBYOPIA.—PARALYSIS OF THE ACCOMMODATION.—SPASM OF THE ACCOMMODATION.

Before speaking of the errors of refraction, we must give a short account of the normal, or *emmetropic eye*, in contrast to eyes affected with an error of refraction, which are called *ametropic eyes*.

Every eye, which is so constructed, that when it is perfectly at rest, parallel rays entering through its cornea are united in a point (focus) on its retina, is called an *emmetropic eye*. (See figure 67).

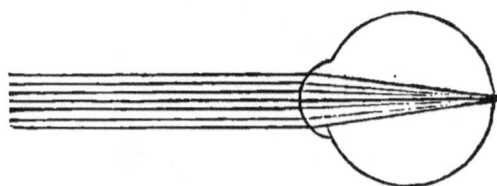

FIG. 67. Shows the way in which parallel rays are focussed on the Retina (yellow spot) in an Emmetropic Eye.

By parallel rays we mean, in practice, such rays as reach the eye from any distant object, and for most purposes we may, without material error, consider rays as parallel when the object from which they emanate is at any distance greater than twenty feet from the eye. The emmetropic eye sees, therefore, any distant object towards which it is directed distinctly and without effort.

Every eye which is not so constructed that, when in a state

# ERRORS OF REFRACTION AND ACCOMMODATION. 175

of rest, parallel rays are focussed on its retina, is an *ametropic eye.*

An eye in which the retina lies in front of its focus for parallel rays, and which therefore cannot in a state of rest see even distant objects distinctly, is called a *hypermetropic eye* (oversighted eye). (See figure 68).

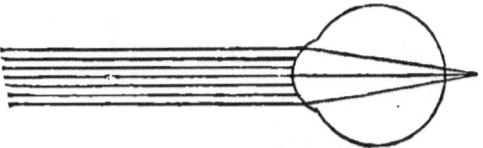

FIG. 68. Shows the way in which parallel rays are focussed behind the Retina of a Hypermetropic Eye.

Every eye, whose retina lies behind its focus for such parallel rays, and which therefore sees near objects distinctly, is called a *myopic eye* (near-sighted eye). (See figure 69).

In other words, when perfectly at rest, the emmetropic eye is focussed for parallel rays, the hypermetropic eye is focussed for convergent rays, and the myopic eye is focussed for divergent rays.

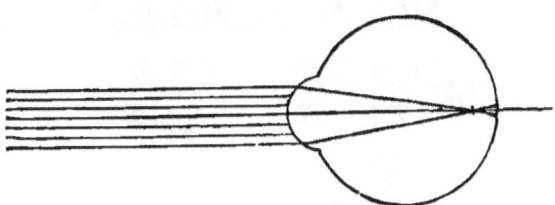

FIG. 69. Shows the manner in which parallel rays are focussed in front of the Retina of a Myopic Eye.

The point for which an eye is focussed, when in a state of rest, is called the *far-point* of that eye. In the case of the emmetropic and hypermetropic eye the far-point is at an infinite distance; in the myopic eye the far-point is at a finite, and often a very short distance from the eye.

For the determination of the acuteness of vision in any eye (See Chapter II.), we make use of test-types constructed after a certain principle. It has been found that an object, in order to be distinctly perceived by the human eye, must be seen under a visual angle of at least 1 minute. The letters, therefore, are arranged in such a manner that at a certain given distance each limb of a letter is seen under this visual angle, and the whole letter under an angle of 5 minutes. The letters are numbered to correspond with the distance in feet, at which each letter should be seen under this angle by the normal eye. Thus the letters which should be seen at 20 feet are marked XX ; at 70 feet LXX, and so on. (See figure 70). If at 20 feet distance an eye can read, for instance, only the letters which a normal

FIG. 70. Snellen's Test Types. A normal eye can read them at 100, 50, and 20 feet respectively.

eye ought to read at 70 feet, we express the visual acuteness (V) of that eye by the fraction $\frac{20}{Lxx}$. (See Chapter II.)

These same test-types are used for the determination of the refractive condition of the eyes. If an otherwise healthy eye can see the letters, which are seen by the normal eye distinctly at 20 feet at that distance, it is emmetropic (or it may, as we shall see later on, be moderately hypermetropic). If such an eye can read these letters as well, or better, when a convex lens is held before it, it is hypermetropic. If a concave lens is required to bring vision up to $\frac{20}{xx}$, the eye is myopic.

Another form of ametropia is caused by an asymetry of curvature in the different meridians of the cornea, or in rare cases of the crystalline lens. Such an eye sees everything blurred and indistinct, and, although, perhaps, improved by convex or concave lenses, it does not by their use alone come up to the standard of the normal eye. We shall later on give further details of this condition, which is called *astigmatism*, because these eyes cannot reunite the rays which emanate from any given point of the object upon any local point within the eye.

We have seen that the eye, when at rest, is focussed for its far-point, which for the normal eye lies at an infinite distance, but the eye has also the power of seeing small, near objects with perfect distinction, or, in other words, it possesses a power of adjustment by which it can focus upon its retina either parallel or divergent rays. This necessarily implies a faculty residing in the eye by which it is enabled at will to increase its refractive power to meet the requirements of near vision. This faculty lies in organs within the eye-ball, and is called *accommodation*. It may be expressed as equivalent to a convex lens, such as would suffice to render the divergent rays coming from the near object parallel, as if they came from a distant object.

The nearest point at which a small object can be seen distinctly by an eye, we call its *near-point*. The difference between the near and the far-point gives us the range of accommodation of an eye.

The accommodative power is, however, not the same throughout life. It diminishes with advancing age, and after the age of 45 or 50 years it is reduced to a small fraction. In consequence of this loss of accommodative power, the near-point gradually recedes farther and farther from the eye, and thus approximates more and more nearly to the far-point.

In every visual act not only must each eye be accommodated singly for the distance of the object, but the axis of the two eyes must be made to converge accurately upon the same point of the object, in order to form identical images upon the maculæ luteæ of the two retinæ. Accommodation is, therefore, intimately associated with convergence, and whenever the one adjustment is called into activity, the other is performed at the same time, even when through some abnormal condition such an association of the two adjustments does not contribute to more perfect vision.

The organs by which the act of adjustment for near objects is performed, are the ciliary muscle and the crystalline lens. *Helmholtz* has explained the action in the following way : When the ciliary muscle, which forms a ring in which the crystalline lens is held by the suspensory ligament (zonule of *Zinn*) is contracted, this ligament becomes relaxed, and the crystalline lens, by its inherent elasticity, assumes a more nearly spherical shape, and is correspondingly increased in refractive power, as if a meniscus had been added to it.

When we observe an eye during the act of accommodation, we see that the pupil becomes smaller, and that the pupillary edge of the iris is slightly moved forwards. Accurate observation has shown that the increased convexity of the crystalline lens during accommodation is due mainly to a change in the form of its anterior surface.

*Hypermetropia*, over-sight or far-sight, exists, as has been stated, when the eye in a state of rest is focussed for convergent rays, and parallel rays entering the eye are refracted towards a point lying behind its retina. In consequence of this condition the retina of such an eye receives only dispersion circles, and the images of distant objects, and still more of near objects must be indistinct. This, as has been stated, can be remedied by the use of convex glasses, and the convex glass which will allow a hypermetropic eye, when perfectly at rest, to unite parallel rays upon its retina gives us the degree of its hypermetropia.

In hypermetropia, if no glass is worn, the deficiency in refractive power is ordinarily, at least for distant vision, supplied by the exercise of the accommodation, and in low degrees of hypermetropia, this may suffice for a time, even for near objects. Low degrees of hypermetropia may thus remain unknown to the patient for years, or until his accommodative apparatus can no longer do its work effectively. This continuous strain of the accommodative apparatus causes, moreover, a permanent contraction of the ciliary muscles, so that they can no longer be perfectly relaxed at will.

It follows, therefore, that in order to find out, whether an eye is hypermetropic, and to what degree it is so, we must relax its accommodation perfectly by artificial means (sulphate of atropia).

The most frequent and characteristic symptom of hypermetropia is *accommodative asthenopia*. The patient may have perfect acuteness of vision, but, when doing near work, such as reading, writing, sewing, etc., his sight which at the beginning was good, becomes indistinct, the letters run into each other, and the eyes feel tired. By indistinctly closing the eyes, and by resting them for a moment, sight appears improved again; but soon this fails to give relief, and pain in the forehead, injection of the conjunctival blood-vessels, and lachrymation are added to the former symptoms, and the work must be laid aside.

These symptoms are usually more pronounced, when the near work is done by artificial light. The patients tell us sometimes that the symptoms have taken their origin from some severe illness, and in fact any weakening influence may suffice to bring them to light.

Occasionally the patients are unable to read at all, and suffer from almost constant head-ache, and not infrequently we meet with a case, in which the patient has been treated for years "on general principles," and has been subjected to all sorts of needless deprivations, where the use of the proper glasses, has sufficed at once to remove all the distressing symptoms.

Hypermetropic children often hold their books close to the eye, as if they were very short-sighted, and thus they strain their accommodation even more than would appear to be necessary for clear vision. This may grow with them into a confirmed habit. The fact, however, that such children can distinguish small distant objects clearly, such as birds, telegraph-wires, etc., will at once reveal the fact, that they are not short-sighted.

It has been stated above, that the function of accommodation and convergence, are closely connected, and it is only after long practice that we can learn to accommodate without converging, or vice versa. The hypermetropic patient, in order to see small objects distinctly, must exert more accommodative effort, than the emmetrope. He will, therefore, also instinctively converge his eyes more, and thus it may easily happen that he converges too much, so that convergent strabismus may be developed. In other words, the hypermetrope will, while using his accommodation in reading, converge his eyes more than is necessary for the distance of the object. He thus loses, of course, the benefit of binocular vision, and also sees the object doubled, and as this diplopia is a source of confusion, he gets rid of it by turning one eye still further inwards, and works only with the other one. Thus the abnormal adduction is thrown entirely into one of the eyes, and the well-known picture of strabismus convergens (cross-eye) is developed.

Patients with a very high degree of hypermetropia do not gain very much in distinctness of vision by squinting; therefore, they, as a rule, do not fall into the habit. Patients with a very moderate degree of hypermetropia do not ordinarily need to sacrifice binocular vision to their fairly distinct perception of small objects. It is, therefore, chiefly in the medium degrees of hypermetropia, that strabismus convergens is observed.

If we examine a patient whose symptoms point to hypermetropia, and we find that his sight at 20 feet is improved by the use of certain convex glasses, the number of these glasses gives us the degree of, what is called, his *manifest* hypermetropia. We know, however, that a hypermetropic patient is in the habit of using his accommodation almost constantly; in order, therefore, to find the *total* degree of his hypermetropia, we must first eliminate the accommodation, and thus find in addition to his manifest hypermetropia which has been hidden by the use of his accommodation, and which is called the *latent* hypermetropia. This is best done by instilling a few drops of a one per cent solution of the sulphate of atropia.

When the accommodation is perfectly paralyzed, we find that the patient needs stronger glasses than before, in order to see the test-types No. XX distinctly at 20 feet, and the glass which now brings his vision to $\frac{20}{XX}$ gives us the exact degree of his *total* hypermetropia.

Although theoretically these glasses ought to be the best, or rather the most useful ones to the patient, since they will remove all undue strain from his accommodative apparatus, we generally find that the old habit of accommodating more than necessary, comes back in some measure, when the effect of the drug has passed off. The patients, therefore, often refuse these glasses at first, and are better satisfied with a number that lies between the degree of their manifest and of their total hypermetropia. Long continued paralysis of the accommodation will do away with the habitual excessive strain of the accommodative apparatus, but it is generally better to begin by giving glasses of such strength as the patient can use with comfort, and to change them later on for stronger ones.

Hypermetropic patients should, as a rule, wear their glasses always, except when their hypermetropia is of a very moderate grade, and their far-vision is comparatively good. In advanced years, when presbyopia is added to the hypermetropia, different glasses for distance and for reading must be used.

*Myopia*, short-sight or near-sightedness, is, as stated above, that condition, in which the eye, when perfectly at rest, is focussed for divergent rays, and in which parallel rays entering through the cornea are united into a point before they reach its retina.

This causes the retina to receive dispersion circles from far objects, and consequently such objects appear indistinct. On the other hand near objects are seen clearly and without accommodative effort.

Concave glasses enable myopic eyes to see distant objects distinct by rendering the parallel rays divergent and the slightly divergent rays more divergent, before they touch the cornea.

In myopia the eye-ball is too long in comparison with emmetropic eyes. This may be a congenital condition, or it may be acquired.

The fact that among uncivilized nations myopia is almost unknown, and that it is pre-eminently an affection belonging to civilized life, shows us that its chief causes are to be sought in early and prolonged application to study, and especially under the unfavorable conditions of small print, badly arranged desks, badly lighted, badly ventilated and over-heated school-rooms, badly arranged or insufficient artificial light, etc. Under such influences the child's eyes, if there is any inherited tendency will certainly become myopic.

Myopia may remain stationary, or it may be progressive. In the latter case symptoms of an inflammatory nature always appear in the posterior part of the eye-ball, and characterize the process as a sclero-choroiditis. With every new inflammatory attack new territory is invaded, and not infrequently the region of the macula lutea is thus rendered blind. Floating opacities in the form of muscæ volitantes, or larger fibrinous flocks, are never wanting.

The pupil is usually larger in myopic, than in emmetropic eyes. To obviate the indistinctness of vision, due to the diffused light admitted through the large pupil, myopic patients get into the habit of partially covering their pupils by squeezing the eye-lids together.

The elongation of myopic eyes causes them to appear full and prominent.

Although distant vision is very indistinct in myopia, the sight for small near objects is excellent (at least where the inflammatory changes have not gone too far), so that small objects which an emmetropic eye can see only by the aid of a weak magnifying glass, may sometimes be seen with ease by a myopic eye. The amount of accommodative power used by a myopic eye is very small, and in this, probably, lies the reason why the converging (internal recti) muscles are also weak and often insufficient for prolonged binocular vision. The elongated shape of the myopic eye-ball is also a mechanical hindrance to convergence. This insufficiency of the internal recti muscles gives rise also to asthenopic symptoms due to fatigue of the external muscular apparatus, and leading to a loss of balance between the internal and the external recti, so that at length one eye refuses the strain on the internal rectus, and becomes passively everted by the unopposed action of the external rectus. To do away with the disagreeable double-images which now appear, and, in order not to give up the feeling of comfort caused by the relaxation of his converging muscles, the patient gradually allows the external rectus muscle more and more liberty of action, and finally a condition of permanent divergent strabismus is established.

Myopes have, as they grow old, a certain advantage over emmetropes and hypermetropes in their partial or total exemption from the necessity of using convex glasses for reading, but they do not, as is often erroneously assumed, become normal-sighted for the distance.

The concave glasses prescribed in myopia ought to be the weakest with which the normal acuteness of vision is obtained. The question whether a patient ought to wear his glasses constantly or only for a distant vision, or whether he should use glasses of different strength for distant vision and for near work, depends mainly on the degree of his myopia, and upon the period of life at which the glasses are prescribed. The sooner accurately correcting glasses are worn, the better it is, as a rule, for the patient, and inasmuch as the corrected eye must use its accommodation for near work, it is usually best to encourage children to wear their correcting glasses constantly. In very high degrees of myopia and in advanced age a glass somewhat weaker than that which perfectly corrects the myopia, should be given.

Synchisis of the vitreous body and detachment of the retina are apt to occur in myopic eyes, as has been already stated.

*Astigmatism*, asymmetry of curvature in the cornea (or crystalline lens), is the condition in which the different meridians of the refractive surfaces have unequal radii of curvature. To a slight degree this inequality exists even in the normal eye. When it is somewhat exaggerated, however, the sight becomes blurred, and details of objects appear more or less distorted for the reason that the unsymmetrical refractive surface can have no perfect focus for the rays which pass through it, but only a series of approximate foci lying along a line which has been given the name of focal interval. (See figure 71).

The name *regular astigmatism* is given to those cases in which the refracting surface is of a regular ovoid form, instead of being a segment of a sphere. In this form of astigmatism we recognize a meridian of greatest and one of least refraction, which two meridians lie at right angles to each other and are called the principal meridians. The astigmatic eye may be emmetropic in either of its principal meridians, in which case it will be either myopic or hypermetropic in the other, and we call this condition *simple myopic* or *hypermetropic astigmatism*. If the eye is myopic in both meridians it is called *compound myopic* or *compound hypermetropic astigmatism*, and if myopic in one and hypermetropic in the other principal meridian, the condition is called *mixed astigmatism*. All forms of regular astigmatism may be corrected by means of a plano-cylindrical lens of the proper radius of curvature, so placed before the eye as to equalize its refractive power in the two principal meridians, and, if any ametropia remains, this may be corrected by grinding the proper spherical surface upon the back of the same lens.

When the curvature of the refracting surface is irregular, we call the condition *irregular astigmatism*. This condition is mostly due to former inflammatory processes in the cornea.

Fig. 71. Focal interval of a bundle of rays having been refracted by a cylindrical surface. (After *Donders*.)

Even in irregular astigmatism vision may sometimes be materially benefitted by spherico-cylindrical glasses.

Regular astigmatism is nearly always congenital.

When the refractive power of the two eyes is not alike, the condition is called *anisometropia*. What glasses are to be used in such cases, must depend on the special requirements of each case. It may be well to give a correcting glass for each eye, if the difference is small; in other cases it is better to give glasses for the same focus for both eyes.

All forms of ametropia can be diagnosticated by the use of the ophthalmoscope, when the patient's and the observer's accommodation are perfectly relaxed, and, if the observer be himself not emmetropic, when his ametropia is corrected.

Although it cannot be expected that every physician shall be able to make an exhaustive examination of the refractive condition of a patient's eyes, he should nevertheless be familiar with the symptoms of ametropia, and especially of asthenopia, so that he may advise the selection of glasses when needed, and, moreover, see to it, that when prescribed, they are worn as directed by the oculist. It is not only young ladies and gentlemen who from vanity often refuse to wear glasses, even though conscious that they are greatly benefitted by them, but frequently the imperfectly educated parents will not allow their children to wear glasses at an age when, perhaps, the child's whole future may depend upon their use.

The common prejudice against the wearing of glasses, and especially of convex glasses, by young persons, is not only unfounded, but it often leads to infinite harm. No one would refuse a patient with crippled legs the assistance of crutches, yet, to refuse the crippled eye the use of glasses is often a much greater wrong.

When speaking of the function of accommodation, it was mentioned that with advancing years this faculty is gradually lost, and that this causes the near-point to recede more and more from the eye. Thus we find that while at 10 years of age the near-point lies at about 3 inches from the eye, at 20 years it is about 4, at 30 years about 6, at 40 years about 9, at 45 years about 12, and at 50 years about 16 inches from the eye. From the fact that the range of binocular accommodation is somewhat less than that of monocular accommodation, the near-point for perfect binocular vision is even further from the eyes than these figures would indicate. The cause of this progressive loss of accommodative power lies in the physiological hardening of the crystalline lens, which renders it less and less capable of changing its form to meet the requirements of near vision.

As soon as the binocular near-point has receded beyond 12 inches from the eyes, reading, especially at night and for fine print, becomes less comfortable. More light is required to see distinctly, and as the book must be held so far away as to allow the lamp to be easily placed between the book and the eyes, this remedy is usually resorted to. The comfort thus received is, moreover, due in part to the contraction of the pupil in bright light, and to the consequent exclusion of dispersion circles.

The same causes which make the near-point recede from the eye may also, although in a less degree, cause the far-point to recede, and may thus bring about an acquired hypermetropia.

These symptoms constitute what is called *presbyopia*, and are usually developed about the age of from 45 to 50 years, so that reading and near work become impossible, except by the aid of convex glasses. The patients often try, however, to read for a time after they have noticed the first symptoms, and then some degree of asthenopia may be developed. In simple presbyopia occurring in an emmetropic person vision for the distance remains perfect; in low grades of myopia it may even improve; in hypermetropic persons distant vision also becomes eventually impaired.

The use of convex glasses to supply the place of the failing accommodative power suffices to do away with all disability and discomfort dependent on presbyopia; they should be worn for all near work. As the patient gets older, his presbyopia will increase, necessitating the exchange of his first glasses for glasses of shorter focus. This change should be made, as soon as the glasses in use prove inadequate for near work.

*Paralysis of the accommodation* brings about the same symptoms as presbyopia, only the pupil is in many cases perfectly dilated, (in other cases unchanged), and while presbyopia always affects both eyes, paralysis of the accommodation may happen either in one or in both.

If paralysis of the accommodation affects a myopic eye, it will (as is also true of presbyopia) cause less inconvenience, than when it occurs in an emmetropic eye. If it occurs in a hypermetropic eye, distant vision also becomes indistinct. Moreover, when in a case of paralysis of the accommodation the pupil is dilated, the diffuse light thus admitted into the eye causes still greater confusion of sight, than in a case in which the pupil is not increased in size.

Paralysis of the accommodation is a sign of some affection of the oculomotor nerve. It may be either an affection of the peripheral branches only, or the symptom of some central lesion. Among the most frequent causes are tumors of the brain, syphilis, and diphtheria of the throat. The loss of accommodative power which occurs in connection with diphtheria, is generally incomplete, and is rather a paresis, than an actual paralysis. This usually comes on several weeks after the diphtheritic process in the throat has run its course; it may be the only paresis following this disease, and it may appear conjoined with paresis of the muscles of the palate, etc. The inability to read in this affection is sometimes mistaken for obstinacy, and thus the child is liable to be misunderstood, and perhaps punished for his supposed fault; the physician should, therefore, always bear in mind this not infrequent sequel of diphtheria of the throat, and should warn the parents that the child's vision may possibly become affected.

In all such cases the child ought to be kept from school, until perfectly well, although the use of a convex glass will enable him to read easily. Tonic treatment and rest will help to get him over the paresis, and, even if nothing is done in the way of medication, a few weeks time will restore him. The instillation of mild myotic agents seems to shorten the time necessary for the recovery.

All drugs which dilate the pupil cause also paralysis of the accommodative apparatus. It sometimes occurs also after an injury.

*Spasm of the accommodative apparatus*, leading to apparent myopia, is sometimes observed, and is usually very troublesome. The treatment must be directed to the full relaxation of the accommodative apparatus, together with the correction of any existing ametropia.

# CHAPTER XXI.

## DISEASES OF THE EXTERNAL MUSCLES OF THE EYE.

NORMAL CONDITION AND ACTION.—DIPLOPIA.—PARALYSIS.—PARALYTIC STRABISMUS.—MUSCULAR STRABISMUS.—CONVERGENT STRABISMUS.—DIVERGENT STRABISMUS.—INSUFFICIENCY OF THE INTERNAL RECTI MUSCLES.—NYSTAGMUS.

The eye-ball can be moved upon its centre, in an infinite variety of directions. This is accomplished by means of three pairs of external muscles, the *rectus superior and inferior*, the *rectus internus and externus*, and *the obliquus superior and inferior*. The four recti muscles, as stated in Chapter I., spring from the apex of the orbit, around the optic foramen, and are inserted upon the sclerotic at different distances from the corneo-scleral margin. The superior oblique muscle also takes its origin at the apex of the orbit, and is inserted in the sclerotic, but only after its tendon has passed around the trochlea. The inferior oblique muscle springs from the inner surface of the orbit near its inferior and nasal margin, and then goes to the eye-ball.

The action of the two oblique muscles is, of course, different from that of the recti, since from their direction from their punctum fixum (trochlea at the inner upper, and origin of the lower oblique at the inner lower orbital margin) is backwards and outwards. The distances from the corneo-scleral margin, at which the several muscles are inserted in the sclerotic, are, according to *Merkel*, the following ones:

| | |
|---|---|
| Rectus superior, | 8.2 millimeters. |
| Rectus inferior, | 7.2 " |
| Rectus internus, | 6.5 " |
| Rectus externus, | 6.8 " |
| Obliquus superior, | 16.0 " |
| Obliquus inferior, | 18.3 " |

These, of course, are average numbers.

# DISEASES OF THE EXTERNAL MUSCLES OF THE EYE.

These muscles may act either singly or in various combinations. When acting singly, the internal rectus turns the eye-ball strictly horizontally inward, the external rectus in the same way turns it outwards; the superior rectus which is inserted somewhat to the nasal side of the median plane of the eye-ball, turns the eye-ball upwards, and slightly inwards, and rotates the upper end of its vertical meridian towards the nose; the superior oblique turns the eye-ball downwards, and outwards, and rotates the vertical meridian of the upper end of the cornea, also towards the nose; the inferior rectus turns the eye-ball downwards, and a little inwards, and rotates the upper end of its vertical meridian towards the temple; the inferior oblique turns the eye-ball upwards, and outwards, and rotates the upper end of the vertical meridian of the cornea also towards the temple.

When the superior rectus and inferior oblique act together, the eye is turned vertically upwards, and by the combined action of the inferior rectus and inferior oblique the eye-ball is turned vertically downwards.

If the eye-ball is turned upwards and outwards, the superior and external recti and the inferior oblique come into play; if downwards and outwards, the inferior and external recti and the superior oblique, etc. Thus in all movements, except those in the horizontal plane, at least two and generally three muscles must act conjointly.

When all the muscles of both eyes act in proper harmony, perfect binocular vision is the result, and two retinal images are perceived by the brain as one object; but if any one muscle refuses to perform its part, the two images will no longer fall on corresponding parts of the two retinæ and double vision (diplopia) must follow. The double or false image may be homonymous, i. e., it may appear on the side of the object looked at, corresponding to the eye in which the double image is perceived, or it may be heteronymous (crossed image), in which case it appears to be on the opposite side of the object. When one of the eyes is turned abnormally inward towards the nose, the false image is homonymous, when one eye is turned abnormally outward towards the temple, the false image is heteronymous.

The oculomotor nerve directs the movements of all the muscles of the eye-ball except the superior oblique and the external rectus. These two muscles have each its own special nerve, namely: the trochlearis nerve for the superior oblique and the abducens nerve for the external rectus. The movements which the eye-ball makes, when certain of its muscles act, being known to us, it is clear that the position of the false image will not only tell us what muscle or groupe of muscles refuse to act, but also which of the cerebral nerves are affected. Thus diplopia is often a symptom of very great value in diagnosticating brain lesions, and even in locating them.

According to the degree of insufficiency of the muscle affected, the false image will, in the positions of the eyes which evoke it, appear nearer to or farther from the real image. The disagreeable consequences of seeing double are greatest when the distance between the two images is small; when this distance is very large, the false image is disregarded, or it may even not be seen at the same time with the real one.

In order to overcome diplopia, the patient will supplement the diminished action of the weakened muscle of the eye-ball by turning his head in the same direction. For instance, if the right eye-ball cannot be abducted in consequence of paralysis of the external rectus, every object lying in this direction will appear double, as long as the patient faces in this direction, but a turn of the head in the same direction will enable him to see single. From this position of the head, which after a while becomes habitual, we can often conclude in which muscle, or groupe of muscles, the affection lies.

Diplopia is most frequently caused by paralysis of one or more muscles, and this again is mostly due either to syphilis to some brain lesion, or to a tumor of the orbit. It has also been observed in cases of malarial poisoning. Paralysis of all muscles of the eye, *ophthalmoplegia*, is seen in rare cases.

In cases of paralysis of one muscle of the eye we find after a while a secondary contraction of the antagonist muscle just as we do in paralysis of other muscles of the body. The affection may thus bring about a form of strabismus which we call *paralytic strabismus*, to distinguish it from the typical or muscular strabismus. In paralytic strabismus the secondary deviation of the healthy eye-ball, when covered, is greater than the deviation of the affected eye, while in typical muscular strabismus the primary and the secondary deviation are equal. (See Chapter II.)

Paralysis of the external rectus is the most frequent cause of diplopia. If partial, the muscle may be able to move the eye-ball somewhat beyond the medium line of the orbit, if total, it cannot move the eye-ball at all, and convergent paralytic squint will soon follow. Diplopia must, of course, exist in all movements of the eye-ball in which the external rectus ought to act. (The method of examining for double images has been detailed in Chapter II). The diplopia, characteristic of paralysis of the external rectus, appears, therefore in the outer half of the binocular visual field. In proportion, however, as the secondary contraction of the internal rectus becomes established, the diplopia extends over the whole field of vision.

Paralysis of the superior oblique causes the double images to appear when the patient looks below the horizontal line. The two images do not stand at an equal height, but the one belonging to the affected eye-ball stands lower than the other, and they converge towards each other at their upper ends. The distance between the images increases when the eyes are converged.

Lesions of the oculomotor nerve may affect all the muscles which it supplies, or any one of them singly. It oftenest affects, however, more than one muscle. (These muscles are the levator palpebræ superioris, the internal rectus, the superior rectus, the inferior rectus, the inferior oblique and the sphincter iridis). If the internal rectus only is paralyzed, we simply find reversed what we had to state with regard to paralysis of the external rectus. Paralysis of the inferior rectus will cause double images in the lower half of the visual field. The false image stands lower than the real one, and slants towards it at its upper end. In paralysis of the superior rectus these conditions are reversed; the double images appear in the upper half of the visual field, the false image stands higher than the real one, and it slants towards it at its lower end. (Paralysis of the sphincter iridis causes dilatation of the pupil, and is mostly combined with paralysis of the accommodative apparatus, of which we have already spoken).

The treatment of paretic and paralytic affections of the muscles of the eye is, in the main, the treatment of the underlying cause, and need therefore not be discussed here. We may only state that in some cases prismatic glasses, in others tenotomy, and in others the advancement of the affected muscle may give some comfort to the sufferer. These operations must, of course, only be resorted to when the paralysis is of long standing, and no longer offers any chance of improvement by internal treatment. In paresis it is sometimes well to grasp the muscle with a toothed forceps, to force the eye-ball to turn in the direction of this muscle, and thus to exercise it passively. (Schmidt—Rimpler).

Paralysis of the muscles is mostly confined to one eye, but it may also affect both eyes at the same time.

*Typical* or *muscular strabismus* almost always appears in early childhood, and is characterized by excessive muscular contraction. This prevents the patient from receiving the image of the object looked at upon the yellow spot in the two eyes. But, while in paralytic squint the eye-ball cannot be moved at all in a certain direction, although there is binocular vision in other directions, the eye-balls move nearly equally well in all directions in the typical muscular squint, only they cannot both fix the same object at the same time, and there is therefore no true binocular vision. Double images must, of course, exist in the beginning of muscular squint, but they are usually either not noticed by the patient, or only for a short time.

Muscular strabismus is practically either *convergent* or *divergent*, although upward and downward squints are seen in rare cases.

The causes to which the occurrence of the squint is usually ascribed by the parents are almost infinite in their variety, and it is not always judicious to try to correct the error. *Donders* first drew attention to the fact that an error of refraction exists in a very large proportion of the cases of strabismus. In another number of cases opacities of the cornea, or in the crystalline lens, or atrophic spots in the choroid and retina are the chief cause of the strabismus. In some cases an abnormal shape of the orbit, or an abnormal distance between the eyes may give rise to squint.

Generally speaking, convergent squint is most frequently caused by hypermetropia. From this fact it is clear, that in either case the timely use of correcting glasses may prevent the development of the strabismus. In practice, however, this is generally not the case, except when the ametropia is corrected, either before the strabismus has shown itself, or at its very incipiency. Later on, when the strabismus has become established, the glasses will no longer cure it, or perhaps only after having been worn for a very long period. All other contrivances, such as opaque spectacles with a small central hole, or spectacles with one half of each glass ground dim, etc., are of no value for the cure of strabismus.

In a great many cases of strabismus we find that one eye (the deviating one) is amblyopic, and the question is, whether this amblyopia is congenital, and so has existed before the squint, or whether the fact that this eye is not used (at least consciously) brings about an amblyopia "*ex anopsia.*" While the former is surely often the case, I do not think the latter should be considered improbable (*Schweigger, Noyes*), as we know of many analogies to it in other parts of the human body. Moreover, not infrequently a crossed eye is observed to become decidedly less amblyopic after an operation for strabismus.

In the beginning strabismus is usually only periodical, and may occasionally remain so for months, or even years; sooner or later, however, it almost always becomes permanent.

Convergent strabismus oftenest makes its appearance within two or three years after birth, when the child begins to employ his eyes in looking intently at small, near objects, toys, pictures, letters, etc. It is said to be sometimes congenital, but this is, to say the least, very rare.

In some cases of convergent strabismus the squint alternates between the two eyes, so that either eye may fix the object, while the other eye is closed. This is called *strabismus alternans.*

As has been already stated, it is not in the highest or the lowest degrees of hypermetropia that we usually find convergent strabismus, but rather in the intermediate grades.

Divergent squint is frequently due to myopia, but it may also occur in hypermetropic and emmetropic eyes. In the latter cases it appears to be due to a congenital excessive power of the external over the internal recti.

*Insufficiency of the internal recti* is always observed before the divergent strabismus becomes pronounced. In this condition the convergence of the eyes in near vision is imperfectly maintained so that the visual axes become relactively divergent, although in distant vision they may be apparently or actually parallel. Divergent squint develops, as a rule, only slowly. It is, moreover, apt to come on at a more advanced age than that at which convergent strabismus usually appears.

Insufficiency of the internal recti may also exist without ever developing in to divergent strabismus, and in these cases the patients can, although with an undue effort, converge enough for binocular vision. This causes asthenopic symptoms to appear, which are often as distressing as the asthenopia which depends upon the undue exertion of the accommodative apparatus in hypermetropia.

The treatment of permanent strabismus, and frequently also of insufficiency of the internal recti, is by operation. The operation for convergent strabismus consists in the division of the tendon of the shortened muscle of the crossed eye, and in most cases of the other eye also. In insufficiency of the internal recti both external recti must usually be divided, and in many cases of conspicuous divergent squint it is necessary to combine with the tenontomy of the externi the operation of advancement of the internus of the deviating eye. These operations ought to be done comparatively early in life. The old story, that the child will outgrow its squint as it gets older, ought to be struck from the list of answers which a physician will give to the inquiring parents in a case of strabismus. The percentage of cases in which a once permanent squint disappears without surgical interference is extremely small, and I do not think it is ever observed after early childhood.

*Nystagmus* is a continuous motion of the eye-balls mostly in a horizontal, but sometimes in a rotatory direction. It is generally observed in connection with congenital amblyopia, cataract, scars on the cornea, albinism, etc., or it may develop in advanced age as a result from brain disease. Is is also observed to attack miners. No treatment is of avail, except in the latter class of cases, in which rest, fresh air, and a tonic treatment are often sufficient to effect a cure.

# CHAPTER XXII.

## ON THE DIAGNOSTIC VALUE OF EYE-DISEASES IN INTRA-CRANIAL AFFECTIONS.

ANÆMIA AND HYPERÆMIA OF THE OPTIC NERVE AND RETINA.—OEDEMA OF THE OPTIC PAPILLA.—OPTIC NEURITIS AND NEURO-RETINITIS.—PROGRESSIVE ATROPHY OF THE OPTIC NERVE.—TUBERCLES IN THE CHOROID.—CONDITIONS OF THE PUPIL.—HEMIANOPIA.

A few years ago it was thought that by the use of the ophthalmoscope an observer could look, so to speak, into the brain, or, in other words, that from the conditions of the optic nerve and retina he could with certainty infer what was going on in the brain. Thus cerebroscopy seemed about to be established as a new branch of medical science. Since then we have learned that the facts do not warrant such enthusiastic anticipations, and we have now a comparatively clear knowledge of what we can expect from ophthalmoscopic and other eye-symptoms as aids to the diagnosis of brain affections. There remains now no doubt that some eye-symptoms help us to diagnosticate certain intra-cranial troubles, and are sometimes of even very great diagnostic value. In a few cases they may even enable us not only to diagnosticate intra-cranial affections, but also to locate them.

Without going further into anatomical details we may here state, that the optic nerve and retina are really parts of the brain, from which they grow during fœtal life, and that their blood-vessels, and their lymphatics are directly connected with those of the brain. Furthermore, we must keep in mind that the sheaths of the optic nerve are directly continuous with the meninges, and that the intervaginal spaces of the optic sheaths correspond to and are in direct communication with the spaces bounded by these membranes within the cranium.

It is evident from these anatomical facts, that an increased or diminished supply of blood or lymphatic fluid in the brain must, when no other affections exist, cause a like condition in the optic nerve and retina.

Although these facts are simply due to the mechanical conditions and cannot be doubted, their diagnostic value is smaller, than we should expect, because even in normal eyes the individual differences in the number, the situation, and the form of the blood-vessels as seen with the ophthalmoscope, are such, that we can hardly venture to diagnosticate a small degree of anæmia or hyperæmia, unless we have had occasion to examine the eyes at a former period. Yet it is in just these cases of incipient hyperæmia or anæmia, that the diagnosis might often be of the greatest value.

When, however, the anæmia or hyperæmia of the optic nerve and retina have reached a high degree, we can easily recognize them, and thus, in combination with the other symptoms present in the case before us, they may help to a diagnosis.

If, for instance, the general symptoms lead to the conclusion that there must be hyperæmia of the brain, a pronounced hyperæmia of the optic nerve and retina may confirm this diagnosis, if all other causes for the hyperæmia of these parts can be excluded.

Or, if we find, in an otherwise healthy individual, pronounced anæmia of the optic nerve and retina (in a case of injury to the head, for instance,) the diagnosis of anæmia of the brain may safely be made.

In other cases the ophthalmoscopic diagnosis of hyperæmia or anæmia of the optic nerve and retina, and consequently of the brain may help us even in the diagnosis of a further affection. For instance, if we find in a case of pertussis (whooping-cough) that the optic nerve and retina are perfectly anæmic, we know that the brain is also anæmic, and this, in connection with the knowledge that the patient's system has been greatly reduced by the disease, may help us to the conclusion that the heart's action especially must be very weak. The latter is, furthermore, proved by the fact already mentioned, that by paracentesis of the anterior chamber and the consequent lowering of the intra-ocular tension, we can bring about a refilling of the blood-vessels of the optic nerve and retina.

Although pronounced hyperæmia, or anæmia of the optic nerve and retina, must necessarily happen quite often, we have much oftener occasion to observe and to utilize for diagnostic purposes certain more pronounced changes of the tissue, namely, œdema of the optic papilla and optic neuritis, for the reason that they are usually combined with more or less important disturbance of vision.

Any intra-cranial affection which causes an increase of the intra-cranial pressure must also cause an increase of pressure in the intervaginal spaces of the optic nerve. This increase of pressure will lead to a dropsical distension of the sheaths of the optic nerve near its entrance into the eye-ball, with venous stasis and œdema of the optic papilla; soon these conditions cause inflammatory symptoms, first in the optic papilla, and then also in the retinal tissue. Whenever, therefore, we find neuro-retinitis in a case in which it is due to an increase of intra-cranial pressure, it must have been preceded by œdema of the optic papilla.

Neuritis optica may, however, furthermore, be caused by a fibrinous or fibrino-purulent inflammation of the sheaths of the optic nerve based on a similar form of meningitis.

This may be due to the fact that exudations resulting from meningitis may simply be forced into the intervaginal space of the optic nerve, or the inflammatory process may itself spread from the intra-cranial meninges to those of the optic nerve.

The result of these inflammations is, as we have seen above, in most cases the total atrophy of the optic nerve.

Œdema of both optic papillæ, or neuro-retinitis in both eyes, give us, therefore, generally a hint, that there is an increase of intra-cranial pressure. Their presence is, however, of little further diagnostic value, (although this hint alone may, under some circumstances be of very great importance), since intra-cranial tumors, hemorrhages, abscesses, and encephalitic and meningitic processes, may all cause these same symptoms at the ocular end of the optic nerve. Yet, we know, that in by far the largest number of cases these symptoms are due to an intra-cranial tumor, and this fact, together with the general symptoms, as well as other functional troubles which may, perhaps, exist in the eye, will in most cases help us to make the diagnosis sure.

The atrophy of the optic nerve caused by neuritis, as has been stated in Chapter XIV, shows in the first period after the inflammatory symptoms have ceased, a more or less characteristic image. We may, therefore, sometimes confirm the diagnosis of a former intra-cranial affection by the presence of such an atrophy of the optic nerve.

Progressive atrophy of the optic nerve may be due to tabes dorsalis or to multiple sclerosis of the spinal cord. The ophthalmoscopic appearance of such an atrophy has nothing that would distinguish it from progressive atrophy due to other causes. The atrophy of the optic nerves may be the first symptom observed in spinal disease. Its existance should, therefore, always lead us to examine for further spinal symptoms. If this atrophy is combined with myosis of the pupil, the diagnosis of a spinal affection is nearly certain. In this case the pupil which is excessively small, will not contract at all when light is thrown into the eye, and but slightly, when the patient accommodates and converges his eyes. This combination of eye-symptoms is considered pathognomonic of a spinal affection. In tabes dorsalis the symptom of color-blindness is generally superadded. Whether the eye-symptoms are due to an affection of special nerve fibres connecting the optic nerve with the cervical portion of the spinal cord, or whether they are simply caused by the same affection from which the medulla suffers, only occurring in other parts of the nervous system, are questions not yet settled.

Tubercles in the choroid were formerly considered to prove the existance of tubercular meningitis. This may hold good, if all other symptoms point to tubercular meningitis. But we know now, see Chapter XII, that tubercular choroiditis may be a primary affection, and we can, therefore, draw no conclusions as to the condition of the meninges, from the simple fact that we find tubercles in the choroid.

Paresis and paralysis of the muscles of the eye-ball may help us to diagnosticate and even to locate, a cerebral trouble as stated in chapter XXI.

The diagnostic value of the condition of the pupil is confined to the fact, that irritation of the sympathetic nerve, as well as paralysis of the oculomotor nerve, cause dilatation of the pupil, while paralysis of the sympathetic nerve and irritation of the third nerve cause contraction of the pupil.

Thus far we have only considered the diagnostic value of objective eye symptoms, we come now to the subjective symptoms, namely, the functional disturbances, and especially *hemianopia*.

Hemianopia is the condition of the eyes, in which one half of the retina is blind, or, in other words, in which one-half of the

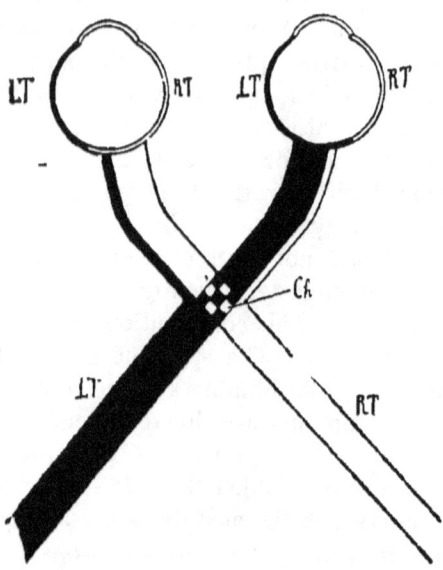

FIG. 72. Diagram Showing the Partial Decussation of the Fibres of the Optic Tracts within the Chiasma. The Crossed Parts (nearly two-thirds of each tract), supply the Inner—the Uncrossed Parts the Outer Portion of each Eye. RT. Right Optic Tract. LT. Left Optic Tract. Ch. Chiasma. The Uncrossed Bundle is drawn too thin; it should be about one-third of the whole breadth.

visual field is wanting. Monocular hemianopia may occur, but is extremely rare.

We have practically only to deal with hemianopia with vertical division of the field. If the left half, or the right half of the visual field of each eye is wanting, we speak of *homonymous hemianopia*. If in one eye the right half and in the other the left half, that is, both the temporal or both the nasal halves are wanting, we call it *heteronymous hemianopia*. In these cases the eyes appear usually otherwise normal and even by the use of the ophthalmoscope we see at least at first no change.

In order to understand in what way hemianopia may be of a diagnostic value in brain affections, we have to consider the origin and the course of the optic nerve fibres.

Each tractus opticus originates in the gray matter of the occipital lobe of the brain around the gyrus angularis. In the chiasma the optic nerves cross each other. The often discussed question in what way this decussation of the nerve fibres takes place is now settled by pathologico-anatomical facts, and also by experimental results. About two-thirds of the fibres of each optic tract are crossed, while about one-third remain uncrossed. The crossed bundle of each optic nerve supplies the inner half of the opposite eye-ball, while the uncrossed one goes to the outer half of the eye-ball which lies on the same side as its tractus opticus. (See figure 72).

From this anatomical fact it is evident that any affection interfering with the cerebral center of vision in the occipital lobe, or with the optic tract of one side between this center and the chiasma will cause blindness of the same half of the retina, that is, the opposite half of the visual field will be wanting for each eye.

This is the most frequent kind of hemianopia. Of the heteronymous forms of hemianopia none is as distinct as the homonymous form, and they must be due to affections in or near the chiasma, while monocular hemianopia from a nervous affection can only be caused by a pathological condition of one optic nerve in front of the chiasma.

If we examine a patient and find one half of the visual field for each eye wanting, we know when this is the left half for each eye, that there must be an in-tracranial affection which interferes with the tractus opticus of the right side, and vice versa. In most cases that have thus far been examined *post mortem*, the lesion has been found to involve the very origin of the tract in the occipital lobe.

# CHAPTER XXIII.

### EYE-AFFECTIONS CAUSED BY DISEASES OF DISTANT ORGANS OR DISEASES OF THE GENERAL SYSTEM.

RESPIRATORY APPARATUS.— CIRCULATORY APPARATUS.— DIGESTIVE APPARATUS.— URO-POETIC APPARATUS.—GENITAL ORGANS.—AFFECTIONS OF THE SKIN.—AFFECTIONS OF THE JOINTS.—INFECTIOUS DISEASES.—INTOXICATIONS.—DIABETES.- SCROPHULOSIS.

*Respiratory Apparatus.*—In affections of the respiratory apparatus, which cause a great deal of hard coughing, and especially in whooping-cough, the rupture of a conjunctival blood-vessel, is sometimes observed. The resultant ecchymosis may, of course, vary greatly in size. No special treatment is required. The same thing may happen during a forcible sneezing attack.

Catarrhal inflammation of the mucous membrane of the nose may extend into the nasal duct, and cause there a swelling and obstruction, and thus give rise to stillicidium (tear-dropping). If the case is an acute one, the sympstoms in the tear-duct may pass away with it. In chronic catarrh of the nasal mucous membrane, the nasal duct becomes frequently permanently obstructed by scar-tissue, or by disease of the bones, due to the diathesis upon which the chronic nasal catarrh is based (syphilis and scrophulosis).

Tumors of the nose, polypi of a benign or malignant character, are apt to encroach upon the orbit, and thus can cause exophthalmus.

Tuberculosis of the choroid has been found in cases of tuberculosis of the lungs.

Hypertrophy of the left ventricle of the heart is apt to produce retinal hemorrhages, or hemorrhages into the vitreous body, and this whether the venous stasis is due originally to an affection of the lungs or of the heart.

*Circulatory Apparatus.*—Diminished arterial pressure, especially when caused by the insufficiency of the aortic valves, may cause pulsation of the arteries of the retina; this pulsation is isochronous with the systolic contraction of the heart.

If the force of the heart's action is considerably reduced, this may cause ischæmia of the optic nerve and retina. The heart in such cases is no longer able to overcome the normal intra-ocular tension, but it can do so again when the tension is reduced by paracentesis of the anterior chamber.

Pernicious progressive anæmia causes anæmia of the optic papilla and retina, and also extravasations into the retinal tissue.

Fibrinous endocarditis may be the cause of an embolism of the central retinal artery, or one of its branches. It is hardly necessary to state that the embolus must be very small to enter this artery.

Pulsating exophthalmus is a symptom which in almost all cases is due to an affection of the blood-vessels, and but very rarely to a pulsating tumor of the orbit. Its most prominent symptom is the exophthalmus, which is often one-sided, and may be very considerable. The upper eye-lid is swollen, and its veins are dilated, and the conjunctiva shows dilated blood-vessels and serous infiltration. The pupil is generally dilated. The eye-ball can be pressed into the orbit without causing pain, but it will protrude again as soon as the pressure is released. Placing the fingers on the eye-ball, it is felt to pulsate, and sometimes the pulsation is even visible. By auscultation pulsatory sounds are heard on the eye and the surrounding regions. Compression of the common carotid artery reduces these sounds or stops them altogether.

Besides the exophthalmus there may be optic neuritis or œdema of the optic papilla. The retinal veins are always considerably enlarged and pulsate. Sight may be very much impaired, and in some cases blindness has been observed. The patients complain chiefly of the continued noise, and sometimes of pain. Paresis of the external muscles of the eye-ball may cause diplopia. These symptoms have but very seldom come on without any known cause; in most cases they have developed after an injury, and for the most part after a heavy fall. They may follow rapidly upon the injury, which is the rule, or they may develop more slowly. When the exophthalmus occurs in both eyes, one eye-ball usually has protruded before the other.

In a few cases the affection has been known to recover spontaneously, but in most cases, when not interfered with, death has been the result. The idiopathic cases of pulsating exophthalmus seem to be more frequent among women, while the traumatic ones have nearly all occurred in men. (*Sattler*).

The anatomical cause of pulsating exophthalmus is sometimes an aneurysm of the ophthalmic artery, but in a large majority of the cases a rupture of the internal carotid within the cavernous sinus, with consequent effusion of arterial blood into this sinus and increase of blood-pressure, causing dilatation and pulsation of the superior ophthalmic vein, and ultimately of all the venous vessels communicating with the superior ophthalmic vein, and also of the inferior ophthalmic vein. The central retinal vein, which empties the blood either into the superior ophthalmic vein, or directly into the cavernous sinus, soon shows therefore the same symptoms of dilatation and pulsation.

The therapeutic measures must, of course, be directed to the primary affection. As we have seen, this is usually a rupture of the internal carotid artery, therefore, continuous digital compression or ligation of the common carotid artery must be performed.

We may here refer also to amblyopia, or amaurosis dependant on the loss of large quantities of blood, to whatever cause it may be due, such as wounds, ulcers of the stomach, the cancerous erosion of a larger blood-vessel, uterine affections, etc. If the patient recovers from the loss of blood, his sight, as a rule, will also gradually be regained.

*Organs of Digestion.*—The congestion to the head caused by chronic constipation, and by hyperæmia of the liver, is sometimes combined with eye-symptoms. These are, in the main, an easily fatigued accommodation, and the appearance of dark or light spots before the eyes. These symptoms disappear with the removal of their primary cause.

Leucæmia causes a form of retinitis which is said to be characterized by a yellow tint of the whole retina.

*Uropoetic Apparatus.*—Diseases of the kidneys give rise to various eye affections. The affection which we call albuminuric neuro-retinitis, and which has been already described in Chapter XIII., is generally due to the shrinking kidney, that form of nephritis in which the specific gravity of the urine is usually low, and in which the albumen is small in quantity, or may at times be wanting altogether. Albuminuric retinitis is also found in acute croupous nephritis, as during scarlet fever, and in cases of amyloid degeneration of the kidneys. The diseases of the kidneys may lead to albuminuric retinitis by causing a hydræmic condition of the blood, which brings on pathological changes in the coats of the blood-vessels. Further symptoms may be due to increased blood-pressure and to the retention of urea. Although this form of retinitis belongs, as a rule, to the latter stages of the kidney disease, it is sometimes the first symptom noticed by the patient, and its characteristic features may thus sometimes lead us to detect a kidney disease when no other symptom is as yet so pronounced, as to suggest the diagnosis.

Another eye-affection due to kidney disease is the so-called uræmic amaurosis. It is seen in all forms of nephritis, but chiefly in acute nephritis from scarlet fever or the nephritis of pregnant women. The blindness usually comes on rapidly during a uræmic attack. The pupils are sometimes dilated. Whether the patient has already been suffering from albuminuric retinitis, or not, makes, of course, no difference as regards the occurrence of such a uræmic amaurosis. The amaurosis may pass off again after a few hours. Sometimes, however, it lasts even several days.

*Genital Organs.*—Amblyopia is sometimes seen after excesses *in venere*. It never lasts long in these cases, and does not give rise to a serious affection. Onanism, especially, when frequently indulged in, causes the same symptoms. It has become to be quite an accepted fact that onanism, as such, may, and is likely to lead to serious eye-affections, and it frequently happens that a patient comes to the physician frightened out of his wits after having read about the serious consequences of this habit. An examination either reveals no eye-affection at all, or one which has nothing to do with their self indulgence, and which in all probability has existed previously.

In rare cases, where onanism is practiced very frequently, it may give rise to chronic conjunctivitis, hyperæmia of the optic nerve and retina, photopsia and blepharospasmus (*Cohn*).

Gonorrhœal pus, brought into the conjunctival sack, causes a most serious purulent conjunctivitis, as stated in Chapter VII. But gonorrhœa may also be the ultimate cause of iritis and choroiditis. In these cases we find usually that a gonorrhœal arthritis has gone before. The treatment is that of iritis, or choroiditis, from other causes.

Uterine diseases are undoubtedly often the cause of eye-affections; yet it is rather difficult to prove the dependance of the eye-affection on the uterine trouble, unless the cure of the latter removes also the former, or the eye disease develops at the same time with the appearance of a uterine trouble. It is well known that women in the climacteric period are apt to suffer from disseminate or chronic exudative choroiditis, and that the suppression of the menstruation at an earlier age may lead to the same disease. Sometimes a detachment of the retina takes place upon suppression of the menstruation, in which case the renewed flow may contribute positively to the cure of the eye-affection. Episcleritis, hyperæmia of the optic nerve and retina, and even neuro-retinitis, have been observed under the same conditions (*Mooren*).

A certain form of asthenopia, which *Foerster* has named kopiopia hysterica, seems to be clearly connected with a chronic atrophic parametritis. This asthenopia is accompanied by pain and photophobia. Convex glasses do not give relief, even although they may correct an existing presbyopia. Such patients are unable to use their eyes for more than a few moments for near-work without pain, although their visual accuteness is usually perfect. The affection yields to no treatment; when left alone disappears gradually, but generally only after a duration of several years.

We may in this place speak also of a disease in which the eye-symptoms are very prominent, and which by many is thought to be due to an affection of the genital organs. I refer to exophthalmic goitre, or *Basedow's* (*Graves'*) disease. (See figure 73).

# EYE-AFFECTIONS DEPENDENT ON OTHER DISEASES. 207

The cardinal symptoms of Basedow's disease are an increased action of the heart, exophthalmus of one or generally of both eyes, and goitre, although one of these three symptoms may be wanting.

The first symptom is usually the increased heart's action. The pulse ranges from 100 to 200 in the minute, the shock at the apex of the heart is felt much stronger than in the normal condition, and can even be seen, although the heart is usually not hypertrophic. The carotid arteries and the veins of the neck pulsate visibly. Any excitement or tiresome work aggravates these symptoms. Sooner or later the thyroid gland be-

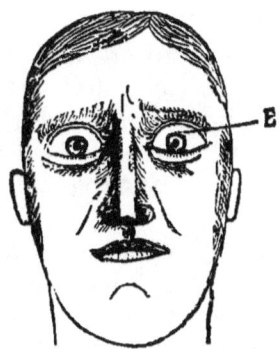

FIG. 73. Basedow's Disease (Grave's Disease). Diagram showing especially Graefe's Symptom—the Loss of Coordination in the Downward Movement of Eye-ball and Upper Eye-lid. E. Exposed Strip of Sclerotic.

gins to swell. The tumor is at first soft, but later on it becomes harder through the newformation of connective tissue, or through deposits of lime. The swelling is not very large, and it may come and go. With the hand a tremor may be felt over the thyroid gland, and with the stethoscope circulatory murmurs can be heard in it. The exophthalmus appears usually as the last of the three cardinal symptoms. The protrusion of the eye-balls is mostly in a forward direction, but sometimes there is divergent strabismus. In most cases the protrusion occurs in both eyes.

Combined with the exophthalmus is a loss of co-ordination in the movements of the eye-ball and eye-lids, so that in downward movements of the eyes the upper lids lag behind and expose a strip of the sclerotic. In the lower eye-lids the same symptom is present, but it is less noticeable. This symptom is considered as almost pathognomonic for this form of exophthalmus, and it is sometimes observed even before the exophthalmus has become very conspicuous. The palpebral fissure is generally very wide, and involuntary nictitation is wanting.

The pupils are often normal, in other cases dilated, the accommodation remains, however, undisturbed. The secretion of tears, at first increased, becomes later on diminished, and a conjunctival catarrh is seldom entirely wanting. The cornea becomes dry, since the eye-lids do not protect it properly, and ulcerations, even the total destruction of the cornea, may be the result. The retinal arteries pulsate.

These cardinal symptoms are attended by a number of varying ones, as chlorosis or anæmia, uterine affections, higher temperature, etc. The palpitations of the heart cause dispnoea, orthopnœa, and even angina pectoris. The digestion is disturbed. Headache and insomnia are almost constant symptoms and help to lower the vital powers.

*Basedow's* disease rarely appears as an acute affection, and it usually takes several years for all its symptoms to become fully developed. Intermissions are the rule, and the characteristic symptoms of the disease may even exist for years, and then disappear. In about 12 per cent of the cases (*von Dusch*) death results from exhaustion, from ascites, or from hemorrhages into the brain, lungs or intestinal tract.

The diagnosis is easy when the cardinal symptoms are all well marked. In the beginning, however, the disease might be confounded with paralysis of the sympathetic nerve.

According to *Mooren*, *Basedow's* disease attacks twelve women to one man. It develops often after other severe, weakening diseases, great losses of blood, undue bodily exertion, etc. Sometimes it seems to be dependent on an hereditary tendency, and and may show itself in several members of the same family.

Anatomical examinations have shown that the heart in *Basedow's* disease may be actually dilated and hypertrophied. The goitre is most frequently a glandular hypertrophy, but in some cases it has been found to be simply due to a dilatation of the blood-vessels of the thyroid gland. The orbital fat is usually hypertrophic and œdematous, and its blood-vessels are dilated. The external muscles of the eye have been found in a state of fatty degeneration, but in a single case which I have had occasion to examine, they were normal. Changes of various kinds in the cervical part of the sympathetic nerve of the neck and its ganglia have been reported in some cases; in other cases no such changes could be detected. Pathological anatomy has, therefore, thus far revealed no common cause for all the symptoms observed in *Basedow's* disease, and it is only upon the clinical symptoms that any rational explanation can be founded.

The palpitations of the heart may be due to irritation of the excito-motory nerves of the heart, which arise from the medulla oblongata, enter the sympathetic nerve, and leave it again with the branches forming the cardiac plexus, or they may be due to paralysis of the inhibitory nerve-fibres coming from the vagus nerve.

Paralysis of the cervical part of the sympathetic nerve will account for the vascular symptoms *Basedow's* of disease, the goitre, and even the exophthalmus; but it produces contraction of the pupil and of the palpebral fissure, while by irritation of the oculo-pupillary fibres of the cervical part of the sympathetic nerve, which spring from the anterior root of the second dorsal nerve, we can produce widening of the palpebral fissure, dilation of the pupil, and exophthalmus. We should, therefore, have to accept two different conditions in the tract of the same nerve in order to explain the more prominent symptoms of *Basedow's* disease on the hypothesis of an origin in the sympathetic nerve.

It would be going too far to give here all theories which have been advanced in order to explain the symptoms of this disease. Suffice it to say, that paralysis of the center for the vagus nerve explains best the majority of the symptoms when combined with paralysis of a special (assumed) center for the blood-vessels of the orbit and thyroid gland, and of the reflex-center for the movements of the eye-lids. From this fact it appears that the symptoms of *Basedow's* disease are due to a brain lesion, and, in fact, *Filehne*, by cutting into the corpora restiformia of rabbits without injuring the fourth ventricle, after having first severed the sympathetic nerve, has produced the cardinal symptoms of this disease.

Tonic treatment of all sorts has been recommended in this disease. The most successful treatment seems to be galvanization, combined with arsenic and iron internally.

If the cornea is endangered by ulceration, the palpebral fissure may be shortened by tarsoraphy.

*Affections of the Skin.*—Erysipelas of the face has in several cases led to optic atrophy through compression of the optic nerve consequent on the extension of the inflammation to the orbital tissues.

Herpes zoster is sometimes found together with herpes of the cornea, and the latter is then considered to be due to a disease of the *ganglion Gasseri*.

*Affections of the Joints.*—Rheumatism, especially articular rheumatism and gout, favor the development of iritis and episcleritis.

*Infectious Diseases.*—Measles in the eruptive stage give rise conjunctivitis. Chronic conjunctivitis conjoined with blepharitis ciliaris, and phlyctænular, and even parenchymatous keratitis, are often seen after measles, and their occurrence is undoubtedly due to the lowering of the whole system by this disease. Optic neuritis and amaurosis have also been observed after measles, but they are extremely rare.

Scarlet fever, by causing nephritis, may bring about an albuminuric neuro-retinitis, or a uræmic amaurosis.

Small-pox may give rise to a great variety of eye-affections, not counting, of course, the fact that pustules may be located on the skin of the eye-lids. The eye-diseases caused by small-pox have, contrary to the general opinion, nothing specific, and their cause is the same as if they were idiopathic eye-affections. Catarrhal, purulent, and diphtheritic conjunctivitis, keratitis, blennorrhoea of the lachrymal sack, iritis and choroiditis are often observed during and after this disease. The most frequent affections, however, are those of the conjunctiva and cornea. The corneal troubles have also been observed to develop some weeks after recovery from the small-pox. They are usually ulcerations and parenchymatous inflammations, which lead to the formation of scars, or even to the total destruction of the eye-ball. Many an eye which has been lost in this manner might have been saved, had the eye-affection been treated in its earlier stages, and, as the treatment is in most cases simply local, and in no way interferes with the treatment of the small-pox, there is no good excuse for neglecting it, even during the active period of the general disease.

Typhus abdominalis may give rise to corneal abscesses or ulcerations, and to paresis of the external muscles of the eye-ball or of the accommodative apparatus.

Amaurosis is sometimes seen after typhus, as it is after other prostrating diseases, and is due to an anæmic condition of the optic nerves. In nearly all these cases sight returns with the improvement of the condition of the general system.

Febris recurrens is said to cause by preference affections of the uveal tract.

Diphtheritis of the throat appears but very seldom to cause diphtheritic conjunctivitis, but in some rare cases the disease reaches the conjunctiva through the lachrymal passages. A much more frequent affection following diphtheritis of the throat is paresis of the accommodation, already referred to in Chapter XX. The physician should at once suspect it, when some weeks, after recovery from the diphtheritic attack in the throat, vision for near objects become weakened or imperfect.

Malarial fever, as has been stated, is thought by many physicians in the Mississippi Valley to cause all sorts of eye-affections. There is no question that chronic conjunctivitis and trachoma, are very frequent in the fever districts, yet, I have not seen that quinine has had any beneficial influence in promoting their cure. Malarial keratitis has been described (*Kipp*) as a special form of keratitis. I have sometimes seen small, point-like infiltrations of the cornea, which have appeared in connection with malarial fever. Malarial optic neuritis and œdema of the optic papilla have been described by *Macnamara*. Paralysis of one or more of the external muscles of the eye-ball may also be due to malarial poisoning.

Pyæmia and septicæmia cause eye-symptoms, which may be due to the thrombosis of the cavernous sinus, or of one of the ophthalmic veins. In other cases, especially in puerperal septicæmia, purulent choroiditis (*choroiditis metastatica*), probably due to embolism, has been observed. I have seen it also caused by a purulent arthritis. A septic retinitis has also been observed and described.

Acquired syphilis shows itself in the eyes in a great many ways, and in all periods of the disease. The part of the eye most frequently attacked by syphilis is the uveal tract. The commonest form of syphilitic eye-disease is iritis. It is usually a simple plastic iritis, which appears at the same time with the skin-symptoms, or at a later period, when other syphilitic symptoms are no longer recognizable. In some cases the iritis is of a recurring type. Such a plastic syphilitic iritis may begin rather quietly and with little pain, and may thus differ somewhat from certain other forms of iritis; yet, as a rule, there is no symptom, which absolutely proves an iritis to be of syphilitic origin, unless it be the formation of a gumma. Gumma of the iris is easily recognized, as has been described in Chapter X. The gumma may remain small, or it may gradually increase in size so as nearly to fill the anterior chamber.

Syphilitic choroiditis may appear as a disseminate choroiditis or as a central chorio-retinitis, or it may be an exudative choroiditis. Gummata have also been observed in the choroid. Syphilitic choroiditis is found in patients of a more advanced age, and occurs mostly at the same time with or soon after the so-called secondary symptoms.

Syphilitic retinitis usually conjoined with choroiditis, and syphilitic neuritis are sometimes met with; also cyclitis, gummata of the ciliary body and of the sclerotic. Atrophy of the optic nerve, and paralytic symptoms in the external muscles of the eye-ball are often due to syphilis; also diseases of the lachrymal apparatus.

Hereditary syphilis is often the cause of a parenchymatous keratitis (often in connection with *Hutchinson's* teeth), and sometimes of iritis.

*Intoxications.*—Lead-poisoning is apt to cause optic neuritis, transient amaurosis, or even atrophy of the optic nerve. The eye affections usually precede the general symptoms.

Progressive atrophy and central scotoma due to alcohol and tobacco intoxication, have been detailed in Chapter XIV.

Toxic effects from eating sausage, meat-pastry or fish (pike), have in rare cases produced a paresis of the accommodation, exactly like that observed after diphtheritis. Sometimes it has been conjoined with amblyopia.

Intoxication with belladonna, hyoscyamus and datura, causes dilatation of the pupil and paralysis of the accommodation.

Morphia and opium intoxication, in the acute forms, causes myosis of the pupil.

Quinine-intoxication has especially of late been found to cause amblyopia and amaurosis. The latter may become permanent, although central vision at least may be re-established. The ophthalmoscope shows anæmia of the optic nerve and retina. The affection usually leaves an impairment of the color-sense and of the light-sense behind.

*Diabetes.*—Diabetes mellitus is sometimes the cause of the formation of cataract. While some operators are afraid to extract such cataracts, and prefer to use the suction-method, others do not acknowledge any special danger from operations for diabetic cataract.

The optic nerve and retina are sometimes found to be inflamed in diabetes mellitus, and the ophthalmoscopic picture is similar to that of albuminuric neuro-retinitis. Furthermore, amblyopia and atrophy of the optic nerve and paralysis of the external muscles of the eye-ball have been found, caused apparently by diabetes.

*Scrophulosis.*—Scrophulosis, strumous habit, is the most frequent cause of phlyctænular affections of the eye, and sometimes of parenchymatous keratitis, or catarrhal conjunctivitis, blepharitis, and affections of the lachrymal apparatus.

# CHAPTER XXIV.

## ON THE DETECTION OF ONE-SIDED SIMULATED BLINDNESS AND CONGENITAL COLOR-BLINDNESS.

METHODS FOR DETECTING SIMULATED BLINDNESS.--HOLMGREN'S METHOD FOR DETECTING COLOR-BLINDNESS.

The oldest and simplest method for the detection of simulated one-sided blindness consists in placing a prism before the eye which is pronounced to be healthy, while the individual is looking at a distant object, and thus to evoke double vision. It is best to hold the prism before that eye with its base upwards or downwards. If the individual under examination acknowledges his diplopia, the eye pronounced blind must necessarily see, and his binocular vision is demonstrated.

In many cases, however, the malingerer is acquainted with this method, and it must then be modified. He is directed again to look at a distant object; then the examiner covers his so-called blind eye, and holds a prism before the so-called good eye in such a manner that the prism covers only about half of the pupillary space, thus producing a monocular diplopia. If the malingerer does not acknowledge this diplopia, he is to be suspected. If he acknowledges it, we proceed to uncover the so-called blind eye, and shift the prism so that it covers the whole pupil, thus changing the monocular into a binocular diplopia. He must, of course, not be allowed to suspect the trick, and if he continues to see double, the so-called blind eye must see.

Another method is to let the malingerer read, and to exclude his so-called good eye from sight by some means, while he is reading. This may best be done by holding a very strong convex glass before it, as but few malingerers will be stupid enough to go on reading, when a dark or ground glass is held before their so-called good eye.

If, further, the malingerer goes on reading undisturbed, and without shifting the book or his head, when a pencil or some such object is held between his eyes and the book, he must see with both eyes.

The so-called good eye may also be excluded from vision by the instillation of a mydriatic. However, but few malingerers will allow anything to be put into their so-called good eye.

*Congenital color-blindness.*—Color-blindness has of late become an important subject in certain branches of modern civilization. The fact that a man is color-blind evidently unfits him for any service in which the prompt fulfillment of important duties depends on his recognizing colored signals.

It has, therefore, become a law in most civilized countries that men applying for positions in the railroad service, or in the marine, must first undergo an examination with regard to their color-perception.

Color-blindness may be total or only partial. In total color-blindness the patient perceives only black and white, and all other colors are to him either white or black or of some intermediate shade of gray. In partial color-blindness the patients generally see two complementary colors besides white and black. In the so-called red-green blindness yellow and blue are perceived; in the so-called blue-yellow blindness red and green are recognized. These two forms are the typical ones of partial color-blindness, yet slight variations are often observed. The visual acuteness of eyes which are color-blind is generally perfectly normal.

Various methods have been devised in order to detect partial congenital color-blindness. The simplest method in common use is that of *Holmgren*. The patient is given a skein of colored worsted, and directed to select from a bundle containing all sorts of colored worsted those skeins which appear to him of the same color as the given one (usually a pale green or a pale pink). If there is any hesitation in matching the color, or if he selects different colors to match the given one, his color-perception cannot be normal.

If, for instance, he matches a light green skein with red, brown or gray, he is surely color-blind. If he is red-green blind, he will mix the colors up on the principle that to him blue and yellow only are distinct colors, and all other colors appear to him as shades of yellow. (*Mauthner*). If he is, however, blue-yellow blind, he will see only red and green as distinct colors, and every other color will to him appear as a shade of red.

Red-green blindness is by far the commonest form of partial color-blindness.

The affection is but very rarely monocular, and nothing is known with regard to its etiology.

# CHAPTER XXV.

### ON THE MOST IMPORTANT OPERATIONS ON THE EYE-BALL AND THE EYE-LIDS.

TENOTOMY.—ADVANCEMENT.—ENUCLEATION.—PARACENTESIS OF THE CORNEA.—ABSCISION OF A CORNEAL STAPHYLOMA.—SCLEROTOMY.—IRIDECTOMY.—IRIDOTOMY. —EXTRACTION OF CATARACT. — DISCISSION OF THE ANTERIOR LENS-CAPSULE. — PTERYGIUM—OPERATIONS. — OPERATIONS FOR THE CURE OF SYMBLEPHARON. — PTOSIS—OPERATIONS.—TRICHIASIS AND ENTROPIUM—OPERATIONS.— ECTROPIUM —OPERATIONS.—CANTHOTOMY AND CANTHOPLASTY.—BLEPHAROPLASTY.

It is intended to give in this chapter only a short description of the most important operations for affections involving the eye-ball and the eye-lids.

*Tenotomy.*—The tenotomy of one or more of the external muscles of the eye-ball is performed for the cure of strabismus. The operation is most frequently done on the internal rectus, more rarely on the external rectus. Tenotomy of the superior or the inferior rectus may also be necessary in rare cases.

When possible, it is best to perform this operation without putting the patient under the influence of an anæsthetic, because the effect of the tenotomy can then be promptly estimated, and, if necessary, improved upon.

After the eye-lids have been separated and are held apart by means of a wire-speculum, or by the fingers of an assistant, the eye-ball is rolled in the direction opposite to the muscle to be cut. The conjunctiva and episcleral tissue is then firmly grasped with strong toothed forceps below the insertion of the muscle and somewhat nearer the corneo-scleral margin. This fold of tissue is then cut by means of strabismus scissors. (See figure 74). If the first clip has not opened *Tenon's* space, this must be done by a second cut. This accomplished, but not before, the strabismus hook (See figure 75) is slipped under the tendon of the muscle through this external incision. The handle of the hook is then raised so as to put the muscle upon the stretch, and the strabismus scissors are introduced, the tendon is cut close to the sclerotic. By then bringing a second strabismus hook

FIG. 74. Strabismus Scissors (bent).

behind the first one, entering it with its point downwards and sweeping the sclerotic with it while turning it upwards, or vice versa, any stray tendinous fibres are detected, and are to be severed. Only when the strabismus hook can under the conjunctiva be moved close up to the cornea-scleral margin, without encountering any obstacle, we may be sure that the muscle is perfectly divided.

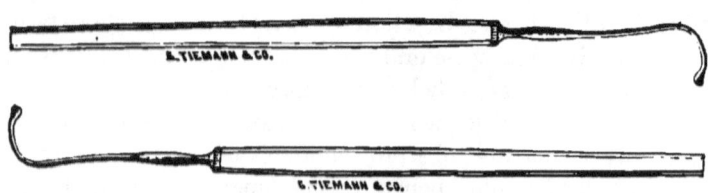

FIG. 75. Strabismus Hooks.

This done, the effect of the operation is to be tested. If the motility of the eye-ball in the direction of the muscle operated upon is greatly reduced, the desired effect is probably attained. If the internal rectus has been cut, the patient ought to be able to move the inner margin of the cornea as far inward as the lachrymal carnucle, and if he can not do this, the effect of the tenotomy may be reduced by drawing the eye-ball by a suture to the inner angle of the palpebral fissure. If the patient can move his eye farther toward the nose, the tendon is not perfectly divided.

If the tenotomy has been performed on the external rectus, the patient should still be able to move the outer margin of the cornea as far as the outer angle of the palpebral fissure; and if he cannot do so, the effect of the operation may be increased by fastening the eye-ball to the outer angle of the palpebral fissure by means of a suture.

Tenotomy has generally to be performed on both eyes. This must, however, never be done at one sitting, when the tenotomy is made to cure convergent strabismus, for an over-correction will result in a divergent strabismus in the place of the convergent one, for which the operation has been performed.

*Advancement.*—In divergent strabismus a simple tenotomy of the external rectus or recti is but seldom fully successful. It is, therefore, necessary in these cases to advance the insertion of the internal rectus to a position nearer the corneo-scleral margin, and thus in effect to shorten the muscle. The operation for the advancement of the internal rectus must nearly always be combined with the division of external recti. In some cases it will be necessary to perform the operation for advancement on both internal recti.

The conjunctiva is first incised over the insertion of the internal rectus in a vertical direction, and the muscle is then grasped with the forceps, or a thread is drawn through it, so as to prevent it from slipping backwards and out of reach when the tendon is cut. This cutting of the tendon is done close to the sclerotic, and the muscle may then be shortened to the required degree. This done, the portion of the conjunctiva which lies between the incision and the corneal margin is undermined with fine scissors, and the internal rectus is drawn under it, and fastened in this position by means of two or three sutures.

The required effect is only reached when immediately after the operation, the eyes show a slight degree of convergence. This apparent over-correction disappears during the process of healing.

*Enucleation.*—The operation of removing an eye-ball by

enucleation should never be performed without having the patient well under the influence of an anæsthetic.

The eye-lids are held apart by a wire-speculum or the fingers of an assistant, and the conjunctiva near one of the recti muscles (I prefer the inferior one) is grasped with the toothed forceps and incised. A strabismus hook is then inserted under the muscle, and all tissue which can be lifted by the hook is divided with the scissors close to the eye-ball, always cutting the conjunctiva first at the corneo-scleral margin. When all the tissue which has been lifted by the first hook is severed, a second hook is inserted behind the first and the tissues lifted by this are cut as before, and so on around the whole eye-ball. When the inferior, external and superior recti tendons have been thus detached, it is best to divide the internal rectus somewhat further back from its insertion so that the stump adhering to the sclerotic can be used in order to rotate the eye-ball outwards during the final step of the operation, which is the cutting of the optic nerve. To accomplish this the eye-ball is turned strongly outwards, and

FIG. 76.     Needle.

a closed, strongly curved pair of scissors is introduced at the nasal side between the loosened orbital tissue and the eye-ball, and is pushed backwards until it has reached the posterior surface of the eye-ball. By moving the point of the scissors up and down, the resistance felt will now enable the operator to make sure of the position of the optic nerve. This ascertained, the scissors are slightly withdrawn, opened and advanced again, so as to catch the optic nerve between the blades. The nerve is then divided by one clip of the scissors, the eye-ball is lifted out of the orbit and the oblique muscles and any further adhesions are cut as quickly as possible, since a profuse hemorrhage takes place as soon as the optic nerve is severed.

*Paracentesis of the cornea.*—Paracentesis (puncture) of the cornea and emptying of the anterior chamber is performed for the relief of an increased intra-ocular tension, or for the removal of pus or other pathological contents from the anterior chamber.

This little operation is usually performed by means of a needle, a stop-needle, (See figure 76.) or a small lance-shaped knife. In puncturing the cornea great care must be taken, not to wound the iris or the crystalline lens, as the former may lead to iritis and the latter will cause a cataract to develop.

*Abscision of a corneal staphyloma.*—Corneal staphylomata are, as a rule, cut off by detaching the lower or upper half of the protrusion with a *Beer's* knife (See figure 77.) and the remaining half by means of scissors.

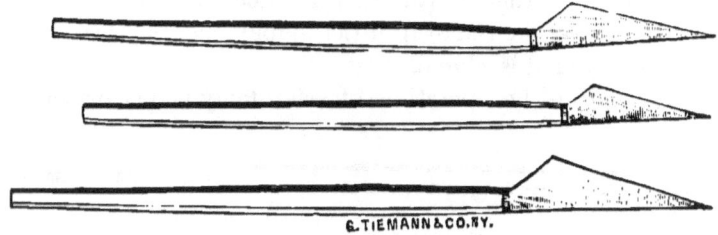

FIG. 77.  Beer's Cataract Knife.

If an eye-ball affected with a total staphyloma of the cornea can for any reason not be totally removed, such a staphyloma may be cut off in the same manner.

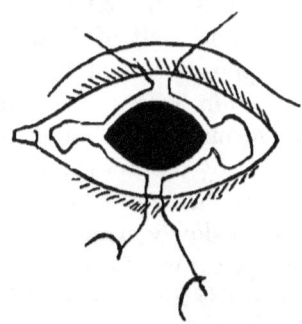

FIG. 78.  Diagram showing Knapp's Method of applying the Sutures in Abscision of a Total Corneal Staphyloma.

If the usually cataractous, crystalline lens is still in situ, it should be removed by the opening of the anterior-capsule.

The wound resulting from this operation may be left to heal

without further interference, or it may be closed by sutures. The sutures must be inserted, ready to be tied, before the staphyloma is removed. This is generally best done by *Knapp's* method. A needle armed with a long thread, is entered under the conjunctiva and episclera above the upper corneo-scleral margin and a little to one side of the vertical meridian, and is brought out somewhat above the horizonal meridian on the same side; it is then entered again a little below this meridian and brought out at point below the lower corneo-scleral margin corresponding to the first point of entrance. (See figure 78.) The same procedure is then repeated on the other side of the vertical meridian. After the removal of the staphyloma the threads are tied and the wound is closed.

*Sclerotomy.*—The operation of sclerotomy is performed to

FIG. 79. Graefe's Cataract Knife.

relieve an increased intra-ocular tension, and has of late been especially recommended as a means of curing certain forms of glaucoma. The operation is generally performed with a *Graefe's* cataract knife. (See figure 79). This knife is entered in the corneo-scleral margin just in front of the insertion of the iris, and is brought out on the opposite side of the cornea, in the corneo-scleral tissue. The section may now be finished, and thus a corneo-scleral flap be formed, or, what is better, because it is less likely to be followed by prolapse and subsequent incarceration of the iris, a narrow bridge of corneo-scleral tissue is left uncut. The knife is then slowly withdrawn.

*Iridectomy.*—The operation of iridectomy, which consists in the removal of a piece of iris-tissue, is one of the operations most frequently performed upon the eye-ball. It is the ordinary operation for artificial pupil to restore sight to an otherwise useless eye, and for the relief of increased intra-ocular tension in cases of primary or secondary glaucoma ; it is also a part of the usual operation for the extraction of cataract.

The cornea is incised by means of a lance-shaped knife or a

*Graefe's* cataract knife in the corneo-scleral tissue. When the knife is withdrawn, the iris may prolapse, in which case it is easily grasped by a pair of iris forceps (See figure 80), gently pulled out and cut off as close to its ciliary insertion as possible. If the iris does not prolapse, the forceps must be introduced through

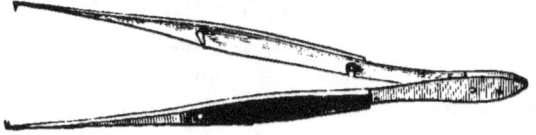

FIG. 80. Iris Forceps.

the corneal incision, in order to grasp and draw it out.

Great care must be taken during this operation not to wound the crystalline lens, as this would cause subsequent formation of cataract; also that no iris-tissue is allowed to remain lying between the lips of the corneal incision.

*Iridotomy.*—The operation called iridotomy or iritomy (*Von Wecker*) is now often executed with the iridotomy-scissors introduced by *Von Wecker* (See figure 81). Its usefulness is most marked in those cases, in which after a cataract-extraction a

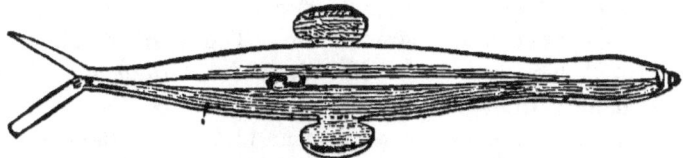

FIG. 81. Iridotomy-Scissors, devised by *von Wecker*.

secondary membranous cataract has been formed, or where in consequence of irido-cyclitis (especially after an injury) the iris and cyclitic membrane together have formed a diaphragm closing the pupil. In these cases the presence of the diaphragm is incompatible with vision, although light-perception and projection are, perhaps, very good; the diaphragm presents, moreover, a serious obstacle to the current of the intra-ocular fluids.

After the cornea has been incised to such an extent that the iridotomy-scissors can be easily introduced into the anterior chamber, the scissors are entered through the corneal incision and the pointed blade is thrust through the diaphragm. Then by closing the scissors a cut is made without appreciable dragging on the ciliary body.

If successfully accomplished the divided tissues retract, open out the slit, and thus a pupil is established. Sometimes it is necessary to make a second cut at an acute angle with the first and thus to isolate a triangular piece of tissue, the apex of which will generally either curl up or become retracted, and so give a permanent opening.

Iridotomy is also performed in various other ways, as for instance, with a sharp narrow knife, like Græfe's cataract knife. By the use of the knife it is possible to avoid dragging upon the ciliary body, and also to dispense with bringing so large an instrument as the iridotomy scissors into the eye-ball.

FIG. 82. Cystotom for Rupturing the Anterior Lens-Capsule in Cataract Extraction.

*Extraction of cataract.* —For the extraction of cataract, a number of methods are in use. The method which is most favored, however, is that introduced by *Graefe* and which bears his name, although, generally somewhat modified. Its first and most important step consists in an incision in the corneo-scleral tissue, generally upwards and forming as nearly as possible, an arc of a great circle. The knife is that already shown (See figure 79.), and the puncture and counter-puncture are made in the corneo-scleral tissue, while the knife is allowed to come out in the corneal tissue, thus forming a low corneal flap of the greatest possible length. The dimensions of the flap are varied according to the operator's estimate of the size and consistency of the cataract which must pass through it. After the corneal incision has been made, iridectomy is performed. Then the anterior lens-capsule is laid open by a cystotom (See figure 82) and finally the lens-substance is gently pressed through the corneal incision out of the eye-ball.

*Discission of the anterior lens-capsule.*—In order to bring the lens-substance in contact with the aqueous humor and to thus cause its gradual absorption within the eye-ball, we must divide the anterior lens-capsule. This may be done in most cases of cataract in persons under the age of thirty years. The little operation is generally executed with a needle, and it must usually be repeated several times before a perfect success is reached. Care must be taken, not to wound the iris, and to make the first division of the capsule very small, as the too rapid swelling of the lens-substance may give rise to glaucomatous symptoms.

A similar operation has to be performed after the extraction of a cataract when the lens-capsule remains clouded, and so interferes with the perfect restoration of vision.

*Pterygium operations.* To remove a small pterygium successfully, it is usually sufficient to separate it from the cornea and to excise with it a little of the conjunctival tissue so as to leave a wound of an approximately rhomboidal shape. The conjunctiva is then stitched together to cover the denuded sclerotic.

Larger pterygia cannot be so easily removed. They may be transplanted into the cul-de-sac of the conjunctiva,(*Desmarres*) or still better by the modified method devised by *Knapp*. The pterygium is first severed from the cornea and sclerotic down to its base, and is then cut into two halves from point to base. The incisions into the conjunctiva are then carried further upwards and downwards into the cul-de-sac, (See figure 33) and this done each half of the pterygium is stitched into the corresponding gap resulting from these incisions. The operation yields lasting results.

A simpler method which has been in use with some operators for many years ( *Galezowsky* ), and has quite recently been warmly advocated, has given me also perfect satisfaction. It is done in the following way: After the pterygium has been dissected from the cornea and sclerotic, down to its base, the conjunctiva at its base is undermined, so that the whole pterygium can be doubled upon itself and folded under it. It is then sewed to the conjunctiva in this position. (See Chapter VII).

*Operations for the cure of symblepharon.* A small bridge-like symblepharon may, as has been already stated, be simply divided with the scissors, but if the union between the eye-lid and eye-ball reaches far down into the fornix, something more must be done to prevent the large wound-surfaces from growing together again. This can be accomplished by transplanting flaps of the conjunctival tissue of the same eye upon the ocular wound surface, or by transplanting a conjunctival flap without pedicle from another human or an animal's eye upon one or both of the two wound-surfaces. Cutaneous flaps have also been successfully made use of. They are taken either from a distant part (arm, *Kuhnt*) and without a pedicle, or from the eye-lid, in which case the skin is drawn through a button-hole-like aperture made in the eye-lid, and stitched to its inner surface.

*Ptosis-operation.*—The operation for congenital ptosis of the upper eye-lid consists in the removal of a horizontal strip of skin from the eye-lid. The effect of this operation may be considerably improved by an iridectomy downwards (*Macnamara*). (See Chapter III).

*Trichiasis and entropium-operations.*—Among the many methods recommended for the cure of trichiasis or entropium of the eye-lids the best seem to be those that have been perfected by *Green* and *Hotz*.

In *Greene's* operation the tarsal tissue is cut through in a horizontal direction, parallel to the lid-margin and somewhat removed from it on the conjunctival surface. Then a narrow strip of skin is removed from the outer surface of the eye-lid corresponding to the tarsal incision. Then sutures are put in, in the following manner: a needle armed with a thread is entered near the ciliary margin and is brought out on the outer surface of the eye-lid at the lower wound-lip, then it is entered again at the upper wound-lip, and after gliding along on the tarsal tissue, it is brought out again through muscle and skin (See figure 14). The ends are then tied. Three such sutures are usually required.

In *Hotz's* operation an incision is made through the skin and muscle of the eye-lid along the orbital edge of the tarsus, so as to lay bare the tarso-orbital aponeurosis. Then a strip of muscular tissue is removed and sutures (three or four) are applied in the following way: the needle, armed with a thread, is entered at the lower wound-lip through the skin and aponeurosis, and is brought out again through aponeurosis and skin at the upper wound-lip. (See figure 15). The ends are then tied so that the skin and aponeurosis may heal together.

*Etropium-operations.*—Slight ectropium of the lower eye-lid may be cured by removing a triangular piece from the tissue adjoining the outer angle of the palpebral fissure, so that the apex of the triangle lies somewhat higher than this angle. Into the apex of the resulting gap the lower eye-lid is then drawn and stitched. (See figure 17). *Kuhnt* most recently recommends to remove a triangular piece of the conjunctiva and tarsal tissue (not including the skin), its base lying at the ciliary margin of the eye-lid, its apex in the fornix of the conjunctiva. This incision is followed by a single suture through the whole lid near the ciliary margin.

When ectropium is caused by the contraction of scar-tissue after a cut or a deep burn, the excision of this scar-tissue may sometimes be sufficient to cure the ectropium. In most cases, however, it requires a more extensive operation, and usually the transplantation of flaps, with or without a pedicle.

*Canthotomy and canthoplasty.*—Shortening of the palpebral fissure sometimes necessitates a surgical interference. If the required effect need not be very large, canthotomy is made. This consists in cutting through the tissues forming the outer commissure of the eye-lids by means of a strong pair of scissors. To increase the effect of this little operation the adjoining conjunctiva is undermined, and then stitched into the gap resulting from the cut.

If the required effect cannot be reached by canthotomy, canthoplasty is called for. The canthotomy being made, the section through the outer canthus is carried further on towards the temple. Then a small flap of skin with its pedicle at the end of this cut is dissected and twisted, so as to fit into the gap caused by the incision. (*Noyes*).

A description of the various methods for partial or total *blepharoplasty* may be found in any modern text-book on operative surgery.

# CHAPTER XXVI.

## ON THE DRUGS MOST COMMONLY USED IN OPHTHALMIC PRACTICE.

ATROPIA.—HOMATROPIA.—PILOCARPINE.—ESERINE.—BORACIC ACID.—ZINC.—TANNIC ACID. — NITRAS ARGENTI. — YELLOW OXIDE OF MERCURY. — REDOXIDE OF MERCURY.—IODOFORM.

The drug most frequently used in ophthalmic practice is the sulphate of atropia. The physician, in prescribing it, ought to be sure that his druggist actually has the neutral salt, sulphate of atropia, in stock, and does not—as too often happens—simply dissolve atropia by means of sulphuric acid. A solution of atropia made with sulphuric acid is almost never perfectly neutral, and when the acid is in excess its instillation causes severe pain. To detect its acidity it may sometimes be necessary to allow the litmus-paper to remain in the solution for several hours.

℞ Atropiæ Sulphatis - - - grs. ij to iv,
   Aq. destill. - - - - - - ʒj.
Sig. To be dropped into the eye.

It will depend on the aim of the physician in the case in hand, how strong the solution must be, and how often it will have to be instilled. In cases of iritis the strongest solution (grs. iv to ʒj) should be used, and the interval between the instillations is to be regulated according to the severity of the case, and the firmness of the adhesions which may have been formed between the iris and anterior lens-capsule.

For milder cases (especially in keratitis) and for the examination of the back-ground of the eye, or for determining an error of refraction, etc., the less poisonous and milder mydriatic, homatropine may be used. The form in which it is prescribed is the following:

R̤ Homatropin. Hydrobromat. - grs. ij to iv.
Aq. destill. - - - - - - - ℥j.
Sig. To be dropped into the eye.

Both mydriatics may be used in solution in oil, or in the form of an ointment, and it is claimed that the effect of the mydriatic is greater, and the quantity needed consequently smaller in these two forms.

After a short period small flocks consisting of minute vegetable formations will appear in the watery solutions of these drugs. They do not impair the action of the drug, yet it is better to remove them by repeated filtering, when they begin to show. Homatropine is as yet a comparatively rare and very costly drug.

To obtain myosis of the pupil we have a mild drug in pilocarpine.

R̤ Pilocarpin. Hydrochlorat. - - grs. ij to iv.
Aq. destill. - - - - - - - ℥j.
Sig. To be dropped into the eye.

If a stronger myotic agent is required, as in glaucomatous attacks, the use of sulphate of eserine is indicated.

R̤ Eserin. Sulphat. - - - - grs. ½ to j.
Aq. destill. - - - - - - - ℥j
Sig. To be dropped into the eye.

The instillation of the sulphate of eserine always causes some pain.

The solution assumes a brownish-red color after a few days, especially when exposed to light. This does not, however, appear to impair its value as a myotic.

In very mild forms of conjunctivitis the use of boracic acid is sometimes indicated.

R̤ Acidi Boracic. - - - - grs. iv to x.
Aq. destill. - - - - - - - ℥j.
Sig. To be dropped into the eye morning and evening

When the use of an astringent drug is required the sulphate of zinc is the most useful.

℞ Zinci Sulphat. - - - - grs. ij to iv.
  Aq. destill. - - - - - - ℨj.
Sig. To be brushed on the inside of the lower eye-lid once a day.

The camels-hair brush used to apply such a solution should be of good size and clean.

The following is another astringent collyrium.

℞ Acidi Tannici. - - - - - grs. x.
  Aq. destill. - - - - - - ℨj.
Sig. To be brushed on the inside of the lower eye-lids once a day.

For caustic treatment *by the physician* himself.

℞ Argenti Nitratis - - - - grs. ij to v.
  Aq. destill. - - - - - - ℨj.
Sig. To be brushed on the inside of the eye-lids once a day.

The following ointments may be used in the treatment of corneal affections.

℞ Hydrargyri Oxidi Flavi - - - grs. ij to iv.
  Cosmoline - - - - - - ℨiij.
Sig. To be rubbed into the eye once a day.

The yellow oxide of mercury must be in an absolutely impalpable powder and must contain no lumps; the ointment must be well mixed. It is best to take the precaution of examining the eye after every application of this ointment, in order to make sure that no larger particles remain lying in the conjunctival sack, as such particles would cause an undue irritation, and may even lead to serious ulcerations.

The red oxide of mercury should never be substituted for the yellow oxide, except when the ointment is used externa'ly, as in blepharitis ciliaris.

℞ Iodoformii. - - - - grs. x to xx.
  Cosmol. - - - - - - - ℨss.
Misce intime.
Sig. To be rubbed into the eye once a day.

# INDEX

| | |
|---|---|
| ABSCESS of the cornea | 95 |
| of the eye-lid, phlegmonous | 34 |
| Abscision of a corneal staphyloma | 221 |
| Accommodation, faculty of changing the focus of the eye | 177 |
| examination of | 26 |
| Accommodative apparatus, ciliary muscles and crystalline lens | 178 |
| Acuteness of vision, examination of | 25 |
| Adenoma of the lachrymal gland | 47 |
| Advancement of the internal rectus for divergent squint | 184 |
| Agnew | 50 |
| Albinism, lack of pigment in the cells of the uveal tract and pigmentary epithelium | 9 |
| Albuminuria | 205 |
| Amaurosis, blindness from disease of the background of the eye | 140 |
| Amaurotic cat's eye, peculiar appearance of an eye affected with glioma of the retina | 133 |
| Amblyopia, reduced vision | 140 |
| Ametropia, condition in which an eye at rest is not focussed for parallel rays | 144 |
| Anæmia of the brain | 197 |
| of the optic nerve and retina | 127 |
| pernicious, progressive | 203 |
| Anæsthesia of the cornea from glaucoma | 158 |
| paralysis of the fifth nerve | 98 |
| Anchyloblepharon, adhesion between the lid-margins or between the eyelids and eye-ball | 88 |
| Aneurism of the ophthalmic artery | 204 |
| Angioma of the eye-lid | 37 |
| Anisometropia | 184 |
| Anterior chamber, space bound by the cornea, iris and anterior lens-capsule | 17 |
| Aphakia, absence of the crystalline lens | 152 |
| Aqueous humor, contents of the anterior and posterior chambers of the eye | 17 |
| Arachnoid sheath of the optic nerve | 13 |
| Arcus senilis, fatty degeneration of the tissue in the periphery of the cornea | 100 |

Arlt - 21
Artery, central retinal - 14
Arthritis, gonorrhœal - 206
Artificial eye, insertion of an - 69
Assistance in eye-operations - 71
Astigmatism, condition in which the meridians of the cornea (or lens) are of different radii - 183
    compound - 184
    irregular - 184
    mixed - 184
    regular - 184
Asthenopia, weakness caused by the strain on the accommodative apparatus from hypermetropia - 170
    of the internal recti from myopia - 182
    from presbyopia - 186
Astringents, use of - 64
Atrophy of the optic nerve after neuritis - 137
    genuine, progressive - 138
Atropia, use of the sulphate of in iritis - 113

**Bandaging** eyes - 70
Basedow's disease, exophthalmus, goitre and palpitations of the heart - 206
Becker - 145
Beer's cataract knife - 221
Belladonna, use of the extract - 114
Blepharitis ciliaris, inflammation of the lid-margin - 30
Blepharoplasty - 227
Blepharophimosis, shortening of the palpebral fissure - 43
Blepharospasmus, spastic closure of the eye-lids, clonic - 42
    tonic - 42
Bone-formation in the choroid
Boracic acid, use of the - 77
Bowman' layer of the cornea - 9
Bowman's probes for dilating strictures of the lachrymal apparatus - 52
Burns of the conjunctiva - 87
    cornea - 102
    eye-lid - 45

**Calomel**, use of - 86
Canalis opticus, short canal through which the optic nerve enters the orbit - 2
Canthoplasty, insertion of a twisted cutaneous flap into the outer angle of the palpebral fissure - 44
Canthotomy, incision through the outer commissure of the eye-lids - 43
Canthus, angle of the palpebral fissure - 3
Caries of the orbital walls - 56
Cataract, opacity of the crystalline lens - 142
    acquired - 146

|  |  |
|---|---|
| complicated | 147 |
| congenital | 144 |
| cortical | 146 |
| diabetic | 147 |
| fluid | 146 |
| hard (nuclear, senile) | 147 |
| hypermature (over-ripe) | 146 |
| immature (unripe) | 146 |
| mature (ripe) | 146 |
| posterior polar (deposit upon the posterior lens-capsule) | 144 |
| pyramidal (anterior polar) | 144 |
| secondary | 149 |
| soft | 146 |
| total | 145 |
| traumatic | 150 |
| uncomplicated | 147 |
| zonular (lamellar) | 143 |
| Caustics, use of | 64 |
| Cellulitis orbitæ, phlegmonous inflammation of the orbital tissues | 56 |
| Chalazion, tarsal tumor | 33 |
| Chemosis, œdematous swelling of the ocular conjunctiva | 123 |
| Chiasma of the optic nerves | 200 |
| Choriocapillary layer | 9 |
| Choroid, anatomy of the | 9 |
| Choroiditis, inflammation of the choroid | 120 |
| areolar | 120 |
| central (chorio-retinitis) | 121 |
| disseminate | 121 |
| fibrino-plastic | 121 |
| metastatic | 123 |
| purulent | 122 |
| serous | 122 |
| Cilia, eye-lashes | 4 |
| Ciliary body | 9 |
| muscle | 10 |
| nerves | 9 |
| processes | 12 |
| Circulatory apparatus, diseases of | 203 |
| Colm | 206 |
| Cold applications | 61 |
| Coloboma fissure of the iris, congenital | 145 |
| rupture of the sphincter iridis, traumatic | 115 |
| Color-blindness, lack of perception of certain colors, congenital | 215 |
| acquired | 140 |
| examination of | 215 |
| Color perception | 26 |
| Cones of the retina | 14 |

## INDEX.

| | |
|---|---|
| Conical cornea | 101 |
| Conjunctiva, anatomy of the ocular | 5 |
|     of the palpebral | 4 |
|     fornix of the | 3 |
| Conjunctivitis, inflammation of the conjunctiva | 75 |
|     catarrhal, acute | 75 |
|         chronic | 76 |
|     croupous (membranous) | 79 |
|     diphtheritic | 80 |
|     gonorrhœal | 78 |
|     granular, acute | 82 |
|         chronic | 81 |
|     phlyctænular | 85 |
|     purulent, acute | 77 |
|         chronic | 79 |
|     of the newly born | 78 |
|     pustular | 86 |
| Constipation | 204 |
| Convergence | 177 |
| Convergent, strabismus | 192 |
| Cornea, anatomy of the | 6 |
| Corneo-scleral margin, anatomy of the | 7 |
| Copper, use of the sulphate of | 64 |
| Crystalline lens, anatomy of the | 16 |
| Cyclitis, inflammation of the ciliary body | 117 |
|     fibirno-plastic | 117 |
|     gummatous | 119 |
|     purulent | 118 |
|     serous | 117 |
| Cyclitic membrane, membrane formed behind the crystalline lens by a fibrino-plastic cyclitis | 117 |
| Cyst of the orbit | 59 |
|     conjunctiva | 91 |
|     iris | 163 |
| **Dakryo-adenitis**, inflammation of the lachrymal gland | 45 |
| Dakryo-cystitis, inflammation of the lachrymal sack, catarrhal | 49 |
|     purulent | 50 |
| Dakryops, cystoid distention of the lachrymal gland | 48 |
| Daturine, use of | 116 |
| Descemet's membrane, posterior limiting membrane of the cornea | 7 |
| Desmarres' lid-retractors | 67 |
| Detachment of the ciliary body from the sclerotic | 117 |
|     retina from the choroid | 129 |
| Diabetes mellitus | 213 |
| Digestive organs, diseases of the | 204 |
| Dilatation of the pupil | 116 |
| Dilator muscle of the iris | 12 |

## INDEX. 235

| | |
|---|---|
| Diplopia, double vision | 189 |
|     examination of | 29 |
| Diphtheria of the throat | 211 |
| Discharge, removal of from the conjunctival sack | 62 |
|     from the eye-lashes | 62 |
| Discission of the lens-capsule | 225 |
| Dislocation of the crystalline lens, congenital | 151 |
|     acquired | 150 |
| Distichiasis, irregular position of the eye-lashes | 37 |
| Divergent strabismus | 192 |
| Duboisine, use of | 116 |
| Dura mater sheath of the optic nerve | 13 |
| **Ectactic** scar | 163 |
| Ectopia lentis, congenital dislocation of the crystalline lens | 151 |
| Ectropium, eversion of the eye-lid | 40 |
|     operations | 40 |
| Electricity, use of in opacities of the vitreous body | 154 |
| Embolism of the central retinal artery | 128 |
| Emmetropia, the condition in which the eye at rest is focussed for parallel rays | 174 |
| Emphysema of the eye-lids | 44 |
|     orbit | 59 |
| Endocarditis, fibrinous | 203 |
| Entropium, inversion of the eye-lid | 38 |
|     operations | 39 |
| Enucleation of the eye-ball | 219 |
| Epiphora, tear-dropping | 48 |
| Episcleritis, inflammation of the episcleral tissue | 104 |
| Erysipelas of the face | 210 |
| Eserine, use of the sulphate of | 116 |
| Examination of the eye, methods of | 20 |
| Excavation of the optic papilla, atrophic | 139 |
|     glaucomatous | 157 |
|     physiological | 14 |
| Exophthalmus, protrusion of the eye-ball | 59 |
|     pulsating | 203 |
| Extraction of cataract | 224 |
| Everting the eye-lids for examination or treatment | 21 |
| Eye-douche | 61 |
| Eye-lashes | 4 |
| Eye-lids, anatomy of the | 3 |
| **Far-point**, point for which the eye at rest is focussed | 175 |
| Far-sight (see hypermetropia) | |
| Fistule of the lachrymal sack | 51 |
| Fluids, course of the, within the eye-ball | 17 |
| Focal illumination (see oblique illumination) | |
| Focal interval of rays refracted by an asymmetrical surface | 184 |

Foerster - - - - - - - - - - - - - 206
Fontana's cavities, anatomy of - - - - - - - - 7
             obliteration of in glaucoma - - - - - 158

Foreign bodies in the ciliary body - - - - - - - 166
               conjunctiva - - - - - - - 67
               cornea - - - - - - - - 165
               iris - - - - - - - - - 165
               lens - - - - - - - - - 165
               vitreous body - - - - - - 166
Fovea centralis of the retina - - - - - - - - 15
Fracture of the walls of the canalis opticus - - - - - 141
             lamina papyracea of the os ethmoidei  59

GANGLION, Gasseri - - - - - - - - - - 210
Galezowsky - - - - - - - - - - - - 91
Gerlach - - - - - - - - - - - - - 2
Glasses, concave for myopia - - - - - - - - 183
       convex for hypermetropia - - - - - - 181
              presbyopia - - - - - - - 186
       cylindrical for astigmatism - - - - - - 184
       protective, against injuries - - - - - - 168
Glaucoma, a disease characterized by an increase of the intra-ocular tension and pathological excavation of the optic papilla - - - - - - - - - - 156
       absolutum, absolute blindness from glaucoma - - 159
       acute - - - - - - - - - - 158
       chronic inflammatory - - - - - - - 158
       chronic simple - - - - - - - - 157
       hemorrhagic - - - - - - - - 160
       secondary - - - - - - - - - 160
Gonorrhœa - - - - - - - - - - - - 206
Gout - - - - - - - - - - - - - - 113
Graefe's cataract-extraction - - - - - - - - 224
          knife - - - - - - - - - 222
Granular eye-lids (see trachoma) - - - - - - -
Granulatious of the conjunctiva (see trachoma) - - -
Granuloma of the conjunctiva - - - - - - - 91
          iris - - - - - - - - 163
Graves' disease (see Basedow's disease) - - -
Green's operation for entropium of the eye-lid - - - - 89
Gruening's magnet for the removal of foreign bodies from the vitreous body - - - - - - - - - - 166

HEART Diseases - - - - - - - - - - 203
Helmholtz - - - - - - - - - - - - 178
Hemeralopia, night-blindness - - - - - - - 131
Hemianopia, blindness of one-half of the eye from brain disease - 200

INDEX. 237

Hemorrhage into the anterior chamber - - - - - - 166
     choroid - - - - - - - 126
     conjunctiva - - - - - - 87
     orbit - - - - - - - - 56
     retina - - - - - - - 133
     vitreous body - - - - - - 155
Herpes zoster - - - - - - - - - - - 210
Hoeurteloup's artificial leech - - - - - - - 62
Holmgren's method for the detection of color-blindness - - - 215
Homatropine, use of the hydrobromate of - - - - - 24
Hordeolum, stye - - - - - - - - - - 32
Horner's muscle - - - - - - - - - - 19
Hotz's operation for trichiasis of the eye-lid - - - - 38
Hutchinson's teeth - - - - - - - - - - 212
Hyaline artery - - - - - - - - - - 17
Hyalitis, inflammation of the vitreous body - - - - 153
Hyoscyamine, use of - - - - - - - - - 116
Hyperæmia of the brain - - - - - - - - - 197
    conjunctiva - - - - - - 74
    episcleral tissue - - - - - - 110
    optic papilla - - - - - - 127
    retina - - - - - - - - 127
Hypermetropia, the condition in which the eye at rest is focussed
    for convergent rays - - - - - - 178
    latent, part hidden by accommodation - - - 180
    manifest, part detected without paralyzing the ac-
     commodation - - - - - - - 180
    total, the sum of the manifest and the latent hyper-
     metropia - - - - - - - 180
Hypertrophy of the left ventricle of the heart - - - - 203
Hypopyum, pus in the anterior chamber - - - - - 97

Incarceration of the iris - - - - - - - - 161
Infectious diseases - - - - - - - - - - 210
Injuries of the ciliary body - - - - - - - - 119
    conjunctiva - - - - - - - 87
    cornea - - - - - - - - 102
    crystalline lens - - - - - - 150
    eye-lids - - - - - - - 44
    iris - - - - - - - - - 115
    optic nerve - - - - - - - 141
Inoculation of pus for the cure of trachoma - - - - 85
Inspergation of medicinal powders - - - - - - 66
Instillation of medicated fluids - - - - - - - 63
Insufficiency of the internal recti muscles - - - - 194
    examination for - - - - - - 29
Intervaginal spaces of the optic nerve - - - - - 198

Intoxication with alcohol - - - - - - - - - 139
     atropia - - - - - - - - - 114
     belladonna - - - - - - - - 213
     datura - - - - - - - - - 213
     hyoscyamus - - - - - - - - 213
     lead - - - - - - - - - - 212
     morphium - - - - - - - - 213
     opium - - - - - - - - - 213
     quinine - - - - - - - - - 213
     sausage-poison - - - - - - - 213
     tobacco - - - - - - - - 139
Intra-ocular tension, examination of the - - - - - 26
Iodoform, use of phlyctænular keratitis - - - - - 86
Iris, anatomy of the - - - - - - - - 12
Iridectomy, removal of a piece from the iris - - - - 222
Iridencleisis, artificial incarceration of the iris in the cornea - - 144
Irideremia, absence of an iris, traumatic - - - - - 164
Iridodialysis, partial detachment of the iris from its ciliary inter-
 tion - - - - - - - - - - - - 116
Iridodonesis, tremulous iris from lack of support from the crystal-
 line lens - - - - - - - - - - - 24
Iridotomy, operation after plastic iritis or irido-cyclitis - - - 223
Iritis, inflammation of the iris - - - - - - - 108
  fibrino plastic - - - - - - - - - 109
  gummatous - - - - - - - - - 112
  purulent - - - - - - - - - - 112
  rheumatic - - - - - - - - - 113
  serous - - - - - - - - - - 111
  syphilitic - - - - - - - - - 112
Ischæmia of the retina - - - - - - - - 127
Isolation - - - - - - - - - - - 66

JEQUIRITY, abrus precatorius, use of the - - - - - 85
KERATITIS, inflammation of the cornea - - - - - 92
    fascicular - - - - - - - - 93
    malarial - - - - - - - - 98
    neuro-paralytic - - - - - - - 98
    parenchymatous - - - - - - - 93
    phlyctænular - - - - - - - 92
    syphilitic - - - - - - - - 94
Kipp - - - - - - - - - - - - 98
Knapp's hook for removing foreign bodies from the eye-ball - - 166
  method of blepharoplasty by sliding flaps - - - 35
     transplanting pterygium - - - - 91
Kopiopia hysterica - - - - - - - - - 206
Kuhnt - - - - - - - - - - - 227

| | |
|---|---|
| LACHRYMAL Apparatus | 18 |
| canaliculi | 18 |
| caruncle | 3 |
| duct | 18 |
| fistula | 51 |
| gland | 19 |
| papilla | 4 |
| puncta | 4 |
| sack | 18 |
| Lagophthalmus, inability to close the eye-lids | 42 |
| Lamina cribrosa of the sclerotic | 5 |
| vitrea of the choroid | 9 |
| Laurence | 54 |
| Leeches, application of | 62 |
| Leptothrix, vegetable parasite found in the lachrymal canaliculus | 49 |
| Leucæmia | 204 |
| Levator palpeqræ superioris muscle | 5 |
| Ligament external palpebral | 4 |
| internal palpebral | 4 |
| pectinatum of the iris | 7 |
| suspensory of the crystalline lens | 16 |
| Limbus of the cornea | 5 |
| Limiting membranes of the cornea | 14 |
| MACNAMARA's method of operating for ptosis of the upper eye-lid | 42 |
| Macula, lutea of the retina, point of acute vision | 15 |
| of the cornea | 93 |
| Madarosis, loss of the eye-lashes | 30 |
| Malarial fever | 211 |
| Malingering | 214 |
| Mauthner | 216 |
| Measles | 210 |
| Meibomian, tarsal glands | 4 |
| Menstruation, suppressed | 206 |
| Merkel | |
| Metamorphopsia, distorted vision from certain retinal affections | 121 |
| Mooren | 105 |
| Motility of the eye-balls, examination of | 28 |
| Muscocele, distension of the lachrymal sack by a mucoid fluid | 50 |
| Muscæ volitantes, spots floating before the eye | 153 |
| Muscles, external of the eye-ball | 17 |
| Mueller's fibres of the retina | 15 |
| Mydriasis, dilatation of the pupil with immobility | 116 |
| Mydriatic agents | 116 |
| Myopia, the condition in which the eye at rest is focussed for divergent rays | 181 |
| Myosis, tonic contraction of the pupil | 116 |
| Myotic agents | 116 |

NASAL Duct for the drainage of the tears - - - - - 18
Near-sightedness (see Myopia) - - - - - - -
Near-point, nearest point for which the eye can accommodate - 177
Necrosis of the orbital walls - - - - - - - 56
Nephritis - - - - - - - - - - - 205
Neurectomy. optico-ciliary, removal of a piece of the optic nerve
          and the ciliary nerves near the eye-ball - - - 172
          of the infra-orbital nerve - - - - - - 42
          supra-orbital nerve - - - - - - 42
Neuritis optic, inflammation of the optic nerve - - - - - 136
       ascendent - - - - - - - - 136
       descendent - - - - - - - - 138
       interstitial - - - - - - - - 136
Neuro-retinitis, inflammation of the optic nerve and retina - - 136
Neurotomy, optico-ciliary, severing of the optic nerve and the ciliary
    nerves from the eye-ball - - - - - - - - 172
Noyes' operation for canthoplasty - - - - - - - 44
Nystagmus, involuntary oscillation of the eye-ball - - - - 194

OBLITERATION of the lachrymal sac - - - - - - - 54
Oblique illumination of the anterior third of the eye-ball by means
    of a convex lens - - - - - - - - - - 24
Oedema of the optic papilla - - - - - - - - 198
Ointments, application of - - - - - - - - 65
Onanism - - - - - - - - - - - 205
Opacities of the cornea - - - - - - - - - 99
          crystalline lens - - - - - - 142
          vitreous body - - - - - - - 153
Ophthalmoplegia, paralysis of all external muscles of the eye-ball 190
Ophthalmoscope, use of the - - - - - - - - 27
Optic foramen, external orifice of the canalis opticus - - - 188
   nerve, anatomy of - - - - - - - - 13
   papilla - - - - - - - - - - 14
Ora, serrata of the retina - - - - - - - - - 14
Orbicularis muscle of the eye-lids - - - - - - - 4
Orbit, anatomy of the - - - - - - - - - 1
Over-sight (see hypermetropia) - - - - - - -
Osteoma of the orbit - - - - - - - - - 86

PANNUS, vascularisation and dimness of the cornea - - - 82
Panophshalmites, inflammation of all the tissues of the eye-ball - 166
Paracentesis of the cornea - - - - - - - - 220
          sclerotic for detachment of the retina - - 130
Paralysis of the accommodation - - - - - - - 186
       external muscles of the eye-ball - - - - 189
       muscles of the eye-lids - - - - - 42
Parametritis atrophica - - - - - - - - - 206
Pediculi. crab-lice, in the eye-lashes - - - - - - 32
Periostitis of the orbit - - - - - - - - - 55

## INDEX. 241

Phlegmonous abscess of the eye-lid - - - - - - - 34
        inflammation of the orbital tissue - - - - 56
Photophobia, dread of light in phlyctænular conjunctivitis - - 85
Photopsia, subjective perception of light-flashes, etc. - - - 171
Phthiriasis (see pediculi) - - - - - - - -
Pia mater sheath of the optic nerve - - - - - - - 13
Pigmentary epithelium, anatomy of the - - - - - - 9
Pigmentation of the retina from choroido-retinitis - - - - 130
Pilocarpine, use of the muriate of in detachment of the retina - 129
Pinguecula, small connective tissue tumor of the conjunctiva - 89
Polypus of the lachrymal canaliculus - - - - - - 49
        nose - - - - - - - - - - 202
Posterior chamber, space bound by the crystalline lens, zonule of
    Zinn, ciliary body and iris - - - - - - - - 17
Presbyopia, physiological loss of elasticity of the crystalline lens
    and, consequent impairment of the accommodation - - 186
Prisms, use of for detecting simulated blindness - - - - 214
Prolapse of the iris through a corneal wound - - - - - 162
Pterygium, triangular fold of conjunctival tissue encroaching upon
    the cornea - - - - - - - - - - 90
    operations - - - - - - - - - - 225
Ptosis of the upper eye-lid, inability to raise it - - - - 41
        atonica - - - - - - - 41
        congenital - - - - - - 41
        paralytic - - - - - - 41
        traumatic - - - - - - 44
        operations - - - - - - 41
Puerperal fever - - - - - - - - - - 212
Pupillary membrane, due to fibrino-plastic iritis - - - - 109
Pyæmia - - - - - - - - - - - - 212

**R**ECURRENT Fever - - - - - - - - - 211
Red-green blindness - - - - - - - - - 215
Refraction - - - - - - - - - - - 174
Remedies in substance, use of - - - - - - - - 64
Respiratory apparatus, diseases of the - - - - - - 202
Retina, anatomy of the - - - - - - - - - 14
Retinitis, inflammation of the retina - - - - - - 131
    albuminuric - - - - - - - - 132
    hemorrhagic - - - - - - - - 133
    leucæmic - - - - - - - - - 204
    pigmentary - - - - - - - - 131
    proliferans - - - - - - - - 154
    syphilitic - - - - - - - - - 132
Retinal purple, substance, secreted by the pigmentary epithelium 9
Rheumatism - - - - - - - - - - - 210
Rods of the retina - - - - - - - - - - 14
Rupture, isolated of the choroid - - - - - - - 125

## INDEX.

| | |
|---|---|
| Sæmisch's operation for ulcer and abscess of the cornea | 96 |
| Salicylate of soda, use of the in iritis | 115 |
| Sattler | 204 |
| Scarlet-fever | 210 |
| Schlemm's canal in the corneal-scleral tissue | 7 |
| Scleritis, inflammation of the sclerotic | 104 |
| Sclerosis of the spinal cord | 199 |
| Sclerotic, anatomy of the | 5 |
| Sclerotomy | 222 |
| Scotoma central, pathological blind spot. | 138 |
| Scrophulosis | 213 |
| Septicæmia | 212 |
| Shrinkage of the conjunctival sack | 82 |
| eye-ball | 164 |
| Silver, use of the nitrate of in conjunctivitis | 76 |
| Skin diseases | 210 |
| Small-pox | 210 |
| Snellen | 176 |
| Spasm of the accommodation | 187 |
| Horner's muscle | 49 |
| Sphincter muscle of the iris | 12 |
| Spongy exudation | 111 |
| Staphyloma, union between a part of the cornea or sclerotic with a part of the uval tract with stretching, of the cornea | 100 |
| sclerotic | 105 |
| Stillicidium lacrymarum, tear-dropping | 21 |
| Stilling's canal in the vitreous body | 17 |
| Strabismus, paralytic | 190 |
| Strictures of the lachrymal drainage apparatus | 51 |
| Suction method of removing a cataract | 148 |
| Symblepharon anterius, union between the lid-margin and the eye-ball | 88 |
| posterius, the union reaches down into the fornix of the conjunctiva | 88 |
| operations | 226 |
| Sympathetic inflammation, an inflammation caused in one eye by a disease usually of traumatic origin in the fellow-eye | 169 |
| irido-choroiditis | 171 |
| irido-cyclitis | 171 |
| iritis | 171 |
| irritation | 171 |
| keratitis | 172 |
| neuritis | 171 |
| neuro-retinitis | 171 |
| Synchisis, liquefaction of the vitreous body | 122 |
| scintillans, containing crystals of cholesterine.etc | 155 |
| Synechia, adhesion of the iris, anterior | 97 |
| circular | 109 |
| posterior | 109 |

| | |
|---|---|
| Syphilis | 212 |
| **Tabes** dorsalis | 140 |
| Tannic acid, use of the in conjunctivitis | 77 |
| Tarsal tissue, anatomy of the | 4 |
| Tarsoraphy, operation for shortening the palpebral fissure | 43 |
| Tatooing the cornea | 100 |
| Teleangiectatic tumors of the eye-lid | 37 |
| Tenon's capsule, anatomy of | 2 |
| space | 2 |
| Tenonitis, inflammation of Tenon's capsule | 58 |
| Tenotomy | 217 |
| Test-types, Snellen's, letters seen under a visual angle of 5 minutes, | |
| used to determine the acuteness of vision | 176 |
| Thrombosis of the central retinal vein | 128 |
| Trachoma, inflammation of the conjunctiva characterized by the | |
| formation of granules | 81 |
| Transplantation of flaps for blepharophasty | 35 |
| the cure of symblepharon | 89 |
| Trichiasis, irregular position of the eye-lashes | 37 |
| operations | 38 |
| Tubercle in the choroid | 124 |
| iris | 116 |
| Tuberculosis of the lungs | 202 |
| meninges | 199 |
| Tumors of the ciliary body | 119 |
| choroid | 124 |
| conjunctiva | 89 |
| cornea | 103 |
| eye-lids | 34 |
| episcleral tissue | 106 |
| lachrymal caruncle | 54 |
| lachrymal gland | 47 |
| optic nerve | 141 |
| orbit | 39 |
| retina | 133 |
| tarsus | 33 |
| Typhus, abdominal | 211 |
| **Ulcer** of the conjunctiva after diphtheria | 80 |
| cornea | 96 |
| eye-lid | 34 |
| Uro-poetic apparatus, diseases of the | 205 |
| Uterine diseases | 206 |
| Uveal tract, anatomy of the | 8 |
| **Vascular** tumors of the eye-lid | 37 |
| Vein, central, retinal | 14 |
| Venae vorticosae | 5 |

| | |
|---|---:|
| Visual field, examination of | 25 |
| Vitreous body | 17 |
| Von Dusch | 208 |
| Von Wecker's operation for iridotomy | 223 |
| **Warm** applications | 61 |
| Warts on the eye-lid | 34 |
| Whooping-cough | 202 |
| Wild hairs | 66 |
| Wire-speculum to hold the eye-lids apart | 68 |
| **Xanthelasma**; small, slightly elevated, yellowish tumors of the skin of the eye-lid | 34 |
| Xerophthalmus, dryness of the eye | 82 |
| **Yellow-blue** blindness | 16 |
| Yellow spot of the retina | 15 |
| **Zinc**, use of the sulphate of in conjunctivitis | 77 |
| Zonule of Zinn, suspensory ligament of the crystalline lens | 16 |

www.ingramcontent.com/pod-product-compliance
Lightning Source LLC
Chambersburg PA
CBHW021343230426
43666CB00006B/393